Global Debates about Taxation

Also by Florian Schui

EARLY DEBATES ABOUT INDUSTRY: Voltaire and his Contemporaries

Global Debates about Taxation

Edited by

Holger Nehring and Florian Schui

palgrave
macmillan

First published 2007 by
PALGRAVE MACMILLAN
Houndmills, Basingstoke, Hampshire RG21 6XS and
175 Fifth Avenue, New York, N.Y. 10010
Companies and representatives throughout the world

PALGRAVE MACMILLAN is the global academic imprint of the Palgrave Macmillan division of St. Martin's Press, LLC and of Palgrave Macmillan Ltd. Macmillan® is a registered trademark in the United States, United Kingdom and other countries. Palgrave is a registered trademark in the European Union and other countries.

ISBN-13: 978–1–4039–8747–1 hardback
ISBN-10: 1–4039–8747–5 hardback

This book is printed on paper suitable for recycling and made from fully managed and sustained forest sources. Logging, pulping and manufacturing processes are expected to conform to the environmental regulations of the country of origin.

A catalogue record for this book is available from the British Library.

Library of Congress Cataloging-in-Publication Data

Global debates about taxation / edited by Holger Nehring and Florian Schui.
p. cm.
Based on a conference on "The transfer of ideas about taxation" held Sept. 16–18, 2005 in Cambridge, England.
Includes bibliographical references and index.
ISBN-13: 978–1–4039–8747–1 (cloth)
ISBN-10: 1–4039–8747–5 (cloth)
1. Taxation–History–Congresses. 2. Finance, Public–International cooperation–Congresses. 3. Finance, Public–Cross-cultural studies–Congresses. I. Nehring, Holger, 1974– II. Schui, Florian, 1973–

HJ2250.G56 2007
336.2–dc22 2006051744

10 9 8 7 6 5 4 3 2 1
16 15 14 13 12 11 10 09 08 07

Printed and bound in Great Britain by
Antony Rowe Ltd, Chippenham and Eastbourne

Contents

List of Tables

List of Figures

Preface

This volume grew out of a conference on 'The Transfer of Ideas about Taxation', held at the Centre for Research in the Arts, Social Sciences and the Humanities (CRASSH), Cambridge, on 16–18 September 2005. The conference itself was a stimulating exchange of ideas, comprising scholars from continental Europe and the United States.

For making this possible, we should like to thank CRASSH, in particular Ludmilla Jordanova; the Centre for History and Economics, Cambridge, particularly its directors Emma Rothschild and Gareth Stedman Jones; as well as the Trevelyan Fund of the History Faculty of the University of Cambridge for providing us with generous funding. Thanks are also due to Catherine Hurley, Nick Swift and Gemma Tyler for the excellent organization of the more practical matters.

Ha-Joon Chang (Cambridge) gave an excellent keynote address which provided us many themes for discussion. Not least, we should like to thank the commentators of the panels, Sunil Amrith (Cambridge), Peter Becker (Linz, Austria) and Christopher M. Clark (Cambridge), as well as the other participants for such stimulating interventions.

We are also very grateful to Julia Moses (Cambridge) for her sterling proofreading efforts. Not least, we would also like to thank Amanda Hamilton at Palgrave for commissioning this volume and Katie Button, Alec Dubber and everyone else at Palgrave who was involved with the production process for their dedication and friendliness.

Holger Nehring
Florian Schui
Sheffield/Egham, July 2006

Notes on the Contributors

W. Elliott Brownlee is Professor Emeritus of History at the University of California-Santa Barbara.

Martin Daunton is Professor of Economic History at the University of Cambridge.

Alexander Grab is Professor of History at the University of Maine-Orono.

Christine Lebeau is Professor of History at the University of Paris – Panthéon Sorbonne.

Frances M. B. Lynch is Reader in French Studies at the University of Westminster, London.

Holger Nehring is Lecturer in Contemporary European History at the University of Sheffield.

Florian Schui is Lecturer in Modern European History at Royal Holloway, University of London.

Miranda Stewart is Associate Professor at the University of Melbourne Law School.

Andreas Thier is Professor of Legal History, Canon Law and Legal Theory at the University of Zurich.

Joseph J. Thorndike is a tax historian and works as an analyst for Tax Analysts, Washington, DC.

1

Introduction: Global Debates about Taxation: Transfers of Ideas, the Challenge of Political Legitimacy and the Paradoxes of State-Building

Holger Nehring and Florian Schui

In March 2005, Alan Greenspan, then still chairman of the American Federal Reserve, argued before the President's Advisory Panel on Federal Tax Reform that 'some useful lessons can be learned by examining earlier systematic reforms of the tax code'.[1] Indeed, the degree to which current debates about taxation and public policy debates more generally revolve around learning from past experiences and from other countries is staggering. The debate about the introduction of a 'flat tax' on income in political circles in the United States, which referred to the implementation of such a tax regime in the Baltic states and which was consequently championed by sections within the British Conservative Party in 2004/5 and by the shadow secretary of the treasury Paul Kirchhof in the German election campaign of 2005, is a prime example of the circulation of ideas about taxation around the globe.[2]

The current interest in the origins of the tax state is closely linked to the question whether, driven by the multiple challenges of budget deficits, considerable public and private debts as well as a general increase in economic and financial interdependencies, the organization of public finance is about to change fundamentally. One characteristic of the current debates about taxation and state finance is that they are concerned with the role of the state and governments in economy and society.[3] They are also closely related to discussions about the transfer of power from nation states to supranational and international institutions under the heading of 'globalization'.[4] The European Union (EU), the World Trade Organization (WTO) and the International Monetary Fund (IMF) are only three of the more prominent examples. Moreover, increasing mobility of capital and individuals has made tax evasion and avoidance a challenge that, some argue, can no longer be addressed effectively in the national context alone.

Structurally, such arguments are not as novel as they might seem, however. Indeed, transfers of ideas about taxation have a long history going back to the Middle Ages. Yet historians of the modern period have remained surprisingly silent in these debates, perhaps because they assume, unlike their colleagues in medieval and early modern history, that death and taxes are certain, as the British proverb has it.[5] While historical research on transnational relations and the transfer of ideas is booming, most historians interested in such processes which transcend the boundaries of the nation states have curiously focused on cultural, rather than on economic and financial issues.[6] Our volume makes a first contribution to fill this gap by bringing together historical, legal and economic expertise.

Indeed, it was common economic and financial challenges, often interpreted by policy-makers as 'crises', which did most to promote the exchanges of ideas about solutions to the perceived problems. Likewise, wars with their impact on more than one nation, have posed common challenges to very different polities. Similarly, the secular growth of welfare states across Western Europe and the world has led to common challenges in raising revenues.[7]

We do not seek to add to the growing body of social science literature on the nature of 'policy learning', its impact, its successes and failures.[8] Instead, we are interested in unveiling the variety of historical experiences with the transfers of ideas about taxation in a number of economic, political and social contexts. Our aim is to encourage a more critical and historically informed approach to problems of state finance in the current situation, by historicizing both the ways in which historical actors thought about taxation and the role which transfers of ideas played in these processes.[9] Hence, rather than presenting an analysis of the structural links between national economies and taxation systems, we seek to bring out the ways in which historical actors have interpreted and conceptualized the challenges posed by economic, political and social developments, and how they have framed and transferred their ideas about taxation accordingly. We define 'ideas' loosely as perceptions of economic, political and social reality (rather than as coherent concepts). The nature of 'ideas about taxation' that were transferred was as diverse as the transfer processes themselves. Three broad categories of 'ideas' can be distinguished: (1) economic thought, which consists largely but not exclusively of economic theorizing and analysis; (2) ethical judgements about taxation, which are based on religious or philosophical considerations but also on specific historical assumptions; (3) administrative knowledge in the form of explicit knowledge, but also in form of experience and know-how. Our chronological focus is on the modern period since around 1750, as it was only from then on that we can speak of nation states and thus of transnational processes.[10]

This volume assembles case studies which trace the interactions between socio-economic challenges and transfers of ideas from a variety of perspectives. Throughout, we highlight the complexities of the transfer processes and conceptualize 'transfers of ideas' primarily as communicative acts and examples of mutual observation. We cannot cover all important developments. For example, our volume lacks essays on Latin America, the Middle East and Asia as well as on the socialist economies of Eastern Europe in the second half of the twentieth century. Many Western and southern European countries have been left out as well. Our volume falls into three sections.

In Part I, the contributors trace the transfer of ideas about taxation in the period from the mid-eighteenth century to the early nineteenth century which, according to Reinhart Koselleck's famous concept of the *Sattelzeit* ('saddle time', literally translated), linked the early modern to the modern period and during which challenges to public finances were primarily derived from warfare.[11] Christine Lebeau examines the circulation of the concept of 'cadastre' between France, the Habsburg Empire, and the duchies and kingdom of northern Italy. Florian Schui assesses the transfer of a whole tax administration from France to Prussia: the so-called *Régie*. And Alexander Grab examines how Napoleon sought to create – and ultimately lost – political legitimacy by using occupied Italy as a tax farm to pay for his European campaigns.

Part II focuses on the challenges and constraints of transfers of ideas between and within federal polities challenged by the double demands of welfare and warfare. Making use of analytical insights from comparative law and legal transfers, Andreas Thier analyses the ways in which ideas about taxation circulated within German Empire from its creation in 1871 to the First World War. Holger Nehring assesses the importance of ideas about taxation from the German Historical School of economists to the American Progressive Movement around 1900 and highlights remarkable similarities in the concepts between German and American Progressive concepts of statehood and the economy. Frances Lynch emphasizes the links between transfers of ideas and the resilience of the nation state in the emerging federal European Union despite tax competition in her detailed assessment of the debates about value added tax in 1950s and 1960s Western Europe and the persistence divergence of Western European tax regimes since then.[12]

Part III presents case studies which assess the ways in which ideas about taxation travelled on a global scale. In particular, they emphasize the importance of considerations of power, race and economic dogma in transfers of ideas within empires and through international institutions. Martin Daunton shows how ideas about taxation which travelled within the British Empire connected to ideas about social and political order and thus often failed to create the political legitimacy in the colonies which they had helped found domestically. Elliott Brownlee presents an in-depth account of the fraught nature of American attempts to install a new tax system in post-Second World War Japan, as ideas about taxation became arguments in election campaigns and as administrative cultures clashed. Miranda Stewart highlights the highly problematic nature of the transfer of tax concepts through the International Monetary Fund (IMF) during the 1980s which served primarily as an instrument for American hegemony and was closely linked to a set of 'neo-liberal' economic ideas. Joseph Thorndike provides us with an analysis of the recent renaissance of ideas about a 'flat tax' in the early twenty-first century, highlighting the interactions between the transfer of ideas,

American power in global economic discourses and the frames of economic dogma.

We do not intend to offer our advice to policy-makers. Indeed, the argument which unites the contributions to this volume is how cumbersome transfer processes were, and how dependent on conditions which lay beyond the policy-makers' control, be they economic, bureaucratic or strictly political. We show how ideas about taxation were linked to perceptions of the economic situation, to administrative cultures and conventions as well as to concepts of a good and stable economic, social and political order, of equity and social justice, and of political legitimacy. Due to the growing complexities of political processes in the emerging modern and highly differentiated societies, the relatively straightforward application of concepts from elsewhere, as they could still be seen in eighteenth-century France and Prussia and in parts of the British Empire during the nineteenth century, became increasingly unlikely. If it did take place, as in the IMF's imposition of a specific type of tax regime in the developing world during the 1980s, it was accompanied by major domestic political upheaval. Our volume seeks to contribute significantly to research on state finance and state-building. We argue that the strength and resilience of the nation state in the modern world are, to a large extent, due to its adaptability to novel political, economic and social conditions. The engagement by governmental policy-makers and society at large with models of public finance from elsewhere played a crucial role in this process: it was by drawing on examples of successes and failures in other countries that populations and governments sought to reassure themselves and bolster their position. Often, models of state finance from elsewhere played a central role in endowing governmental proposals for reform with legitimacy which would otherwise have been lacking.[13] Building on previous research, we intend to make three contributions to historical research. The following sections of this introduction provide an overview of how our volume contributes to the broader research on transnational history, fiscal history and state-building as well as political legitimacy.

Transnational and national fiscal history: the paradoxes of state-building

The first contribution of our volume lies in the way in which we conceptualize the transfer of ideas about taxation. Taken together, the essays assembled in this volume introduce transnational history to one of the historical topics – the study of statehood – which has been most resilient to this historical approach. The reason for this resilience is obvious: while studies of statehood have been concerned with the very history of the ways in which bureaucracies, governments and the state structures they formed became clearly identifiable political, social and economic actors, the very concern of transnational history has been to undermine the understanding of states and nations as 'containers' closed to interaction with the outside world.[14] Tax historians argue that fiscal administrations in particular played an important part in the process of defining the limits of the state externally against other states and internally against other social and political spheres. Externally, the geographic boundaries of the 'new, hard-edged nation states' of the modern world were in large part defined by the control that fiscal administrations exercised over territory and borders.[15]

Yet the opposition between transnational and national history has an artificial flair about it, which impedes historical understanding. There is a risk of applying transnational approaches regardless of period and topic and to forget that the term 'transnational' itself has strong value-laden roots in nineteenth-century progressive thinking.[16] Too often, transnational historians seem to forget that understanding '*trans*national' has to come with the understanding of the national processes they transcend.

Historians have, therefore, applied transnational approaches unthinkingly to time periods where the gains of such an approach seem to be minimal. A recent book on the German Empire, for example, assembles an array of wide-ranging and highly stimulating essays. But the editors and authors remain conspicuously silent about the importance of these findings for our general understanding of this period which was characterized by the significant bolstering of nation states and found its culmination in the First World War. Similarly, C. A. Bayly's highly stimulating volume, *The Birth of the Modern World*, is rather unhistorical in its selection of examples and perception of the literature.[17] But for all the parallels and links which Bayly's study uncovers, the really interesting issue to explore is not the characteristic of this age as global, or transnational. It is how, in such a global and interconnected world, national bureaucracies and the state began to play such a key role and interacted with transnational developments.[18]

Our approach is pragmatic and seeks to make sense of this paradox. We are interested as much in understanding the success of the transfer of ideas as in specific failures. Thus, we intend to historicize what 'transnational' meant for each of the cases, in each of the concrete historical and economic situations we examined. Exchanges involving ideas, experiences, tax experts and taxpayers from different nations were important for the historical development of the tax state. But their impact is far more complex than most transnational historians would have us believe. They were deeply embedded in complex processes of appropriation and rejection which permitted exchanges between academics and public officials and make economic theories and their implications for tax policy available to a wider public.[19]

The term 'transfer' is, like its twin brother 'diffusion', rather problematic. It suggests an almost automatic and mechanical process in which distinct packages of ideas are passed around.[20] As the essays assembled in this volume show, the fact that such packages existed was itself part of fiscal discussions, and the construction of such packages as related to specific nations was itself highly arbitrary. There was a great variety of engagement and encounter with ideas from elsewhere: rejection, appropriation, affirmation, revision and reinvigoration.[21] And most of this took the form of second-order observation.

Despite these problems, we decided to adhere to the well-known terminology for lack of a better term. We identified three kinds of 'transfer': observation, direct communication and assimilation. Observation may take place through the reading of publications, of public and of secret documents, or through direct encounters. The gentlemanly grand tour of the early modern period and the fact-finding missions of the nineteenth, twentieth and twenty-first centuries are examples of transfers through observation.

Direct communication entails a conscious bilateral process in which opinions, theories and experiences are verbalized and exchanged. This process might take place through epistolary exchanges or direct discussion. Expert missions which contain important elements of observation will most often also include direct communication about fiscal matters. Finally, assimilation is the form of transfer that is most difficult to capture. In particular, where administrators and experts from different contexts work together, many transfers of ideas and experiences take place tacitly, without being verbalized or leaving many traces for the historian. All three types of transfer may occur at the same time and they will often be inseparably intertwined.

As it was our aim to historicize assumptions about transnational history, each of our authors came with very different assumptions about what 'transfer of ideas' meant – and we regard the importance of this variety as one of the main contributions of this volume. The chapters by Christine Lebeau on the cadastre system and Florian Schui on the import of French tax administrators to Prussia in the first section make use of an approach that can be characterized as connective history, which has gained important impulses from historians of cultural transfers in Germany and France and which seeks to explore connections that were part of historical reality.[22] Lebeau and Schui use this approach to overcome national limitations of fiscal history, to explore the flows of ideas and the institutional impact of transfers of ideas and to develop the comparative historiography of taxation further. They conclude that the concept of the 'tax state', which is central to many comparative works and the present volume, is itself a category that requires more critical scrutiny than it has received so far. The term 'tax state' suggests a degree of institutional homogeneity and uniformity in the historical development that was absent from historical reality. Lebeau's and Schui's essays explore the contemporary perceptions and languages associated with the complex historical processes that are often lumped together under the heading of the 'tax state'.

While Lebeau's and Schui's essays emphasize direct observation and adaptation, several other contributions stress the importance of mutual observation and communications through various forms. This self-referential character of more recent discussions becomes particularly clear in Joseph Thorndike's essay on the flat tax debate in the late 1990s and early 2000s, as well as in

Frances Lynch's chapter on tax convergence in the European Union. From around 1800, the expansion of bureaucratic practices across Europe made observing others much easier. Yet, at the same time, it made the adaptation of the observed models much more cumbersome and, often, impossible: the transfer of a complete tax administration from France to Prussia, a story told by Florian Schui, was associated with great difficulties in the eighteenth century and simply not feasible in later periods. This had to do with questions of political legitimacy: Alexander Grab's examination of the transfer of tax systems within the Napoleonic Empire significantly ends with the defenestration of the Napoleonic tax official. Likewise, Martin Daunton's chapter shows how cumbersome transfers of ideas about taxation were within the British Empire. And Miranda Stewart's account of the introduction of a value added tax in Ghana in the 1980s shows the enormous constraints and serious problems which policy-makers faced. An analysis of tax transfers in the post-colonial context shows, from a new angle, the problems which the imposition of European models of statehood caused in the former colonies.[23]

But, as the chapters of Andreas Thier, Holger Nehring, Elliott Brownlee and Frances Lynch make clear, another constraint of transfer through adaptation lay in the resilience of bureaucratic norms and knowledge. This resilience made it almost impossible to think of adaptation, as the standards for counting and accounting, of calculating income and indeed the very assumptions behind statistics differed significantly.[24]

Redefining fiscal history and the paradoxes of state-building

Our second contribution relates to the implications of this transnational perspective for the predominant accounts of fiscal history and state-building. Our conceptualization of transnational history enables us to contribute to an examination of fiscal developments since the mid-eighteenth century which is more sophisticated than approaches which build on modernization–theoretical models and posit different phases of fiscal development. Our transnational approach sits uneasily with explanations that have identified several stages of the emergence of the modern tax state and have, following the nineteenth-century German political economist Adolph Wagner, identified this development with a 'law of increasing state expenditure'.[25] Unlike medievalists and early modernists, most modern historians have not given tax history the attention it deserves. They have left the field to economists, legal scholars and financial sociologists and have frequently been all too pleased to write history from the perspective of the rich nineteenth-century literature in this field. If modern historians have paid attention to the importance of the topic, they have addressed it from the perspective of state-building. These historians have tended to single out taxation as one of the crucial elements of modern statehood.[26]

They argue that one of the characteristics of the nation states which developed in the period from the mid-eighteenth century onwards was their claim to pursue goals that benefited the whole nation and not only a ruler or a dynasty. In order to achieve these goals, the revenue base of the state had to be broadened: the domains of the ruler became insufficient as sources of state revenue. The ability to tax became also one of the most important expressions of the power of nation states and a defining characteristic of the boundaries of national territories. Fiscal administrations were among the most important components of the 'administrative machinery' through which states asserted control over the nation's territory and population.[27]

Following the historicist assumptions of the nineteenth-century economist Joseph Schumpeter, these historians have diagnosed the rise and consolidation of the 'tax state'. According to Schumpeter's now classic definition, the 'tax state' is an organization of public finance in which the resources for the common tasks of a society are mainly raised by taxing the economic activity of the members of that society. Schumpeter developed the concept of the tax state in contrast to other forms of government finance in which governments engage directly in economic activity in order to generate revenue. Examples include the early modern practice of domains managed by the state and, in the twentieth century, socialist forms of economic organization.[28]

Richard Bonney and William Ormrod have tried to introduce some dynamic elements into this approach. They distinguish between earlier and later forms of the tax state and argue that the tax state was followed, historically, by what they call a 'fiscal state'. This fiscal state is, they argue, characterized by high levels of expenditure, particularly for the military and for welfare, by a comprehensive system of direct taxes, such as on income, as well as by an efficient system of public debts. Bonney and Ormrod claim that, in a process of self-sustained growth, such fiscal states had the tendency to grow further.[29]

Although these characteristics are of some use for defining tax states in the nineteenth and twentieth centuries, Bonney and Ormrod's model shares the problematic assumptions of all modernization–theoretical approaches.[30] It implies the construction of specific phases, characterized by clearly identifiable characteristics. Yet models such as this explain transformation by looking at the results, the transition to a new phase. And only very rarely have there been attempts to justify the notion that financial organizations are systems in themselves, within which various institutions, such as financial markets and investors, interact rather than exist side by side.[31] The emphasis which historians have placed on the emergence of the 'tax state' has, therefore, done little to illuminate what distinguished the form of statehood that emerged over the course of the sixteenth to the eighteenth centuries from that of the nineteenth, twentieth and early twenty-first centuries. Moreover, the question of historical change since around 1800 has been mostly absent from historical accounts. Hence, the 'tax state' has tended to become an ahistorical concept, devoid of any contextualization.[32] Comparative approaches have only reinforced thinking in terms of historical models.[33]

Examining processes of change in more detail, without assuming transitions from one phase to the next, appears to us to be the more rewarding option for historians. And within these processes of change, transfers of ideas played a central role. But ideas cannot have an impact by themselves. They need to find resonance within specific political, social and economic systems. In particular, they have to find resonance within policy-making institutions.[34] Different forms of fiscal ideas were associated with different groups of individuals who participated in the evolution of fiscal systems: taxpayers, fiscal experts, administrators and politicians are some of the most important actors in the transfer of fiscal ideas.

Such ideas also had to be perceived as related to the 'hard facts' of economic and political life. Broader religious, philosophical, economic and political debates are inseparable from controversies about taxation. Equally, the imperatives of economic reality and interests cannot be neatly separated from the impact of fiscal ideas. 'What prevails in real life', John Kenneth Galbraith writes about economic and political decision making, 'is not the reality but the current fashion and the pecuniary interest.'[35] It is precisely the interaction between 'the current fashion' of fiscal ideas and 'the pecuniary interest' associated with economic considerations that needs to be explored if the impact of ideas on fiscal history is to be fully understood. Fiscal ideas, just like economic development, transcended national borders.

Transfers of ideas about taxation have rarely resulted in direct implementation. If a tax system or a tax model was indeed transferred, it was frequently distorted and the adaptation did not resemble the original model. Like earlier fiscal sociologists, we found that public finances and taxation have been a central area in which economy, society, politics and culture met. Global debates about taxation reveal political and economic as well as social and cultural changes.[36] They frequently destabilized political systems and stimulated or retarded economic systems. They were connected to specific and clearly identifiable political decisions in which certain models were chosen and others rejected. They were, most importantly, linked to economic challenges. Frequently, wars and the financial resources they required provoked governments to look for models of state finance.[37]

These observations on the development of 'tax states' also imply a more complex conception of statehood, which historians of taxation in the nineteenth and twentieth centuries have been quite slow to adopt. The assumption which underpins the contributions to this volume is that the tax state should be unpacked. We intend to counter a tendency in some historical and sociological research on statehood to regard 'states' as reified entities.[38] States are neither natural organisms nor metaphysical beings. They are intellectual concepts which have come about in processes of political power and human action. 'States' only exist as notional units on paper and as historical abstractions: no one has ever seen 'the state'. We can only glimpse at its bureaucracies as symbols of state power, and we know its sovereignty as a claim to authority of those wielding political power.[39] The historian's task is to unveil the dynamic in the development of these processes and the historical flavour of the controversies that surrounded it. Hence, we argue that we cannot understand the emergence of modern forms of state- and nationhood in their entirety if we do not take account of the ways in which governments and bureaucracies have engaged with the ideas and models produced and implemented by other governments and bureaucracies. Paradoxically, however, this engagement with others often led to the strengthening of governments and bureaucracies at home.[40] It is this paradox, we argue, that defines the characteristic of modern statehood in the realms of taxation and public finance. The essays assembled in this volume examine the parameters which influenced these processes. They show that the process of emergence and consolidation of 'tax states' as notional units was itself highly dynamic and contested, and it was here that transfers of ideas about taxation played a key role.

The main reason for the paradoxical character of this development is that, historically, debates about fiscal reform have often developed simultaneously in several countries or in regions on either side of a border as responses to the same international economic situation. Yet, as Niall Ferguson as shown, this 'cash nexus' was never deterministic, but was mediated by many other factors.[41] Processes of mutual observation were often related to wars which involved more than one nation. Since policy-makers perceived the ability to raise revenue as decisive for the outcome of wars, fiscal competition has often been part and parcel of warfare. The imitation of fiscal practices of opponents and allies alike constituted an important part of institutional innovation in periods of warfare. Like wars, other 'national emergencies' such as natural disasters and fundamental economic transformations do not stop at national borders. All this means that the picture which emerges from our accounts is a highly ambiguous one in which the resilience and strength of governments, bureaucracies and nations are coupled with a surprising permeability of national borders for models and ideas. The transfer of ideas about taxation across and within national borders has, therefore, today become more complicated than ever.

Transfers of ideas about taxation and political legitimacy

The contributions to this volume show that transfers of ideas about taxation cannot be divorced from questions of political legitimacy. This is the third contribution of our volume. It has mostly been in battles for political legitimacy at home that governments have looked abroad for expertise and know-how. And often, the mutual observation which emerged from these processes was used as arguments in battles for political legitimacy, even when no concrete matters had, in fact, been transferred. This made transfers of ideas about taxation such a cumbersome and unpredictable affair. As Michael Braddick, Martin Daunton, Niall Ferguson and Hans-Peter Ullmann have shown, the quest for political legitimacy played a crucial role in shaping fiscal developments.

Taxation was intimately connected with the nature of the political systems of European states. This connection was not predetermined, but the result of complicated political negotiations.[42] Economic theories of legitimacy with regard to taxation are, therefore, insufficient explanations of fiscal developments. They either assume that politicians wish to maximize tax revenues and spend more, and that voters and taxpayers wish to minimize their payments and spend less (the approach of the Virginia School of public economics), or that individual taxpayers make rational choices when deciding whether or not to pay taxes.[43] But as the chapters in this volume show, what was decisive was how political actors perceived political legitimacy, and that was often not directly related to hard economic facts and state policies.[44]

This process itself has been conditioned by the growth of the modern bureaucratic and fiscal state and the ideas which underpinned it. Until around 1800, bureaucratic practices and concerns for legitimacy still allowed for processes of direct adaptation. Yet, from the 1800s onwards, the questions of political legitimacy, established bureaucratic practices and norms, as well as, not least, economic and financial conditions worked against the direct transfer of ideas as distinct units. From the mid-nineteenth century to the present, the transfer of ideas about taxation drove developments more by way of being used as a political argument in discussions rather than through the direct transfer of personnel or administrative techniques.

Thus, the transfer of ideas about taxation became intimately linked to processes of social and political self-observation which have characterized modern societies. The explanations about the development of fiscal systems which economists and legal scholars have produced since the mid-nineteenth century have been part of this process.[45] Likewise, the production of statistics about revenues and expenditure, classified according to different social and economic criteria, has served to reify the much murkier and much more fluid economic, political and social realities.[46] From the mid-nineteenth century, as nationhood and statehood became intertwined, national characteristics were introduced to these transnational debates about taxation.[47] As Julia Moses has shown, specific social welfare developments as well as fiscal and tax systems were now endowed with national characteristics which served as arguments in political discussions. They gradually condensed into national 'models' which served as arguments in fiscal–political discussions since at least the 1850s.[48] The idea of a 'model' implies a modernization–theoretical view of history. The assumption is that progress towards a specific end can be achieved if certain measures are implemented.[49] Frequently, such arguments were deeply embedded in political and economic competition between nation states.[50] Indeed, mutual observation became part of the competition between nation states, and the thinking in terms of national models served to illustrate national superiority or an inferiority which had to be overcome. Thus, descriptions of the other became crucial features of national identity, and increased mutual observations only made this possible.[51]

Foreign models could be used to bolster the case for development, or to represent it as a threat. Governments and policy-makers have looked abroad for models and advice at times when they could not find support at home for their ideas. The classic case for this is the Prussian *Régie* in the mid-eighteenth century, which was still very much in continuity with medieval and early modern forms of tax transfers.[52] In colonial and post-colonial settings, by contrast, the transfer of ideas without adequate political legitimacy, such as the transfer of value added tax (VAT) to South Korea and Ghana in the 1970s and 1980s respectively, has often had disastrous results, for the financial situation of the governments concerned, for their political legitimacy and, thus, for the political stability of these countries.

As Frances Lynch's essay shows, the nation state in Western Europe has still not been replaced as a 'decision space' and an 'identity space'.[53] In fact, the character of the debate has merely changed to another and much more complex form of mutual observation and communication. Lynch shows that current governments have moved from influencing economic matters directly to merely communicating about how best to influence markets. It was this communication which led to the engagement with ideas from other countries and to certain fashions with regard to tax regimes, such as the introduction of value added taxes in Western Europe since the 1960s. Expert knowledge increasingly figured in these developments. Experts came to play a crucial role in policy formation.[54] But experts no longer merely acted as providers of information and also came to act as resources for political legitimacy. Expert advice came to serve as a resource for political power that endowed specific decisions with the necessary legitimacy.[55] Arguments which made use of foreign models hid, however, that the motives for engendering change were home-grown and crucially linked to specific economic and social interests as well as political ideologies and parties.

As Martin Daunton demonstrates, an exception to this trend was the British Empire, which imposed its own ideas about tax regimes onto the colonies, albeit often with disastrous results for its political legitimacy.[56] It is significant that, as Elliott Brownlee shows in his essay on the US's Shoup mission to Japan after the Second World War, the success of the American Empire in generating legitimacy for its goals was not crowned by success and resulted in a political debate about the merits of the 'Americanization' of the Japanese economy.

Conclusions

Our volume seeks to provoke questions and debates more than to give rough-and-ready answers. Can we learn from these stories? They send a call of caution to policy-makers within the IMF, the World Bank and within national governments. Only an understanding of the intricate mechanics of bureaucracies, economies, societies and political systems as a whole makes it possible to introduce new tax regimes. Policy-makers, economists, fiscal sociologists and, not least, historians should open the black box of the state and pay more attention to the 'little tools of knowledge'[57] as a source of political and economic power as well as legitimacy when looking for lessons from the past and from other countries.

Notes

1 Alan Greenspan, 'Testimony before the President's Advisory Panel on Federal Tax Reform', Washington, DC, 3 March 2005 http://www.federalreserve.gov/BOARDDOCS/TESTIMONY/2005/20050303/default.htm (accessed 1 Sept. 2006).

2 Cf., for example, 'A taxing solution', *The Sunday Times*, 21 August 2005, p. 13; W. Elliot Brownlee, *Federal taxation in America* (Cambridge, 1996), p. 183.

3 Cf., for example, Christian Seidl, 'The tax state in crisis', in idem (ed.), *Lectures on Schumpetrian economics* (Berlin, 1984), pp. 89–109; Paul Kirchhof, *Der sanfte Verlust der Freiheit* (Munich, 2004), p. 1.

4 Cf. as one example among many with references to further literature: Daniel W. Drezner, 'Globalization and policy convergence', *International Studies Review*, 3 (2001), pp. 53–78. On the general issue: T. V. Paul, G. John Ikenberry and John A. Hall (eds), *The nation-state in question* (Princeton, 2005).

5 For a first and very stimulating analysis of the various factors cf. F. Neumark, 'Internationale Gemeinsamkeiten und nationale Eigenarten der Finanzpolitik', *Kyklos*, 2 (1948), pp. 317–48.

6 Cf. Jürgen Kocka, 'Comparison and beyond', *History and Theory*, 42 (2003), pp. 39–44; Jürgen Osterhammel, 'Transnationale Gesellschaftsgeschichte: Erweiterung oder Alternative?', *Geschichte und Gesellschaft*, 27 (2001), pp. 464–79; Johannes Paulmann, 'Internationaler Vergleich und interkultureller Transfer', *Historische Zeitschrift*, 267 (1998), pp. 650–85 and the special issue on 'political transfers' of the *European Review of History*, 12, no. 2 (2005). For a rare contribution to the political and economic aspects of transnational history cf. Patricia Clavin, 'Introduction: defining transnationalism', *Contemporary European History*, 14 (2005), pp. 421–39.

7 Pierre-Cyrille Hautcoeur, 'Cash or account? A plea for a comparative history of European financial systems', *Contemporary European History*, 12 (2003), pp. 345–58, here p. 358.

8 Cf. on this Peter A. Hall, 'Policy paradigms, social learning and the state. The case of economic policymaking in Britain', *Comparative Politics*, 25 (1993), pp. 275–96; Michael J. Oliver and Hugh Pemberton, 'Learning and change in 20th-century British economic policy', *Governance*, 17 (2004), pp. 415–41 and Hugh Pemberton, *Policy learning and British governance in the 1960s* (London, 2004).

9 For a similar approach cf. Jim Tomlinson's work, in particular his 'The British "productivity problem" in the 1960s', *Past and Present*, 175 (2002), pp. 188–210 and his *The Labour governments 1964–70*, vol. 3: *Economic policy* (Manchester, 2004).

10 Cf. Wolfgang Reinhard, *Geschichte der Staatsgewalt. Eine vergleichende Verfassungsgeschichte Europas von den Anfängen bis zur Gegenwart* (Munich, 1999), p. 340; James C. Scott, *Seeing like a state: how certain schemes to improve the human condition have failed* (New Haven and London, 1998).

11 On this concept cf. Reinhart Koselleck, 'A response to comments on the *Geschichtliche Grundbegriffe*', in Hartmut Lehmann and Melvin Richter (eds), *The*

meaning of historical terms and concepts: new studies on Begriffsgeschichte (Washington, DC, 1996), p. 69 and idem, *Futures past: on the semantics of historical time* (Cambridge, Mass., 1985).

12 For historical examples of tax competition in Germany cf. Mark Spoerer, *Steuerlast, Steuerinzidenz und Steuerwettbewerb. Verteilungswirkungen der Besteuerung in Preußen und Württemberg* (Berlin, 2004).

13 On the more general point cf. Jim Tomlinson, 'Managing the economy, managing the people: Britain c. 1931–70', *Economic History Review*, 58 (2005), pp. 555–85.

14 Cf. Peter Evans, Dietrich Rueschemeyer and Theda Skocpol (eds), *Bringing the state back in* (Cambridge, 1985).

15 Rudolf Braun, 'Taxation, socio-political structure and state building: Great Britain and Brandenburg-Prussia', in Charles Tilly (ed.), *The formation of national states in Western Europe* (Princeton, 1975), p. 301.

16 On these problems cf. Martin H. Geyer and Johannes Paulmann (eds), *The mechanics of internationalism* (Oxford, 2001). On the links to progressivism in ideas and historical practice, cf. Akira Iriye, 'The internationalization of history', *American Historical Review*, 94 (1989), pp. 1–10, especially pp. 9–10.

17 Sebastian Conrad and Jürgen Osterhammel (eds), *Das Kaiserreich transnational* (Göttingen, 2004); C. A. Bayly, *The birth of the modern world, 1780–1914* (Oxford, 2004); cf. also the project 'Exchanges of Economic and Political Ideas since 1760' at the Centre for History and Economics, Cambridge, http://www-histecon.kings.cam.ac.uk/research/hex/index.htm

18 Cf. Jürgen Osterhammel, *Die Entzauberung Asiens. Europa und die asiatischen Reiche im 18. Jahrhundert* (Munich, 1998).

19 Cf. Hugh Heclo, *Modern social politics in Britain and Sweden* (New Haven, Conn., 1974), pp. 304–22.

20 Cf. David Dolowitz and David Marsh, 'Learning from abroad: the role of policy transfer in contemporary policy-making', *Governance*, 13 (2000), pp. 5–23; for a critique, cf. Oliver James and Martin Lodge, 'The limitations of "policy transfer" and "lesson drawing" for public policy research', *Political Studies Review*, 1 (2003), pp. 179–93. Cf. also the special issue of the *Journal of Public Policy*, 11, no. 1 (1991).

21 Cf. the astute insights by Percy Ernst Schramm, 'Deutschlands Verhältnis zur englischen Kultur nach der Begründung des Neuen Reiches', in Walther Hubatsch (ed.), *Schicksalswege deutscher Vergangenheit: Beiträge zur geschichtlichen Deutung der letzten hundertfünfzig Jahre: Festschrift für Siegfried Kaehler* (Düsseldorf, 1950), pp. 289–319 and Rudolf Muhs, Johannes Paulmann and Willibald Steinmetz, 'Brücken über den Kanal? Interkultureller Transfer zwischen Deutschland und Großbritannien im 19. Jahrhundert', in idem (eds), *Aneigung und Abwehr: Interkultureller Transfer zwischen Deutschland und Großbritannien im 19. Jahrhundert* (Bodenheim, 1998), pp. 7–20.

22 Michel Espagne and Michael Werner, 'Deutsch-Französischer Kulturtransfer im 18. und 19. Jahrhundert', *Francia*, 13 (1985), pp. 502–10; Michael Werner and Bénédicte Zimmermann, 'Vergleich, Transfer, Verflechtung', *Geschichte und Gesellschaft*, 28 (2002), pp. 607–36. This may in part be due to the fact that academic exchange programmes, structures of research funding and the general political climate of the post-war period have encouraged cooperation of German and French historians. The merits and problems of comparative and transfer history have been discussed extensively. See for example: Hartmut Kaelble, 'Die Debatte über Vergleich und Transfer und was jetzt?', *Geschichte Transnational*,

8 February 2005, http://geschichte-transnational.clio-online.net/forum/type=artikel&id=574. Cf. for a different context William O'Reilly, 'Genealogies of Atlantic history', *Atlantic Studies*, 1 (2004), pp. 66–84, here p. 80.

23 Cf. Dagmar Engels and Shula Marks (eds), *Contesting colonial hegemony. State and society in Africa and India* (London, 1994); Robert H. Jackson, *Quasi-states: sovereignty, international relations and the Third World* (Cambridge, 1990).

24 Cf. Peter Becker, 'Überlegungen zu einer Kulturgeschichte der Verwaltung', *Jahrbuch für Europäische Verwaltungsgeschichte*, 15 (2003), pp. 311–36. Cf. also Bernhard S. Silberman, *Cages of reason. The rise of the rational state in France, Japan, the United States and Great Britain* (Chicago and London, 1993).

25 Reinhard, *Staatsgewalt*, p. 306.

26 Cf. Richard Bonney (ed.), *Economic systems and state finance* (Oxford, 1995); Martin Daunton, *Trusting Leviathan* (Cambridge, 2002), p. 2; John Brewer, *The sinews of power: war, money and the English state, 1688–1783* (London, 1989).

27 Reinhard, *Staatsgewalt*, p. 309.

28 Schumpeter, 'Die Krise des Steuerstaats', pp. 341–52.

29 Richard Bonney (ed.), *The rise of the fiscal state in Europe, c. 1200–1815* (Oxford, 1999); W. M. Ormrod, Margaret Bonney and Richard Bonney (eds), *Crises, revolutions and self-sustained growth* (Stamford, 1999); and the critique by Hans-Peter Ullmann, 'Überlegungen zur Transformation des Systems der öffentlichen Finanzen in Deutschland seit dem 18. Jahrhundert', *Jahrbuch für Wirtschaftsgeschichte*, 1997, no. 2, pp. 169–78.

30 Cf. especially Martin Daunton's chapter in this volume for a differentiation of this approach.

31 Cf. Franklin Allen and Douglas Gale, *Comparing financial systems* (Cambridge, Mass., 2000).

32 Cf. Kersten Krüger, 'Public finance and modernisation', in Peter-Christian Witt (ed.), *Wealth and taxation in central Europe* (Leamington Spa, 1987), pp. 49–62; Hans-Peter Ullmann, *Der deutsche Steuerstaat. Geschichte der öffentlichen Finanzen* (Munich, 2005), pp. 8–9.

33 Cf. for example, Orhan Kayaalp, *The national element in the development of fiscal theory* (London, 2004); Eckart Schremmer, 'Taxation and public finance: Britain, France, and Germany', in Peter Mathias and Sidney Pollard (eds), *The Cambridge economic history of Europe*, vol. 8 (Cambridge, 1989), pp. 315–494; Sven Steinmo, *Taxation and democracy: Swedish, British and American approaches to financing the modern state* (New Haven, 1993); Carolyn Webber and Aaron Wildavsky, *A history of taxation and expenditure in the western world* (New York, 1986).

34 Cf. Mary O. Furner and Barry Supple, 'Ideas, institutions, and state in the United States and Britain: an introduction', in idem (eds), *The state and economic knowledge. The American and British experiences* (Cambridge, 1990), pp. 3–39.

35 John Kenneth Galbraith, *The economics of innocent fraud* (London, 2004), p. 5.

36 Cf. Gustav Schmoller, 'Historische Betrachtungen über Staatenbildung und Finanzentwicklung', *Schmollers Jahrbuch*, 33 (1909), pp. 1–64; Werner Plumpe, 'Gustav von Schmoller und der Institutionalismus', *Geschichte und Gesellschaft*, 25 (1999), pp. 252–75; John L. Campbell, 'The state of fiscal sociology', *Annual Review of Sociology*, 19 (1993), pp. 163–85.

37 Cf. Alan Milward, *The European rescue of the nation-state* (London, 1992); William Wallace, 'Rescue or retreat? The nation state in Western Europe, 1945–1993', *Political Studies*, 42 (1994), pp. 57–76.

38 For critiques cf. Timothy Mitchell, 'The limits of the state: beyond statist approaches and their critics', *American Political Science Quarterly*, 85 (1991), pp. 77–96; and idem,

'Society, economy, and the state effect', in George Steinmetz (ed.), *State/culture: state formation after the cultural turn* (Ithaca, NY, 1999), pp. 76–97; Andreas Osiander, 'Sovereignty, international relations, and the Westphalian myth', *International Organization*, 55 (2001), pp. 251–87.

39 Reinhard, *Staatsgewalt*, p. 18; Thomas J. Biersteker and Cynthia Weber (eds), *State sovereignty as social construct* (Cambridge, 1996); James J. Sheehan, 'The problem of sovereignty in European history', *American Historical Review*, 111 (2006), pp. 1–15.

40 Cf. Patrick Karl O'Brien, 'State formation and the construction of institutions for the first industrial nation', in Ha-Joon Chang (ed.), *A world of differences: institutional diversity and development* (Tokyo, 2006, forthcoming).

41 Niall Ferguson, *The cash nexus. Money and power in the modern world 1700–2000* (Harmondsworth, 2002), p. 14.

42 Michael J. Braddick, *The nerves of state: taxation and the financing of the English state, 1558–1714* (Manchester, 1996), pp. 180–201; Daunton, *Trusting Leviathan*, p. 5; Ferguson, *Cash nexus*, pp. 81–106; Ullmann, *Steuerstaat*, pp. 10–11; Matthew Vester, 'The political autonomy of a tax farm: the Nice-Piedmont gabelle of the Dukes of Savoy, 1535–1580', *Journal of Modern History*, 76 (2004), pp. 745–92.

43 Cf. Daunton, *Trusting Leviathan*, pp. 8–9 and James M. Buchanan and Gordon Tullock, *The calculus of consent: logical foundations of constitutional democracy* (Ann Arbor, 1962); Geoffrey Brennan and Loren Lomasky, *Democracy and decision: the pure theory of electoral preference* (Cambridge, 1993). For a critique cf. Ferguson, *Cash nexus*, pp. 224–42.

44 For a theoretical approach cf. Kenneth G. Binmore, *Game theory and the social contract: playing fair* (Cambridge, Mass., and London, 1994) and Margaret Levi, 'The state of trust', in Valerie Braithwaite and idem (eds), *Trust and governance* (New York, 1998), pp. 77–101; Robert D. Putnam, *Making social democracy work. Civic traditions in modern Italy* (Princeton, 1993); idem, *Bowling alone. The collapse and revival of American community* (New York, 2000) and the sophisticated critique by Simon Szreter, 'The state of social capital: bringing back in power, politics, and history', *Theory and Society*, 31 (2002), pp. 573–621.

45 Cf. Erik Grimmer-Solem, *The rise of historical economics and social reform in Germany 1864–1894* (Oxford, 2003).

46 Cf. Silvana Patriarca, *Numbers and nationhood. Writing statistics in nineteenth-century Italy* (Cambridge, 1996); J. Adam Tooze, *Statistics and the German state, 1900–1945. The making of modern economic knowledge* (Cambridge, 2001), idem, 'Imagining national economies: national and international economic statistics, 1900–1950', in Geoffrey Cubitt (ed.), *Imagining nations* (Manchester and New York, 1998), pp. 212–28; Lawrence Goldman, *Science, reform, and politics in Victorian Britain: the Social Science Association, 1857–1886* (Cambridge, 2002).

47 Cf. on the general issues John Breuilly, *Nationalism and the state* (Manchester, 2nd edn, 1993); Istvan Hont, 'Permanent crisis for a divided mankind: "Contemporary crisis of the nation" in historical perspective', *Political Studies*, 42 (1994), pp. 166–231.

48 Cf. J. M. Moses, '"Foreign" models, welfare politics, and the nexus of modernity in Imperial Germany' (forthcoming); Silvana Patriarca, 'Indolence and regeneration: tropes and tensions of Risorgimento patriotism', *American Historical Review*, 110 (2005), pp. 380–408.

49 For more recent examples, cf. David C. Engerman et al. (eds), *Staging growth: modernization, development, and the global Cold War* (Boston, 2003).

50 On tax competition *within* the German Empire in the nineteenth century, cf. Mark Spoerer, 'Wann begann der Fiskal- und Steuerwettbewerb? Eine Spurensuche

in Preußen, anderen deutschen Staaten und der Schweiz', *Jahrbuch für Wirtschaftsgeschichte*, 2 (2002), pp. 35–59.

51 Cf. J. M. Moses, 'German national identity and the international development of social welfare, 1880–1916' (unpublished M. Phil. thesis, University of Oxford, 2004); Mark Hewitson, *National identity and political thought in Germany: Wilhelmine depictions of the French Third Republic, 1898–1914* (Oxford, 2000); Harold James, *A German identity, 1770 to the present day* (London, 1989).

52 Ferguson, *Cash nexus*, p. 57; Christopher Dyer, *An age of transition? Economy and society in England in the later Middle Ages* (Oxford, 2005), pp. 111–13.*****

53 Cf. Charles S. Maier, 'Consigning the twentieth century to history: alternative narratives for the modern era', *American Historical Review*, 105 (2000), pp. 807–31.

54 Cf. Michael J. Lacey and Mary O. Furner, 'Social investigation, social knowledge, and the state: an introduction', in idem (eds), *The state and social investigation in Britain and the United States* (Cambridge, 1993), pp. 3–62; Lutz Raphael, 'Die Verwissenschaftlichung des Sozialen als methodische und konzeptionelle Herausforderung für eine Sozialgeschichte des 20. Jahrhunderts', *Geschichte und Gesellschaft*, 22 (1996), pp. 165–93; Margit Szöllösi-Janze, 'Wissensgesellschaft in Deutschland. Überlegungen zur Neubestimmung der deutschen Zeitgeschichte über Verwissenschaftlichungsprozesse', *Geschichte und Gesellschaft*, 30 (2004), pp. 277–313; Lawrence Goldman, 'Experts, investigators, and the state in 1860: British social scientists through American eyes', in Lacey and Furner (eds), *The state and social investigation*, pp. 95–126; for a more recent period, Alexander Nützenadel, *Stunde der Ökonomen. Wissenschaft, Politik und Expertenkultur in der Bundesrepublik 1949–74* (Göttingen, 2005).

55 Cf. Stephen Hilgartner, *Science on stage. Expert advice as public drama* (Stanford, 2000).

56 On the importance of information gathering in the British Empire, cf. C. A. Bayly, *Empire and information. intelligence gathering and social communication in India, 1780–1870* (Cambridge, 2000).

57 Peter Becker and William Clark (eds), *Little tools of knowledge. Historical essays on academic and bureaucratic practices* (Ann Arbor, 2001).

Part I
Challenges of War and Occupation

2

Regional Exchanges and Patterns of Taxation in Eighteenth-Century Europe: the Case of the Italian Cadastres

Christine Lebeau

In the first half of the nineteenth century, a large number of European states (France, Austria and the greater part of the German Confederation – England being a notable exception) carried out geometric land surveys in order to establish a land tax. Indeed, the first International Congress of Statistics (1853) passed a resolution in favour of establishing cadastral surveys and valuations based on land maps. The creation of such cadastral surveys as a basis for the introduction of industrial and land taxes can be examined in terms of national history alone, but it can also help us trace the protracted history of administrative transfers which accelerated after 1750 in connection with major fiscal reforms.[1] Antonella Alimento and Jean Nicolas have noted the occurrence of 'a number of similar decisions taken across Europe and underwritten by the same financial, administrative, centre-driven and modernizing forces'.[2] Financial burdens on European states first began to increase with the War of Spanish Succession (1705–14), which the traditional source of state revenue, the domain (*regalia*), alone could no longer sustain. The political crisis was exacerbated by the installation of new dynasties which upset the traditional use of the domains and encroached upon church properties. Taken together, these factors explain some of the similarities of the decisions. But they do not address the questions of, first, how the agents of public finance came to implement detailed surveys of land rather than levy excise duties; second, by what means and through which conduits individual exchanges gave way to the circulation of ideas and objects; and, third, more generally, how public practices became objects of scientific inquiry.[3]

This chapter aims to explain how an Italian practice, closely linked to the war situation, came to be improved and then adopted as an administrative model after 1750. This chapter will show how it spread first from place to place, and how, through a complex web of diplomatic ties and literary exchanges, it later succeeded in becoming common practice and public knowledge, abandoning the barrier of secrecy which had protected cadastral debates in earlier decades. Thus, through processes beyond state borders, geometric and cadastral surveys came to be used as political instruments by the administrators against the opinions of economists.

From the Kingdom of Piedmont to the Milan region: exchange by degrees

The idea of raising revenue from holdings rather than people goes back a long way. If one takes the example of Piedmont, one of the more important territories in the politically fragmented north of Italy, two edicts (issued on 27 March 1584 and on 1 May 1600 respectively) recommended establishing a register of land and landholders. Despite the vigilance of the Auditor's Office and the development of an audit book by the chief auditor Capré, the first Piedmont cadastral offered but a poor reflection of reality since it came without a detailed map. These Italian or Franco-Italian practices, which the intendant Bouchu tried to implement in Dauphiné, explain the renewed interest in land surveying in Italy and France at the end of the seventeenth century.[4]

Contiguity appears to be the reason for the Milanese decision of 1718.[5] In 1709, the Count de Pras, of Piedmont origin, approached Eugène, the Austrian governor of the state of Milan, with a proposal for a levy. In fact, it was no more than a plagiarized version of Marshal Vauban's *Résumé de la Dîme royale* ('A project for a royal tythe').[6] The marshal, a member of the French Academy of Sciences since 1699, had helped fortify the Savoy border on the French side and had established direct contact with the Turin court.[7] In spite of the clandestine nature of the book, which was in fact hostile to the undertaking of a land survey because of its prohibitive cost and its ephemeral nature, the *Dîme royale* was received with shock in 1707, and the book's infamous reputation grew further after the death of its author.[8] The communities of Parma ultimately exposed the Count de Pras' unacknowledged borrowing of Vauban's text. As Pras' brothers served as French diplomatic intermediaries in Turin, they described it as a French plot to raise tax.[9] Thus, while the plagiarized text initially provoked debate, it later brought about reform, the very aim assigned to the *Dîme royale* by its author. The communities in the state of Milan vented their discontent and agreed to have a commission set up by the end of 1718 in order to update the cadastre, which dated back to Charles V, rather than to implement a new tax.

The Milanese type of cadastre also played a considerable role in the subsequent land surveys in Piedmont. Between 1699 and 1711, the Piedmontese administration verified the size and calculated the value of land as well as of the taxable revenue in the Duchy of Nice and the Piedmont provinces of Cuneo and Mondovi without drawing land maps, setting aside the seigniorial and ecclesiastical rights. The cadastral land surveys in Piedmont resumed after two edicts in 1728 and 1731 only to be interrupted again by the war. As a consequence, an edict dated 5 May 1731, stipulated that a register be kept in Turin and Chambéry, listing and describing all the parcels of land according to their size and the types of crops they produced, as well as the name of their holders. The edict also stipulated that a map in the form of a detailed geometric survey had to be included. Contemporaries denounced the impenetrable secrecy surrounding the valuations.[10] As the people distrusted the new tax, they faked names, withheld information on joint ownership, or absented themselves as a means of evasion. The survey also failed to take into account the land valuations, altitude variations, the aspect of the land, the types of crops and the access to roads and markets. The Piedmont land cadastre was characterized by its empirical nature, but also by its dithering methods and the various amendments which allowed big differences to appear between the practices in Piedmont itself, where valuations applied to the members of the communities rather than the land. This had been the practice in both Savoy, where a comprehensive but flawed land survey had taken place, and the newly annexed provinces of 1738, where the valuations had been done according to the Milanese method.

The Piedmont map had been drawn by a team of land surveyors and mathematicians brought together by a commission from Milan.[11] The technical know-how was first developed in the Italian domain. The Milanese land surveyors met in Perugia for the first time. Here, Andrea Chiesa oversaw the detailed land survey. They also met in Bologna, where Giovanni Cantoni, Boncompagni's main collaborator, developed the Milanese type of cadastre. Lastly, they met in France, when land experts arrived who had been engaged in the Milanese and Piedmont general cadastral surveys. The Milanese type of cadastre thus came to play a considerable role in the subsequent land surveys in Piedmont and in cadastral surveys more generally.[12]

Two factors deserve consideration here: first, the composite nature of the state in the modern age which encouraged an administrative culture to develop and which facilitated the movements of state administrators at a time when the science of finance per se was not codified; second, the importance of contiguity, which Marc Bloch mentioned as a factor worthy of investigation.[13] Indeed, Savoy, attached to the Kingdom of Piedmont, was next to the Dauphiné, while the Milan region under Austrian rule lay next to the Kingdom of Piedmont. In spite of shaky political relations, ideas and techniques moved gradually within a restricted area which can here be identified as Italianate.

At the beginning of the eighteenth century, the implementation of cadastres as fiscal instruments was not feasible in either Vienna or Paris. Charles VI and later Maria-Theresa ordered a review of their existing land registers, but these reviews entailed no more than an updating of the existing lists. The French administrators were weary of the idea of a cadastre and favoured a *taille tarifée* ('indexed land tax') instead. The different forms of *taille* were the most important direct taxes in France. The *taille tarifée* was a reform project which aimed at a more equal distribution of the tax burden through changes in the assessment of the different types of income and through a limitation of fiscal privileges.[14] Other factors intervened before the idea of using the land survey as a tool spread beyond the Italian domain.

Political economy and taxation policies

From the mid-eighteenth century onwards, books on economic topics came to play a larger role in the training and thinking of those who initiated administrative transactions. Henry d'Ormesson, the organizer of the French mission to Piedmont and Sardinia, still only relied on Velly's *Histoire de France* for his financial information.[15] However, Trudaine de Montigny, the co-organizer of the 1763 mission, owned a very large collection of books on political economy. The same was true of Ludwig von Zinzendorf, the president of the Auditor's Office in Vienna, who dispatched his brother Karl to Italy in order to look up the Milanese cadastre. How did political economy contribute to the theory of taxation since Vauban?[16] What views did it express on the question of a land cadastre?

Justi, a professor of cameralistic sciences (political economy) at the Theresianum in Vienna, was the first to propose a comprehensive financial-science manual which was used by Karl von Zinzendorf when he was a member of the Trade Council of Lower Austria before he left for Italy.[17] The volume gave no specific examples. Its purpose was to analyse the nature of taxation. Such an analysis, it claimed, could no longer be limited to the domain and had therefore to be extended to the subjects of the state. In the rural states that mostly made up Germany, such a tax was, necessarily, to be based on land, a certain source of revenue. Moreover, according to Justi, only a cadastre could allow fiscal equity.[18]

The cadastre Justi imagined had the following characteristics. Along with the *Fund- und Lagerbücher* (registers of landholders), the register was to include a comprehensive survey of the parcels of land, executed by surveyors under the authority of the prince, as well as an indication of the number of houses.[19] These findings were to be reviewed every eight or ten years by a special commission, while a new cadastral survey of land would have to be undertaken every 40 years.[20] The aim was to classify the estate into three categories: mediocre, average and good, taking into account their situation, particularly with regard to a princely home. The purpose of this exercise was to determine whether the contribution should be a quarter, a fifth or a sixth of the net land product.[21] In a publication which came out in 1762, Justi took Vauban to task: not only did the *Dîme royale* not guarantee fiscal equity in his eyes, but, above all, its perceived complexity seemed to him to be an insuperable obstacle.[22] Such positions remained isolated, however, even in Vienna where banking solutions were put into place to finance the Seven Years War, and even more so in France where other ways of thinking prevailed.[23]

In Italy, Carlo Antonio Broggia, in his *Trattato dei Tributi* ('Treatise about duties') published in Naples in 1743, remained sceptical about the accuracy of the former Italian registers.[24] Gian Francesco Pagnini, on the other hand, in his *Della Decima* ('Of the tythe'), published in 1765, claimed to be favourable towards a general cadastre, but argued for one based on the declarations of the landholders in order to avoid the cost of surveying.[25] Pagnini's attention had been drawn to the transactions conducted by the Marquis d'Enseñada, most probably by Gerónimo de Ustáriz, whose books were found in Italian libraries. He built his argument around references taken from Charles de Montesquieu's *Esprit des lois* ('Spirit of the laws'), David Hume's *Political Discourses* and Claude-Jacques Herbert's *Essai sur la police des grains* ('Essay about the order of the grain trade'). He never mentioned the Piedmontese or Milanese cadastres, or even the *Relazione* by Pompeo Neri, which describes the Milanese cadastre.[26] One must note, however, that the *Della Decima* represented an attempt at fiscal reform in Florence, as well as a hostile view on the cadastral survey.[27]

The question which arises from this Italian side of the story is whether the information about cadastres was any more developed in France. There, the topic was debated in the 1750s in the double context of an aggravation of the financial crisis and the reform of the *vingtième* ('twentieth') imposed by the finance minister, Machault d'Arnouville.[28] Claude-Jacques Herbert favoured a general cadastre which, in his view, could serve as a basis for all administrative transactions. But this entailed no more than a list of land parcels put together according to the landholders' declarations, after the model of the English land tax.[29]

François Veron de Forbonnais in his *Considérations sur les finances d'Espagne* ('Considerations on Spain's financial situation') analysed the causes of Spain's decline in terms of 'the principle' of its finances.[30] Relying on the information given by the Spanish economists (*arbitristas*), this was, in fact, his first manual on the science of finance, before his *Considérations sur les finances de la France* ('Considerations of the state of French finances').[31] While Forbonnais gave a description of the Spanish fiscal system, he was also somewhat critical of it. Indirect taxes, he thought, were inadequate because they were not proportionate to the taxpayers' incomes. Sharing the views of the English economist Charles Davenant, he stressed the considerable burden placed on the taxpayers by the consolidated debt and the increase of the internal excise duties, which led to exorbitant benefits for the French financiers over the taxpayers. Forbonnais went on to demonstrate that indirect taxes and land taxes were complementary: 'the proposal of a single tax will not be as favourable to the people as many seem to think'. He then discussed the 1749 declaration which had established a special commission with the purpose of devising a new land tax as well as pursuing investigations, declarations and verifications: over 20,000 people were employed and a million *piastres* spent per year.[32] The rest of Forbonnais' argument was taken up by a rather poor historical rendering of the Catalonian cadastre, known as the *patiño*. He neither described the mode of verification of properties, nor that of land valuation.[33]

He unequivocally rejected the single tax, and while he did not wholly discard the idea of a cadastre, its implementation was relegated to a somewhat distant future, to a time when one would be in a position 'to conduct a scrupulous examination'.[34] Conversely, the Marquis de Mirabeau, whose *Théorie de l'impôt* ('Theory of taxes'), was published in 1760, praised the single tax but avoided discussing the idea of a 'cadastre' which seemed to him on the whole unworkable in an 'exhausted state'.[35]

The economists' cadastre remained mostly a concept for the administrator. Most European countries experienced different types of land tax regimes, however, and established some sort of rudimentary cadastre. While the concept of a cadastral survey in the eighteenth century represented a move towards equity, it still had to invent the means of achieving its aim.

Publicizing a reform: the birth of a republic of administrators

The question now is why the Piedmont and Milanese cadastres (rather than the Catalan one) were taken as models. This had less to do with their quality than the publicity that surrounded them. What had really changed in the eighteenth century was the administrators' reliance on public opinion as a force to which they could appeal to promote their ideas. In the course of the journey which took him, via Portugal, from Paris to London, Karl von Zinzendorf only managed to get hold of Zavala's treatise, a work already known to European administrators thanks to Forbonnais' *Considérations*.[36] The greatest mystery, however, surrounded the Castilian cadastre which had just been reintroduced. Conversely, the Milanese cadastre was bolstered by the publicity it received when Pompeo Neri discussed it in his *Relazione*, which was published in Milan in 1749 at the request of the Italian council in Vienna.[37]

Centred on a vigorous attack against the 'bad local administrators', the *Relazione* offered no formula, but presented a rigorous description of the administrative process. The work was presented as a gift by the Count Firmian, the Austrian plenipotentiary in Milan, to the administrators journeying through Milan, notably Count Karl von Zinzendorf, brother of the president of the Audit Chambers in Vienna, Lord Shelburne, the English prime minister, and François-Joseph Harvouin, the French envoy. Turgot, then intendant and later the finance minister, already had a copy in his library.[38] Once in Milan, Harvouin studied it for a week before submitting a detailed questionnaire to the Milanese administration and requesting to see 'the main directives of the operation, such as the first decisions taken to set it up, the first principles established to serve as a basis to draw out instructions for all operations relating to the communities, and their officers, as well as the handling techniques and valuations'.[39]

Such lacunae were partially provided for by the *Relazione del Censimento dello stato di Milano* ('Report on the census of the state of Milan'), drawn up by Gian Rinaldo Carli, before he took over the direction of the Economic Council of the state of Milan in 1765.[40] Indeed, in addition to retracing the history of the Milan cadastre compiled by Neri, this volume also mentioned the geometrical aspect of the undertaking: the land measuring and map making. It also provided answers to the questions put forward by Harvouin with regard to the settling of litigation, as it described the establishment of tribunals in order to deal with the matter, and the administrative reform which followed in its wake. The purpose of the work was, however, different. It aimed to promote the fiscal reform in the state of Milan and the abolition of the tax on commodities. Carli's *Relazione* sought to influence both the Milanese and Parisian political scenes. During his stay in Paris in the company of Cesare Beccaria, Alessandro Verri distributed a number of volumes of the *Relazione* and later had a case of them brought over. Verri's mission was to make the 'Milan School' known in Paris, and in so doing to consolidate the trend of reforms in Milan.[41]

The publicity surrounding the Milan cadastre was not just an appeal to local public opinion, but targeted more specifically the administrators.[42] The world of the administrators was built on opinion and, like in Plato's cave, where the flow of information was impeded, individuals had to be careful not to confuse the actual information with the publicity surrounding it. The Milanese, or rather the Austrian administrators, gave full prominence to their project, echoed in that by the French administrators.[43]

A new information system, halfway between international relations and exchanges within a Republic of Letters, started to develop. The French sources insisted on the role of the Bailli de Solar, Sardinia's ambassador to France from 1758 to 1765. The preparatory note to Harvouin's journey stated:

> The [land tax] exists everywhere in the Milan region. The King of Sardinia has established it in his States. The operation took ten years, and the present ambassador in France has great praise for it and says it keeps nations happy. It would be important to have good and instructive historical data on this nation [. . .] The Sardinian ambassador among others seems well disposed to give all the information requested.[44]

The inquiry begun by Marie-François-de-Paule Lefèvre d'Ormesson and Daniel Trudaine cannot be explained without taking account of the diplomatic issues at stake here. The King of Sardinia expected support from France in his claims on the Duchy of Piacenza as he hoped to find new markets for his salt marshes.[45] The requirements of peacetime encouraged demands for money, but also created a new mobility and fluidity in the relations between the various powers. Vienna's goodwill was also manifest and underscored by the entente between France and Sardinia.[46]

Administrators started to appear in the diplomatic networks. The dispatch of specific envoys pointed to the desire to push aside, albeit with great care, the diplomats and, probably, the minister Choiseul, in order to prevent them from gaining some of the knowledge occasionally provided in the dispatches.

It is, therefore, possible to draw a parallel between the dispatch of Harvouin to Italy and the journey of Karl von Zinzendorf around Europe. Zinzendorf '[was] one of the few people to know both Italy and the Netherlands', two regions which fell under the control of the State Chancellery in Vienna and thus escaped the control of the Auditor's Chambers. The investigation set out among French diplomats by the finance intendant Jean-Louis Moreau de Beaumont legitimized sending Karl von Zinzendorf to Europe.[47] Of course, the ambassador remained the proper intermediary in terms of codes, use, protocol, diplomatic conjectures and local politics. But administrators sought to open new channels of communication which ambassadors clumsily tried to control. Thus, the French ambassador in Turin, the Marquis de Chauvelin, willingly spoke of the 'Parent affair', named after the civil servant who had unlawfully secured Piedmont maps in order to put together a rival report to that of Harvouin.[48] This allowed the administrative offices of the allied powers sharing common interests to engage in a public debate about 'models', and this despite the 'dirty tricks' of officious planners. The transactions in Piedmont required a four-month stay, while the matter was dealt with within a month in Milan.

There was nothing systematic in these individual transactions which only occasionally took an administrative route. However, the Italian models gave rise to a common political culture validated by the tacit agreement of all concerned within the Republic of administrators, under the control of various brokers. Among these brokers were Count Firmian, Austrian plenipotentiary in Milan and purveyor of Pompeo Neri's *Relazione*, as well as Trudaine de Montigny, intendant in charge of the taxation department and creator of literary reputations in Paris by way of providing the translated works of various authors. Administrators sought to legitimize their models by exposing them outside their national borders. Even if the Milan cadastre was viewed as the most accurate, the praise for the Piedmont cadastre was based on the quality of the documents provided to the French administration and the European administrators.

Pompeo Neri's arguments in favour of a cadastre were based on the documents provided to him by Harvouin relating to the evaluations of the newly acquired provinces.[49] The latter gave an account in Turin of his dealings with Neri and most likely provided a copy of the report by Neri.[50] Harvouin also turned over to Karl von Zinzendorf the material he had collected on the Sardinia cadastre, which included the questionnaires he had carried out, and his analysis of the *Relazione*, in return for reports on the financial affairs of England.[51] The Piedmont cadastre later became the focus of criticism and praise both in France and across Europe, when Jean-Louis Moreau de Beaumont published his description of the fiscal systems.[52] This tract informed Adam Smith and inspired the *Recueil méthodique des lois, règlements, instructions et décisions sur le cadastre de la France* ('Collection of the law, rules, instructions and decision about the cadastre in France').[53]

Comparison and adaptation

Models evolved partly through a web of tenuous channels both at institutional and informal levels, partly through a series of opportunities, personal contacts, acquisitions from book dealers and, above all, on the basis of give and take. This web of exchanges also enabled intellectual concepts to evolve, most notably regarding the feasibility of a comparative project. The editor of the second edition of the *Mémoires concernant les impositions et droits en Europe* ('Treaty about taxes and custom duties in Europe') reminds us of this, in his praise of Jean-Louis Moreau de Beaumont: 'M. de Beaumont doesn't stop at presenting the shape of things alone, he also develops their organizing principle [. . .] The administrator who thought he was only dealing with a picture or a story finds himself suddenly filled with ideas and foresights.'[54] As a consequence, many reformers sought to turn their know-how into a 'governmental science'. Secrecy no longer underscored power, science did, but science understood as a rational gathering of facts and experiments, not science as a prior accumulation of knowledge by the scientist who would then 'disclose' the process.[55] In the dispute which pitted economists against administrators, the latter regained the upper hand.

While the new French finance minister, Laverdy, tried to quell the dispute relating to the general cadastre by ordering silence, André Morellet, the economist, focused on the importance of a public discussion in economic matters. Debate had to be permitted, he asserted, in order to counterbalance the instability and inconsistency of the administrators' position.[56] Discussion, acting as a kind of platform, should enlighten the minister about the current important written works and prevent the good reports from falling into oblivion.

The administrators had none of this. They broke away from the planners and constituted themselves into a group, specifically with the purpose of exchanging material. Working with non-governmental experts was also hampered by the lack of expertise. Faced with a Genovese project planner who had 'invented' a cadastre, Harvouin first tried to find out the nature of its secret. But, having discovered the invention to be conceptual rather than mechanical, he decided that it was accessible to all. According to Harvouin, the administrator's task was to gather descriptive models (registers, accounts, maps, handling techniques) which would act as evidence. Armed with a set of instructions, mostly technical questionnaires, Harvouin relentlessly tried to sort material already published from documents that could prove useful to the French administration. In possession of 'much considerable material', gathered by the King of Sardinia's estate, in the state of Milan and from President Neri, he could afford to ignore the interested offers of the Genovese project maker.[57] Similarly, Neri's ambition was to write a general treatise since he felt that the criticisms addressed to Vauban and the Abbé de Saint Pierre came from individuals who had 'more wit than experience', which is to say very little precise knowledge in the matter.[58] In the Physiocratic *Ephémérides du citoyen*, a clear distinction was established in the preface to its 1769 edition between experts and amateurs. Henceforth, access to dictionaries, precis and journals would be set aside for non-specialists.[59] As Neri had pointed out, the difficulty met by the renewed proposal of a cadastre lacking the support of the 'vocal tradition', the writing of treatises was to be the way by which administrative memory would be constituted, and it would also mark the start a new cultural practice of supplying proofs to back up principles.[60] The answers provided by Pompeo Neri to Harvouin, the French envoy, met this objective.[61]

The question of a comparative study underwrote the whole process. Peace allowed the late implementation of Montesquieu's method through the instructions given to Harvouin who informed Choiseul of the decision to send 'intelligent individuals' or specialists in every foreign country where a cadastre had been established to 'gather more precise details as to the manner in which the process was conducted and the advantages or inconveniences which can ensue, relating to the difference in climate, laws and customs which rule the countries under different dominations'.[62] A comparative knowledge of the European states, thus far the prerogative of the diplomats, was now brought into the administrators' sphere. Harvouin first visited the former Sardinian ambassador to France, on the grounds that the latter knew the French Constitution intimately. This would assist him in preparing for future discussions with Neri on that topic.[63]

The principles were now being reviewed from the perspective of the administrators. No matter what differences might have existed between the various levies, the main tax had to be based on a land cadastre, that is, on a description of the actual estate of the various landholders and calculated proportionally to their net revenue, without excluding the recourse to other forms of levies besides the land tax.[64] Apart from the very influential school of Physiocrats, a clear vision emerged which was built around a common technical base, distinguishable from a fiscal policy. As a jurist well versed in Roman law, Neri could then go on to develop an entire system which took into account the structure of the society and the constitution of the country.

From handwritten memoirs, Neri's *Lettre* and Harvouin's *Mémoire*, to printed papers by Jean-Louis Moreau de Beaumont and Hennet, the jurists also contributed to the creation of a sphere of influence away from that of the economists.[65] They, too, entered into a debate with the economists based on the comparison of the experience they had gathered in their respective fields. The difference in constitutions was no longer an obstacle but now served as an encouragement: 'the neighbouring states have given us the example of cadastres: England, Germany, Hungary, Italy have adopted this method a long time ago and have concentrated their energies on perfecting it'.[66] The cadastral survey, accredited as an administrative technique within the republic of administrators, could now at last impose itself as a reality in the national manuals on the science of finance.[67]

The transfer of geometrical and administrative techniques which allowed the development of land surveys appeared at first as a pioneering attempt, due to a set of exceptional circumstances (peace, financial pressures, composite structures of the state), which caused men and techniques to circulate. The transformation of a well-tested practice into a public administrative principle testifies, however, to a profound change in the intellectual approach to administrative reforms. It was the principle of exchange between experts which enabled first the gathering of evidence and which then legitimized the administrators' stance against the opinion of economists. After comparison and reflection on the merits, these different principles and models could be applied in different European contexts. The scientific rationale which articulated and demonstrated the need for the principle to be based on evidence took over from the political logic of prudence and secrecy.

Notes

1 The decision was taken in the Kingdom of Piedmont in 1698, in Catalonia in 1714–15, in the state of Milan in 1718, in the Duchy of Savoy in 1728, in Spain in 1749. Projects were discussed in France after 1763, in the Margrave of Baden and in the Grand Duchy of Tuscany in the 1770s, and by the Habsburg monarchy from 1785. The land parcel cadastre was established in the Austro-Bohemian countries in 1817 and in Hungary in 1849. After a first attempt by the French administration in 1810, the Tuscan cadastre was established in 1817. In France, it was completed by 1850. For the national perspectives, cf. Guido Quazza, *Le riforme in Piemonte nella prima metà del settecento* (Modena, 1957); Sergio Zaninelli, *Il nuovo censo dello Stato di Milano dall'editto del 1718 al 1733* (Milan, 1963); Renato Zangheri, 'I Catasti', in Ruggiero Romano and Corrado Vivanti (eds), *Storia d'Italia* (Turin, 1973), V, pp. 761–806. For a critique of the national perspective, cf. Leandro Conte, 'Il Catasto Lorenese', in Aldo Fratoianni and Marcello Verga (eds), *Pompeo Neri* (Castelfiorentino, 1992), pp. 377–90.

2 Jean Nicolas, *La Savoie au XVIIIe siècle. Noblesse et bourgeoisie* (Paris, 1978), I, p. 126. A more general presentation by Antonella Alimento, 'Entre justice distributive et développement économique: la lutte pour la création de cadastres généraux au 18e siècle', in Luca Mannori (ed.), *Kataster und moderner Staat in Italien, Spanien und Frankreich (18. Jh.)* (Baden Baden, 2001), pp. 1–28.

3 In the eighteenth century, excise was far from meeting with general approval. See Florian Schui's essay in this volume and Andreas Schwennicke, *Ohne Steuer kein Staat. Zur Entwicklung und politischen Funktion des Steuerrechts in den Territorien des Heiligen Römischen Reichs (1500–1800)* (Frankfurt/Main, 1996), p. 309.

4 Intendants were high-ranking royal officials who were *inter alia* responsible for large parts of the fiscal administration in the provinces.

5 Zaninelli, *Il nuovo censo*, pp. 18–20.

6 Text reproduced by Sergio Zaninelli, 'Un progetto d'un nuovo sistema di Taglia da pratticarsi nello Stato di Milano del 1709', *Archivio storico Lombardo*, 87 (1960), pp. 535–86, here pp. 562–9.

7 Michèle Virol, *Vauban. De la gloire du roi au service de l'État* (Seyssel, 2003), p. 285.

8 Vauban, *Projet d'une dîme royale*, in Eugène Daire (ed.), *Economistes financiers du XVIIIe siècle* (Paris, 1843), p. 37.
9 Zaninelli, 'Un progetto' and Archives du Ministère des Affaires Étrangères (AAE), Paris, Correspondance Politique (henceforth CP) Sardaigne 237.
10 Isabella Ricci, 'Perequazione e catasto in Piemonte nel secolo XVIII', in Carlo Carozzi and Lucio Gambi (eds), *Città e proprietà immobiliare in Italia negli ultimi due secoli* (Milan, 1981), pp. 133–52 (with a few map reproduction); Daniele Borioli, Magda Ferraris, Antonio Premoli, 'La perequazione dei Tributi in Piemonte sabaudo e la realizzazione della riforma fiscale nella metà del XVIII secolo', *Bollettino storico-bibliografico subalpino*, 88 (1985), pp. 131–211 and Nicolas, *La Savoie au XVIIIe siècle*, I, p. 127.
11 Renato Zangheri points out that in fact measurement techniques date back to the eighteenth century, 'I catasti', pp. 764–5.
12 The 1731 Edict was promulgated by Charles III, son of Vittorio Amedeo II. Ricci, 'Perequazione', p. 137. Nicolas, *La Savoie*, p. 126. The process is precisely described by Borioli et al., 'La perequazione', pp. 174ff.
13 Marc Bloch, 'Pour une histoire comparée des sociétés européennes', *Revue de synthèse historique*, 28 (1928), pp. 15–50.
14 Mireille Touzery, *L'invention de l'impôt sur le revenu. La taille tarifée, 1715–1789* (Paris, 1994).
15 'Notes sur la jurisprudence et les finances tirées de l'Histoire de France de l'abbé Velly et de Villaret', 'Notes sur les finances de l'histoire de France de Garnier', 'Notes sur les finances tirées de l'histoire de France de l'abbé Velly', Paris, AN, Archives Lefèvre d'Ormesson, 144 AP 126–128. In 1774 Henry IV-François-de-Paule Lefèvre d'Ormesson (1751–1808) succeeded his father Marie-François-de-Paule Lefèvre d'Ormesson (1710–75), chief intendant of finance since 1756. He became Contrôleur Général of Finance in 1783. Françoise Mosser, *Les intendants des finances au XVIIIe siècle. Les Lefèvre d'Ormesson et le département des impositions (1715–1777)* (Geneva, 1978).
16 Books on economy represent 7 per cent of the sale catalogue of Trudaine de Montigny's library, cf. *Notice des douze premières vacations des livres de la bibliothèque de feu M. Trudaine* (Paris, 1777). On the use of the book on economy by Karl von Zinzendorf, Christine Lebeau, *Aristocrates et grands commis à la Cour de Vienne (1748–1791). Le modèle français* (Paris, 1996).
17 Johann Heinrich Gottlob von Justi (1717–71) started his career as an economist while he was a tutor in the household of Count Haugwitz, the father of Austrian reform in 1748. The latter entrusted him in 1751 with the teaching of cameralistic sciences at the Theresianum, the noble academy founded by Maria-Theresia. Discharged from his duties, he tried to find a position in Saxony where he resided between 1756 and 1760. Eventually, he entered the Prussian administration before being sent to prison for embezzlement.
18 Johann Heinrich Gottlob von Justi, *Staatswirtschaft oder systematische Abhandlung aller oekonomischen und Cameral-Wissenschaften, die zur Regierung eines Landes erfordert werden* (Leipzig, 1755), II, pp. 287ff.
19 Ibid., § 236.
20 Ibid., § 241.
21 Ibid., § 239.
22 Johann Heinrich Gottlob von Justi, *Ausfürhliche Abhandlung von denen Steuern und Abgaben nach ächten, aus dem Endzweck der bürgerlichen Gesellschaften abfliessenden Grundsätzen und zur Wohlfahrt der Völker dienlichen Maassregeln* (Königsberg and Leipzig, 1762), p. 20.

23 On the loan as a means of financing the War of the League of Habsburg, Lebeau, *Aristocrates*, and Peter George Muir Dickson, *Finance and Government under Maria Theresia 1740–1780* (Oxford, 1987).
24 His work is recorded in Germany: 'Notizie', in Pietro Custodi (ed.), *Scrittori classici italiani di economia politica, parte antica* (Milan, 1803–5), IV.
25 (Gian Francesco Pagnini), *Della Decima e di varie altre gravezze imposte dal comune di Firenze. Della moneta e della mercatura de' Fiorentini fino al Secolo XVI* (Lisbon and Lucca, 1765), I. Gian Francesco Pagnini had been finance secretary to the Grand Duke of Tuscany since 1744. On Pagnini, Luigi Dal Pane, 'Uno storico dell'economia nella Toscana del Settecento: Gian Francesco Pagnini', in *Studi in memoria di Gino Borgatta* (Bologna, 1953), I, pp. 143–69.
26 Pagnini, *Della Decima*, chap. II to IV, especially pp. 31–2.
27 G.B. Nelli's point of view in favour of the cadastral survey and the polarization of the debate on these two viewpoints in Florence between 1769 and 1770, Conte, *Il Catasto Lorenese*, pp. 382–3.
28 The *vingtième* was a proportional and declaratory tax which was applied not just to the revenues from the land but also to revenues from industry.
29 Claude-Jacques Herbert, *Essai sur la police générale des grains, sur leurs prix et sur les effets de l'agriculture* (Berlin, 1755) (Paris, 1910 edn), pp. 123–4. On the land tax, William Reginald Ward, *The English land tax in the eighteenth century* (Oxford, 1953); John Vincent Beckett, 'Land tax or excise: the levying of taxation in seventeenth and eighteenth century England', *English Historical Review*, 100 (1985), pp. 285–308. We know little about the career of Claude-Jacques Herbert (1700–58). A fiscal administrator, he was ruined by his son-in-law's bankruptcy and committed suicide in 1758. The *Observateur Littéraire* claims, in a letter dated 14 July, 1758, that he owned a library of 12,000 volumes.
30 François Duverger Véron de Forbonnais (1722–1800) comes from a family of linen merchants from Le Mans whose interests he represented while on tour in Spain in 1749. In 1756, he became 'inspecteur général des monnaies de France', then chief adviser of Moreau de Séchelle and Silhouette. He had links with the Encyclopedists circle.
31 François Véron de Forbonnais, *Mémoires et considérations sur le commerce et les finances d'Espagne, avec des Réflexions sur la nécessité de comprendre l'étude du commerce et des finances dans celle de la politique* (Amsterdam, 1761), p. 81. Forbonnais bases his argument on the free translation he did of Gerónimo de Ustáriz's work, *Théorie et Pratique du commerce et de la marine* (Paris, 1753), published in Spain in 1724 and, for the Catalonian cadastre, on Miguel de Zavala y Auñon's *Miscellanea económico-política, ó Discursos varios sobre el modo de aliviar los vassallos con aumento de el real erario* (Pamplona, 1749).
32 Ibid., pp. 168–9.
33 Ibid., p. 79.
34 Ibid., p. 185.
35 Victor de Riqueti, Marquis de Mirabeau, *Théorie de l'impôt*, 1760 (n.d., n.p.), p. 266.
36 Karl von Zinzendorf, 6 July 1767, Vienna, Haus-, Hof- und Staatsarchiv, Tagebuch Zinzendorf, 1767 (hereafter Zinzendorf, Tgb).
37 (Pompeo Neri), *Relazione dello stato in cui si trova l'opera del censimento universale del ducato di Milano, nel mese di maggio dell'anno 1750. Divisa in tre parti . . .* (Milan, 1750). Pompeo Neri (1707–76) came from a privileged family of citizens in Volterra. His grandfather was Ferdinand de Medici's astronomer and his father counsellor to the grand duke and professor of public law. In 1728, Pompeo took over the chair

from his father. In 1739, he became a member of the Council of Finance of Tuscany before presiding over the *giunta del censimento* in Milan from 1749 to 1758. In 1758, he returned to Florence and became in 1765 *ministro degli Interni*, then, in 1769, president of the Council of State.

38 Takumi Tsuda (ed.), *Catalogue des livres de la bibliothèque de Turgot: d'après un catalogue manuscrit conservé dans la Bibliothèque nationale* (Tokyo, 1974–75).

39 'Premier Journal de la route et du travail de Mr Harvouin Receveur general des finances a compter du 9 juillet 1763', Paris, Archives Nationales, Archives Lefèvre d'Ormesson, 144 AP = 156 Mi 72, 2 (henceforth: Harvouin, 'Premier Journal').

40 Gian Rinaldo Carli, *Relazione del censimento dello stato di Milano*, in P. Custodi (ed.), *Scrittori classici italiani di economia politica* (Milan, 1803–5), Parte moderna, XIV.

41 Pietro to Alessandro Verri, from Milan, 13 November, 1766, *Carteggio di Pietro e di Alessandro Verri dal 1766 al 1797* (Milan, 1923 edn), I, p. 60. On the preparation of the journey by Pietro Verri, C. Capra, *I progressi della ragione: Vita di Pietro Verri* (Bologna, 2002), p. 265.

42 Sandro Landi, *Il governo delle opinioni. Censura e formazione del consenso nella Toscana del Settecento* (Bologna, 2000).

43 One must therefore modulate slightly the exclusively French perspective proposed by Antonella Alimento, 'Le rêve de l'uniformité face à l'impôt: le projet du premier cadastre général en France', *Histoire & Mesure*, 8 (1993), pp. 387–416.

44 Instructions données pour sa mission à M. Harvouin, Paris, Archives Nationales (AN), Archives Lefèvre d'Ormesson, 144 AP = 156 Mi 72, 2.

45 Paris, AAE, CP Sardaigne 237 and 238.

46 Harvouin, 'Premier Journal', 19 October 1763. Cf. Zinzendorf, Tgb, 23 July 1766.

47 Ludwig to Karl von Zinzendorf, 3 July 1766, Vienna, Deutschorden Zentralarchiv, MS 64.

48 15 October 1763, AAE, CP Sardaigne 240.

49 Harvouin, 'Premier Journal', 7 March 1764.

50 Harvouin, 'Premier Journal', 27 March 1764.

51 Zinzendorf, Tgb, 2 and 21 January 1769.

52 Jean-Louis Moreau de Beaumont, *Mémoire concernant les impositions et droits en Europe* (Paris, 1768–69).

53 Albert-Joseph-Ulpien Hennet, *Recueil méthodique des lois, décrets, règlements, instructions et décisions sur le cadastre de la France* (Paris, 1811), p. 12.

54 Jean-Louis Moreau de Beaumont, *Mémoires concernant les impositions et droits en Europe*, Nicolas-Juste Poullin de Viéville (ed.) (Paris, 1787), pp. iv–v.

55 On the development of scientific methods in France in the second half of the eighteenth century, Christian Licoppe, *La formation de la pratique scientifique. Le discours de l'expérience en France et en Angleterre (1630–1820)* (Paris, 1996) and Olivier Ihl and Martine Kaluszynski, 'Pour une sociologie historique des sciences de gouvernement', *Revue française d'administration publique*, 52 (2002), pp. 229–43.

56 André Morellet, *Réflexions sur les avantages de la liberté d'écrire et d'imprimer sur les matières de l'administration, écrites en 1764, à l'occasion de la déclaration du Roi du 28 mars de la même année, qui fait défenses d'imprimer, débiter aucuns écrits, ouvrages ou projets concernant la réforme ou l'administration des finances* (London and Paris, 1775), p. 4.

57 Harvouin, 'Premier Journal', 31 March and 1 April 1764.

58 Harvouin, 'Premier Journal', 23 March 1764.

59 *Éphémérides du citoyen ou Bibliothèque raisonnée des sciences morales et politiques*, 1769, I, preface.

60 Neri, *Premier mémoire*, p. 9. Similarly Morellet noted that the administrators' versatility stemmed from the fact that the previous ways of doing things had been forgotten.

61 This involves seven memoirs, on respectively the translation in French of the *Relazione*, the different types of *taille* (tax), the reform of the communities, the setting up of an office for a general cadastre in Paris, the surveying of land, the general valuation, the benefits and disadvantages of a cadastre. Turin, Archivio di Stato, Archivio di Corte, Materie economiche, Perequazione del Piemonte, mazzo I di Prima Addizione, n. 5, Copia di lettera scritta dal presidente Neri a mons. Harvoin deputato dal Re di Francia, che l'aveva richiesto di diverse notizie riguardo delle operazioni fattesi per il censimento di Milano, 27 March 1764 (henceforth: Copia di lettera scritta dal presidente Neri).

62 A Monsieur le duc de Praslin, 2 June 1763, Paris, AN, Archives Lefèvre d'Ormesson, 144 AP = 156 Mi 72, Dossier no. 2. Montesquieu's method which we refer to here leads us to look at relationships between the laws of a country and various factors including climate, the political system in which people live, and the mores; cf. Charles de Montesquieu, *Esprit des Lois*, 1748, XIV and XIX.

63 Copia di lettera scritta dal presidente Neri, p. 36.

64 'Cioé sopra une descrizione reale dei beni stabili di chiaschedun possessore stimati in proporzione della rendita netta', Memoria seconda sopra le differenti nature di Taglie, Copia di lettera scritta dal presidente Neri, p. 14.

65 'La constitution de l'Etat, les loix rendües sur la matiere des impositions, les tribunaux créés pour en connoitre les usages différens, les privilèges du clergé et de la noblesse, et ceux attachés aux offices, ainsy qu'une depense considerable, sont autant d'obstacles à vaincre pour établir le cadastre en France', Copie du mémoire remis à la Commission des Finances par M. le contrôleur général au sujet de l'établissement du cadastre, de la répartition et de la perception des impositions dans les Etats du Roi de Sardaigne, Paris, AAE, Mémoires et documents France, 1365, fos 239–69.

66 See entry 'Cadastre', *Encyclopédie méthodique 'Finances'* (Paris, 1784–87), I, p. 152.

67 See Charles Ganilh, *De la science des finances et du ministère de M. le Cte de Villèle* (Paris, 1825); Ludwig Heinrich von Jakob, *Die Staatswissenschaft theoretisch und praktisch dargestellt und erläutert durch Beyspiele aus der neuern Finanzgeschichte europäischer Staaten* (Halle, 1821); Carl August von Malchus, *Handbuch der Finanzwissenschaft und Finanzverwaltung* (Stuttgart and Tübingen, 1830).

3

Learning from French Experience? The Prussian *Régie* Tax Administration, 1766–86*

Florian Schui

In 1766, some 350 Frenchmen reached Berlin. They were not the first immigrants to arrive in Prussia, nor were they the last foreigners who contributed to the fascinating rise of the Prussian state over the centuries. The Frenchmen who arrived in the capital in 1766 were different from most of the other immigrants who had passed through the gates of Berlin previously. They were not religious refugees or makers of silk, hats or gloves like many of their compatriots. They were not in the business of making goods but rather in the business of taking them: they were tax administrators. During the following 20 years they created a completely new tax administration for indirect taxes in the Prussian states, commonly known as the *Régie*. While the new institution had the support of Frederick II, it was also widely criticized: the French tax administrators were perhaps the most controversial public figures in Prussia in the period. The opposition against them remained strong and when Frederick II died in 1786, his successor dismissed the French advisers. However, many of the changes which they had introduced had a lasting impact; the creation of the *Régie* must count as one of the most important turning points in Prussia's financial history.[1]

The importance of immigration for the economic and cultural development of Prussia in the eighteenth century is well studied. Also, the relevance of fiscal development for state formation in Prussia has been examined at least to some extent. However, little is known about the significance of transfers of individuals and ideas for the development of the most central institutions of the Prussian state. The archival material about the creation of the *Régie* illuminates the transnational context of the progress of the Prussian tax state and opens up new vistas on aspects of the social and economic history of Prussia in the period. Four interrelated arguments will be explored here. First, this essay examines how the Prussian fiscal development after the Seven Years War was influenced by transfers from France. The reign of Frederick II was a crucial period for the rise of the tax state in Prussia: revenues from taxation and domains balanced each other in the state's budget. This essay argues that Prussia made substantial progress in addressing some of the problems associated with the transition from domain to tax state, in particular in the areas of universality and horizontal equality of taxation, because it learned from the experience of the French fiscal system through the officers of the *Régie*. The essay thus seeks to set the development of the tax state in Prussia in a transnational European context.[2]

Second, the analysis of fiscal change in the period is used as an inroad to illuminate the political process of state-building in Prussia. The creation of the *Régie* as a homogeneous fiscal administration for almost all territories of the Hohenzollern monarchy was a crucial step in the process of state-building in Prussia. Paradoxically, this development towards a Prussian state was made possible and was in large part shaped by a transfer of fiscal ideas and administrators from another country. This illustrates the dialectical relationship between transnational tax state and state-building in the Prussian context. Moreover, it also contributes a new aspect to the answer of the question 'What is Prussia?' The heterogeneity of the Prussian territory and the important contributions of immigrant communities are a challenge for historians who seek to explain the rise of the Prussian state. Prussia was in many ways less than the sum of its parts. The developments associated with the *Régie* support the view that the modern Prussian state was above all unified by economic, political and military imperatives.[3]

Third, the opposition to the *Régie* also sheds light on a crucial period of social development in Prussia. The new fiscal administration did not only escalate the long-standing conflict between Crown and estates but also illuminates the increasing importance of a new social paradigm. The creation of the *Régie* was an important step towards an increasingly sharp distinction between the state, the sphere of economic activity and an emerging public sphere. At the same time the fiscal administration was also one of the most important areas where these spheres overlapped and where conflicting interests clashed. An important part of the social conflicts that led to the end of the *Régie* derived from an emerging bourgeois protest against the interference of the fiscal administration in spheres of production and consumption that were increasingly considered to be private.

Fourth, the chapter illuminates the nature of the transfer processes involved. Ideas are rarely transferred without undergoing change in the process. Even where transfers are initiated voluntarily, they often result in unintended outcomes. In the case of the *Régie*, some of the actors sought to recreate parts of the French fiscal model in Prussia, but the outcome was more complex. The French administrators arrived with views that were formed in response to the French fiscal reality rather than with the intention to copy it. These views were then further transformed in a process of political communication between the French advisers, Frederick II, the Prussian administration and different social groups. The exchanges were set in the larger context of cultural transfers between France and the German states, but they also differed from other forms of transfers because they had a direct impact on the institutional structure of the Prussian state.[4]

Exchanges of ideas about taxation, 1750–1848

The case of the *Régie* fits into the wider context of fiscal transfers in the period. The intense exchange between France and Prussia was an outstanding but not unique development. In the second half of the eighteenth century and the first half of the nineteenth, a tightly knit web of international communication about taxation developed in Europe and the Atlantic world. In the period from 1763, which followed the Seven Years War, most European states' finances were extremely strained and the threat of 'general bankruptcy' loomed over Europeans' thoughts.[5] The war escalated a long-standing structural problem: the 'increasing expansion of public and particular state activities' could no longer be accommodated within the existing fiscal framework. This was also the contemporary view. 'In all advanced countries', noted Voltaire, 'the taxes are very high because the tasks of the state are very heavy.' Tax revenues did not increase sufficiently to allow for this augmented state activity, mainly due to military expenses. The War of Austrian Succession (1740–48) and the Seven Years War (1756–63) had involved the European states in almost continuous warfare between 1740 and 1763. The wars were costly for winners and losers alike.[6] Military expenses escalated the crisis but other spending equally increased the financial needs of governments. Prussia is a case in point: it maintained the largest army in Europe – relative to its population – and also actively promoted economic development with subsidies, loans and tax reductions. During Frederick's reign, a total of 2.8 million thaler was spent just in *direct* subsidies for manufacturing, and the Prussian government was involved in the creation of 1302 manufacturing businesses in the period after the Seven Years War alone. Other economic development efforts included expenditure for the recruitment and settlement of foreign colonists and the building of roads, canals and similar infrastructure. In addition, even at the comparably frugal court of Frederick II, considerable expenses emerged for buildings, art and court entertainment. As a result, the Prussian budget increased during Frederick's reign from 7 to 20 million thaler. While the military and economic development efforts of Prussia were outstanding, similar patterns of expenditure can be found in most European states.[7]

Faced with dramatically increased expenditure, an intense debate about fiscal reform developed across Europe and the Atlantic world. A multitude of issues was discussed, but the universality of taxation was at the centre of contemporary concerns. Across Europe, genuine and fake tax privileges reduced the tax burden of nobility, clergy and other groups. Writing about taxation during a stay in Berlin in 1786 and 1787, the later hero of the French Revolution and noted Physiocratic economist Mirabeau summed up the problem. 'In most European countries some classes such as the nobility, or the clergy, or other mixed corporations whose interests are opposed [to that of the state] are too predominant.' Mirabeau was writing about this European problem in Berlin, but it was certainly most dramatic in his native France. Aristocrats did not even face the heavily reduced tax burden. Patronage, corruption and inefficient tax collection substantially reduced their tax payments. The Duke of Orléans, one of the richest men in France, effectively only paid about 0.2 million livres of the 2.4 million that he owed annually. 'I pay more or less what I like', he famously said, thus impressively confirming Mirabeau's assessment.[8]

This unsolved conflict and an ever-worsening state of public finance put France at the centre of the international debates of the period. The country became a fertile ground for fiscal theory and fiscal reform projects which were widely discussed in Europe and beyond. Boiguilbert, Maréchal de Vauban, Abbé de Saint-Pierre, Voltaire, the Physiocrats and Necker are only some of the most prominent authors who proposed far-reaching fiscal reform in the course of the century. While their projects differed in many respects, they had two concerns in common: the reduction of fiscal privileges and a more equal distribution of tax payments. Intellectual and political elites discussed fiscal reform, but also lower-level administrators, less prominent authors and taxpayers exchanged their views on necessary change. An example of this is the projects that were received by the so-called 'bureau of dreams'. The same Duke of Orleans who later displayed a rather nonchalant approach to taxation had established the office during his regency as a part of the larger financial reform projects which also included John Law's bank. A common concern with the reduction of fiscal privileges emerged from nearly all proposals.[9]

The extraordinarily prolific discussion about the French fiscal crisis coincided with the inability of the French political system to implement fundamental change. The history of the ministries of Maynon, Terray, Turgot, Calonne, Brienne, Necker and other finance ministers of the period is a history of attempted fiscal reforms which were blocked, delayed or modified by the hardened opposition of the *parlements* and the social groups which they represented. The Crown made some progress in taxing the privileged in particular in the context of the Seven Years War. However, the revenue generated remained too limited to solve the budget problems, while the conflict over universal taxation damaged the ties of loyalty between estates and Crown, a process which contributed significantly to the political destabilization of the French monarchy.[10]

Despite the many problems of the French fiscal system, France became a fiscal laboratory for Europe and the Atlantic world in the eighteenth and early nineteenth centuries. In order to understand this paradoxical development, it is important to grasp the complexity of transfers. Fiscal transfers were rarely attempts to copy the French system as a whole. Instead transfers developed for different motives and in different areas. One of the reasons that led to fiscal transfers from France was the high level of administrative skills of the French fiscal administration. Many transfers were attempts to learn from the sophisticated techniques employed by French tax officials. From a technical point of view, the French General Farm remained one of the most efficient fiscal administrations of the time. Furthermore, in many cases it was not French practices that were transferred but fiscal ideas from France that had been formed as a reaction to these practices. France was a fertile ground for debates about fiscal reform precisely because of the flaws of the French fiscal system. France had some of the most advanced economic thought, a lively culture of public debate and perhaps the greatest fiscal problems of any country of the period: together these developments made France the most prolific producer of innovative fiscal thought. While the political situation in France prevented the application of most reform proposals, French debates were followed outside France with great attention and influenced fiscal thought and evolution in other countries. Finally, the French case also influenced fiscal developments in Europe because it served as a warning. The flaws of France's fiscal system and the collapse of the Bourbon state over a fiscal crisis impressed the importance of fiscal matters on governments and observers across Europe and beyond. Even after the revolution and throughout the first half of the nineteenth century, France remained at the centre of international transfers of fiscal ideas and practices. The Napoleonic occupations and the administrative reforms introduced in this period changed fiscal systems in many European countries. The essays of Christine Lebeau and Alex Grab in this volume explore further aspects of the importance of France for European fiscal development.

Transfers between France and Prussia after the Seven Years War

Some of the most intense fiscal transfers in the eighteenth and nineteenth centuries developed between France and Prussia after the end of the Seven Years War. This was a phase of heated debate about fiscal reform in both countries. 'People no longer speak but of these [tax] edicts', noted a Parisian lawyer in 1763. In France the *parlements* vigorously resisted an increase of *vingtième* and *capitation*, two universal taxes, but eventually had to give in to the pressure of the Crown. The French controversies about universal taxation were linked to the European context in more than one way. They formed a part of the experience that the administrators of the *Régie* brought to Prussia. In the years before they became fiscal advisers of Frederick II, these administrators had been involved in an important step in the evolution of the French fiscal administration towards more universal taxation. Marc Antoine de la Haye de Launay, the director of the *Régie*, had been a high-ranking official of the French General Farm in the Languedoc region. He was also part of the 'fiscal aristocracy' of France. He was related to the la Haye and the de Launay families. Members of both families were repeatedly among the General Farmers, the consortium of 40 financiers who, for the payment of a lump sum to the Crown, acquired the right to collect most taxes. Other directors of the *Régie*, such as Joseph Trablaine de Candy, also had held important posts in the French administration. However, while French debates influenced developments in Prussia, they were themselves influenced by the fiscal situation of other European countries. The language of the *parlements* included frequent references to 'Anglican principles' and the fiscal prerogatives of the English parliament. The Crown, too, argued from a European perspective. The finance minister Bertin claimed that the reluctance of the *parlements* to approve new taxes undermined France's ability to borrow from European financiers and thus jeopardized the country's chances to win the war. On the one hand, observation of other fiscal systems and arguments borrowed from foreign authors were a commonplace in these controversies. On the other hand, the actors in these debates expected other European monarchs, administrators, military leaders, financiers and taxpayers to observe them in the same way that they observed developments abroad. Contemporaries, it seems, took the transnational nature of fiscal development much more for granted than modern historians.[11]

In 1763, fiscal change was also high on the agenda in Berlin, the Prussian capital. Mirabeau points to this year as a turning point in the economic policies of Frederick II. All parts of Prussia had been occupied by foreign troops at one point or another during the war. In the still largely agrarian country, many fields had not been sown for several years. The population had dropped by half a million, a decline of more than 10 per cent in seven years. In this situation, the king decided to undertake a fiscal reform. The objectives were a limited increase in tax revenue, approximately 300,000 thaler, and a fiscal structure that promoted economic development. However, on 10 June 1765 the king met von Massow, the vice-director of the General Direktorium, the council of the heads of the different branches of Prussian administration, who flatly refused to execute the king's orders.[12]

The conflict did not come completely as a surprise. It had developed since Frederick was crowned in 1740, and, at the centre of the king's differences with his administration, was the implementation of the excise. The Prussian excise was a confusing mix of different taxes. It consisted mainly of consumption taxes, tolls and tariffs on the products of the cities. Collection of the excise had become extremely lax in the times of war and occupation. However, collection was also inefficient because the tax was much disliked by the beneficiaries of fiscal privileges who had considerable influence in the administration. The reason for the opposition of the aristocracy and other privileged groups to the excise can be gleaned from the debates which surrounded the introduction of the tax in Prussia in the seventeenth century. The excise was introduced in the context of the Thirty Years War, following the example of the Netherlands, where indirect taxes were applied with great success. A number of arguments for the excise can be found in contemporary debates: the excise was easy to collect; it was a 'stealth tax' because it was paid in small increments, so the level of taxation was easy to adjust; the tax was less intrusive than direct taxes; and the tax provided – in modern terms – a good 'handle' for the taxation of the growing sector of manufacturing. But most important was another argument: the excise was a way to circumvent fiscal privileges because it was paid by all consumers and could be introduced without the consent of the estates. Perhaps the most enthusiastic defender of the excise was the German author Christoph Tenzel who praised the universality of the tax in his pamphlet 'The discovery of the goldmine that is the excise'. The excise, he wrote, was a duty that was also paid by those who 'lived in luxury'. Nobody, he added, would feel pity to see 'aristocrats', 'priests' and 'scholars' finally taxed.

In Prussia and other parts of Europe, the enthusiasm for the excise continued well into the second half of the eighteenth century. The regressive character of flat indirect taxes was not viewed negatively at the time. It mattered more that the privileged contributed to public expenditure at all. Also, the regressive tendency was limited in the only partly monetized economies of the seventeenth and eighteenth centuries. The excise was only levied on goods that were traded for money on markets. These goods also tended to be more refined and of higher quality. There was no excise on goods that were produced for home consumption or were bartered. Through this mechanism, the excise was levied to a greater extent on the consumption of the elites. In addition, the tariffs on different products were often differentiated in order to tax progressively. As we will see, this was an important aspect of the Prussian reforms. However, the features of the excise that led to some people's enthusiasm for it were also the reason why it met with resistance in other quarters. As Mirabeau pointed out, it was 'very difficult' to convince aristocrats that it was to their advantage to pay taxes. As a consequence, a dual system developed in Prussia. The cities paid the excise, and the countryside paid a direct land tax. Most city dwellers preferred the excise because it seemed just to them and because it was associated with less governmental intrusion into their business activities. The countryside continued to be taxed based on a land tax from which some of the biggest landowners were exempt. However, perhaps the biggest flaw of the fiscal system was that the administration of taxes was inefficient. Despite the considerable changes introduced by the Great Elector and Frederick William I, Frederick II still inherited an administration in which representatives of the estates exercised significant influence.

This prevented an efficient collection of taxes in many instances, in particular when taxpayers and administrators belonged to the same social group. The refusal of the administration to implement a fiscal reform which was bound to offset the status quo against its interest can therefore hardly be surprising. However, as much as this conflict was typical of European societies at the time, the solution was a typically Prussian one. When the Prussian administration opposed Frederick's plan, the monarch decided to recruit French civil servants. The king's was a bold decision. It put the Prussian monarch, his administration and a large part of the elite of the country in open conflict. However, this decision was also part of Prussian normality. On the one hand, the conflict between estates and the Hohenzollern was a constant feature of the Prussian polity. On the other hand, the king's decision needs to be seen in the context of a long history of immigration to Prussia. It was not unusual to recruit foreigners to carry out tasks that Prussians could not handle. Swamps were drained by Dutch engineers, silk manufactures were created by immigrants from France, and the underdeveloped Prussian financial sector progressed with the help of Viennese Jews. Foreigners also served the Prussian state before as army officers, inspectors of factories and in other positions. However, the *Régie* officers also stand out by their numbers, their visibility to the population and the fundamental administrative change which they brought about. For the purposes of this essay three sets of questions with regard to the *Régie* will be examined: first, why did the Prussian king recruit French tax experts? Second, how did taxation change in Prussia in this period, and how did the experiences and views of the French administrators influence this change? Third, why was the *Régie* abolished and what was its lasting influence?[13]

Why France?

Frederick's choice to recruit tax administrators in France may surprise the modern reader. After all, France was only little more than 20 years away from a fiscal collapse, while the English fiscal system of the late eighteenth and nineteenth centuries is today widely seen as one of the more successful approaches. Part of the answer to this question lies in the different perspectives of contemporary policy-makers and historians. Judgements about the French and English fiscal systems were in large part formed by events that occurred after the reign of Frederick II, namely the French Revolution and Britain's military and economic successes in the nineteenth century. Moreover, the choice of French advisers also has to be seen in the context of the close association of fiscal systems with the social and political structure in which they develop. A plan for fiscal reform is always a statement about the nature of the society that one believes one lives in or that one wishes to build. It is indicative that the only other fiscal administration that Frederick studied attentively in the period before the creation of the *Régie* was that of Austria. Frederick's efforts to improve Prussia's fiscal system through observation and imitation concentrated on Austria and France because their social and political structures as well as their fiscal problems were similar to those of Prussia. A transfer of fiscal ideas and experience from England would have been more difficult and certainly less desirable from Frederick's point of view because they would necessarily also have included the transfer of certain 'English' political ideas and structures. As in the French debates, representatives of the estates were much more likely to lay claim to English principles of taxation than central governments. Finally, the choice of French advisers was also the result of the superior quality of French fiscal administration. As contemporaries were well aware, the most sophisticated and skilled tax administrators were to be found in the French General Farm. This was linked to a more general contemporary admiration for

France in many areas. French ideas, art, products, lifestyles and not least the French language were sought after and imitated almost everywhere in Europe and in particular in Potsdam. It is not a coincidence that many of the officials of the *Régie* came through the recommendation of a man who also brought some of the latest tendencies of French thought to Prussia. Helvétius, who had stayed in Potsdam in 1765, was not only one of the most prominent authors of the Enlightenment but he had also been one of the General Farmers until 1751.[14]

No less intriguing than Frederick's motives for the recruitment of French administrators are the reasons that led de Launay and his colleagues to leave France and settle in the comparably primitive circumstance of the Prussian provinces. Nothing suggests that any of the *Régisseurs* were forced to leave France. De Launay was from an influential family of financiers and, during his stay in Prussia, he did not completely cut his connections to France but arranged marriages with French financiers for both of his daughters. The migration of fiscal officers from France to Prussia took place in a wider context of migration of officials of the French General Farm. Jean-Claude Waquet describes the migration of French officials to Italy: around the middle of the century, French administrators were called to Tuscany, Parma and Milan in order to establish tax farm operations. The developments in Italy were also directly linked to the reforms in Prussia: one of the directors of the *Régie*, de Lattre, had previously been a tax farmer in Florence. He arrived later than most of his colleagues in Prussia and his migration was most likely related to the end of the French administration in Tuscany in 1767. The migration of French officials to Prussia therefore needs to be seen in a wider context of European fiscal transfers which also included officious fiscal fact-finding missions such as that of the Austrian Zinzendorf and the migration of fiscal adventurers in the mould of John Law.[15]

The impact of French administrators and experience on fiscal reform in Prussia

Whatever might have been the individual motives of the French administrators to leave France, their arrival in Berlin heralded crucial changes in Prussia's fiscal development, of which only a small part can be discussed here. Most of the French administrators arrived in 1766, but some of the directors, including de Launay, had arrived already in 1765. At this stage the king and the Frenchmen negotiated the exact nature of the fiscal reform project. Up to this point it had only been clear that some form of fiscal reform was to be implemented but the details – the geographical areas, the kind of taxes, the form of involvement of the foreign administrators – had not been elaborated.

The first and perhaps most important contribution of French experience to the development of the Prussian fiscal system was made at this early stage. Frederick proposed to de Launay the creation of a fiscal administration based on the French model: a General Farm was to pay a yearly lump sum to the Crown for the right to collect all taxes in the country. The king expected the farm to pay the tax revenue of 1764/5 plus 300,000 thaler. This was clearly an extremely advantageous offer. The war had only ended in 1763 and tax revenues in 1764 were still extraordinarily low. The intention to establish a tax farm may also have been another reason for Frederick's decision to recruit officials from the French General Farm for his administration. It would have been very difficult to raise the required sums on the rudimentary Prussian capital market, and the king may have had in mind a solution which was backed by General Farmers similar to the operations that were established in Italy at the time. The unavailability of credit from Prussian financiers was a crucial consideration for Frederick's fiscal policy. Even the wealthiest Prussians would have been unable to raise the necessary sums. Moreover, most of the important entrepreneurs in Prussia – with the exception of the Westphalian province – were closely associated with the government. They received government subsidies and credits and were often also military suppliers. Under such conditions, they could hardly offer substantial credit to the government. Foreign creditors could have supplied credit to the Prussian government. However, this possibility was uncertain and could interfere with foreign policy, as the experience of the Silesian loan had demonstrated. Frederick therefore preferred to accumulate a war treasury where possible rather than to finance wars through credit.[16]

However, de Launay refused the offer and insisted that the new administration be run directly by the government or in the *régie* of the government. The Frenchman thus gave the informal name to the new administration and saved Prussia from one of the most hated institutions of the *Ancien Régime*. De Launay refused the offer because it was much to the disadvantage of the state. He also argued that the system of tax farming itself was flawed because the tax farmer had of necessity *intérêt au pressoir*, an interest to extract as much tax from the taxpayers as possible without any regard to justice, fairness or legitimacy of taxation. As a former tax farmer, de Launay knew these problems well. In France, the General Farm was much hated and was seen as yet another way in which the fiscal system benefited the wealthy. By becoming members of the consortium of the General Farmers, rich financiers were tax exempt and made a profit from the tax payments of the masses. 'The Farmers General', one historian of eighteenth-century France points out, 'were probably the most unpopular men in the country.' Consequently they were also the best represented of any social or professional group on the scaffolds of the revolution.[17]

Roughly at the time when de Launay prevented the Prussian king from introducing tax farming, the problems associated with this institution had also become clear to government officials in France. In 1780, Necker attempted to reduce the importance of the General Farm in France and substitute it in part with a *Régie*-type fiscal administration. However, the reforms came too late and remained incomplete. The transfer of de Launay and his colleagues to Prussia thus meant that government officials learned from French experience more quickly and more efficiently in Berlin than in Paris. The payment for the directors of the Prussian *Régie* was eventually agreed to be a fixed sum with only a 5 per cent share in any revenues after the year 1765/6.[18]

A second set of decisions in which the French officials had significant influence related to the new excise tariffs. In 1766, after consultations between de Launay and Frederick, a declaration patent announced a provisional reform of the excise tariffs and the creation of a commission which was to decide on the final tax structure. The principal aim of the reform was a change of the tariff structure and administration; the increase of revenue was a secondary objective. The declaration patent stated that the new tariffs were to bring 'just' and 'proportional' taxation and that tax payments should be shared in proportion to wealth. The document outlined the broad guidelines of the reform and established a commission which elaborated the details of the new tariffs. The tariff commission was the principal place of confrontation between the king's new advisers and the old Prussian administration, including members from the provinces which were close to the interests of the estates. However, with the support of the king, de Launay and his colleagues were able to push through most of the changes, and the new tariff of 1769 followed closely the recommendations of the declaration patent. De Launay thus became, in Mirabeau's words, 'in reality a kind of minister of finance' for all Prussian states at a time when that position did not yet exist in Prussian government. The new excise tariff was based on what would later be called the 'ability to pay' approach. In the present context the tariff changes can only be discussed in summary fashion because of the great number of different tariffs on different goods. Only some characteristic examples will be cited. In order to achieve their objectives, the king and de Launay discussed a number of measures to 'de-tax the poor' by reducing tariffs on basic foodstuffs. The abolition of the grain excise was agreed, and, with a similar intention, the lowest quality of beer was not taxed any more. It was to be sold exclusively to the poor and to soldiers.[19] These tax reductions were to be offset by an increased taxation of wealthier consumers. 'One must take from the rich', de Launay argued, 'what the people cannot pay [in taxes] on its necessities.' The better varieties of beer, brandy, some types of meat and luxury goods were taxed at a higher rate. In this context, much of the debates about the new tariffs did not focus on the question whether 'luxury goods' should be taxed more highly, but which goods counted as 'luxury goods'. There was some disagreement as to how meat should be treated; de Launay maintained that it was a luxury good because the common people did not eat meat anyway, but Frederick did not want to hear anything about a higher meat tax. In the end, a compromise was reached, and a new tax was levied on meat with the exception of pork, which was seen as the meat of the poor. For most luxury goods, the tariff of 1766 confirmed the excise increases that Frederick had already decided in the tariff of 1749, which had multiplied tariffs on many luxury goods. The real change that was felt by consumers was that the *Régie* began to collect the higher tariffs with more efficiency. In fact, the decision of the king to reform the administration of the excise must be seen in the light of the inefficient application of the tariff reform of 1749.[20]

The *Régie* also worked to reduce fiscal privilege in Prussia by systematically controlling the legal bases of the claims to tax exemption. This was a third area in which the new administration developed extraordinary activism. Privileges were mostly associated with social status and geography. In general, the countryside was not submitted to the excise, and certain groups such as aristocrats and clergy were exempt from the duty. Many of the privileges were not clearly defined, and the line between genuine privileges, privileges which had slowly been extended beyond their original scope, privileges that were claimed without legal basis and simply inefficient tax collection was blurred. The *Régie* began systematically to control the legality of privileges and generally tried to reduce all forms of tax exemption. The attempts to reduce fiscal privilege were apparent less in tariffs and regulations, but mainly in administrative practices. A great number of disputes over privileges and complaints about the operations of the *Régie* at the provincial and local levels illustrate conflict which continued throughout the existence of the new administration. The position of the administration in these confrontations was considerably strengthened by the creation of a separate court system for disputes regarding the *Régie*. The creation of these courts led to continuous protests by taxpayers who were subject to the decisions of the courts and objected to their legitimacy, magistrates who expected the courts to rule against their interests and existing courts who saw their competencies limited. In part, the increasing number of conflicts over privileges were also the result of the more efficient tax collection by the *Régie*, which made the issue of tax exemption more important.

The attempts of the *Régie* to reduce fiscal privilege went beyond the explicit will of the monarch, who had given instructions not to interfere with any genuine privileges. The *Régie* developed a considerable activism in this area and, in many cases, went beyond a control of the legality of tax exemptions. The French officers wanted to increase fiscal pressure on the privileged but they also sought to create a homogeneous fiscal administration for all Prussian states and all inhabitants of Prussia. The eagerness of the *Régisseurs* in this area also needs to be understood in the context of their experience. Fiscal centralization and homogeneity were far more advanced in France and were, in their view, cornerstones of an efficient fiscal administration. It was also part of their experience that, in France, many of the Crown's achievements against the privileged were accomplished through more aggressive operations at the administrative level.[21]

With the new tariffs, more efficient collection and the reduction of privileges, the excise affected a great number of taxpayers but, above all, it became a tool for the Prussian state to tap the incomes of the elites on a larger scale than previously. Schmoller and his disciples saw this as a form of 'socialism' on the part of Frederick. However, they also made sure to add that this socialism was quite different from that of their own time. In their view, Frederick's 'socialism' was a well-measured concern with the fate of the poor paired with a profound respect for the historically grown social status quo. In this description, the philosophy behind Frederick's 'socialism' exhibited some remarkable similarities to the social concerns of the Historical School. However, it seems anachronistic to look for socialist or redistributive motifs in the thought of the Prussian king or the directors of his fiscal administration. The principal concern remained to collect the necessary funds for the expanding activities of the Prussian state where they could be found. The ability to pay was the main reason for the more progressive taxation of the *Régie*, but it was also influenced by concerns with justice and legitimacy of taxation. For de Launay, stable tax revenue could only be generated if taxes were paid voluntarily. One way to ensure consent to taxation in the absence of any political mechanisms which could fulfil this function was to tax mainly 'superfluous' luxury products which consumers could renounce. In this way, de Launay argued, the tax collector could tell the taxpayer at any moment: 'It is not necessity or constraint that forces you to pay, it is your free will that makes you pay [taxes].'[22]

A fourth area of innovation was only indirectly linked to the function of generating revenue for the state. The declaration patent stated explicitly that the promotion of industry was one of the principal goals of the fiscal reform. The new administration contributed significantly to influence consumption habits, gather statistical information and control quality standards in manufacturing. Frederick and de Launay pursued a policy that would later be called 'infant industry protection'. The term is associated with the nineteenth-century economist Friedrich List, but the concept and even the language to describe it were familiar to Frederick and his advisers. In discussion with de Launay, the king once pointed out that the new tariffs should afford protection for 'industries that were still in their cradle'. To this end, the *Régie* became a tool in the 'politics of taste'. Frederick complained that even the 'meanest servant' aspired to wear foreign silk and consumed other imported luxuries. This reduced demand for Prussian industries that were in fact mostly still in their 'cradles': many products of domestic manufacturing compared poorly with imports. In order to increase demand for domestic industry, the *Régie* imposed higher taxes on many foreign goods. Some imports were even banned completely. While most of the measures for the protection of domestic manufacturing were developed together by de Launay and the king, there was a strong disagreement about import bans. De Launay warned against the loss of tax revenue but Frederick insisted that the promotion of domestic industry took precedence over all fiscal objectives. The disagreement illustrates that short-term fiscal consideration played a comparably small role among the motivations for the fiscal reform.[23]

The *Régie* also took an active role in the creation of new manufacturing businesses. One of the objectives that Frederick wanted to achieve with the new tariffs was to prevent a negative balance of trade. De Launay agreed with the 'bullionism' of the monarch but went further in his reasoning: only if expenditure for all of consumption – domestic and imported – were limited, would Prussians be able to 'preserve enough wealth in order to use it to acquire more of it'. The tax on luxury goods was, therefore, also intended to deter Prussians from consuming and induce them to save and invest in new manufacturing businesses. However, this mechanism for the promotion of industry was insufficient in many instances. The king complained to de Launay that his subjects were often too poor or unwilling to change traditional ways of production in order to create new industries. Even the offer of generous subsidies was often not enough: 'I was obliged to force my factory owners in Berlin to create a similar one in Bromberg', Frederick complained to de Launay.[24] Where his subjects were unable or unwilling to take economic initiative, Frederick considered it his duty to step in: 'You have to understand', he told de Launay, 'that in my realm there are things that are above the strength of my subjects. It is my duty to shoulder these expenses and allow them to collect the fruits.'[25] Wolfram Fischer and Adelheid Simsch have rightly emphasized the importance of this type of flexible cooperation of the Prussian state with private entrepreneurs for Prussia's economic development. For the period after 1766, it emerges that many measures for the promotion of industry were either funded by revenues from the *Régie* or even used the *Régie* for direct interventions. 'I knew about all these details', de Launay described his role in the promotion of industry, 'because he [the king] put me in charge of everything and he even ordered me to make a plan for silk factories.' The connection between fiscal administration and the promotion of industry was institutionalized in 1786 when the administration of the excise and the Fifth Department of the General Direktorium which Frederick had created in 1740 for the promotion of industry were merged into one department.[26]

The *Régie* also contributed to economic development by producing some of the first reliable information about production and consumption. One of the instances when Frederick had complained loudly about his old excise administration was when his top administrators could not answer the question of how much coffee was consumed by his subjects annually. Along with the professional French administrators, modern methods of accounting and statistics arrived in Prussia. For the first time, the king learned details about the volume, origin and type of commerce at Prussia's most important fair in Frankfurt on Oder. For a government as concerned with controlling and fine-tuning economic development as that of Frederick, this kind of information was of the highest value. In other areas, the *Régie* also worked as a quality control. In order to protect consumers, the new tax tariffs regulated, for example, how much grain was to be used in order to brew a certain quantity of beer.[27]

The changes introduced by the *Régie* resulted in a total increase of tax revenue of about 27 million thaler. The exact increase is difficult to quantify. The sources are incomplete, and the increase in revenue associated with the *Régie* is hard to separate from the fluctuations of economic activity. Much of the contemporary debate about the success or failure of the *Régie* and, indeed, the arguments of many historians, have focused on the question of how much surplus the *Régie* generated. However, this question may not only be difficult to answer but also misleading. The more durable impact of the *Régie* was associated with the structural change that it brought about. In the wake of the Seven Years War, Prussia made important steps towards a fiscal system that prioritized the joined economic development of all Prussian provinces over social privilege. The Prussian fiscal administration increasingly interacted with taxpayers, regardless of their social status and regional origin, and thus contributed not only to the economic development of Prussia but also to the construction of a Prussian state.[28]

The end of the *Régie*

Frederick II died in 1786. One of the first decisions of Frederick William II was to suspend de Launay and the creation of a *Revisions Kommission*. The findings of the commission resulted in changes mainly in three areas. First, the French officers were dismissed and replaced by Prussians, many of whom had been trained in the *Régie*; second, specific tariff changes were repealed, among them the abolition of the grain excise, and, third, the powers of the excise officers to carry out inspections and searches were limited. However, the administrative and tariff structures which had been introduced by the *Régie* remained largely unchanged. Some of the most important administrative changes with a long-term impact were the introduction of a single administration for most indirect taxes for almost the entire Prussian province; the development of a body of skilled civil servants who were specialized in the administration of indirect taxes; the elaboration of clear and functional rules for the administration, including control mechanisms, individual accountability and collegiality; the implementation of customs controls on the borders of the Prussian territories, thus reducing controls at city gates and other places within the provinces. The most important legacy of the *Régie* in the area of tariffs is perhaps the harmonization of tariffs in almost all Prussian provinces. Moreover, even after changes introduced in 1787, the tariff structure reflected the objectives for which it had been designed: to prioritize economic development, fiscal justice and tariff harmonization over fiscal privileges, short-term increases in tax revenue and local special interest.

The question why the *Régie* was partly abolished despite its substantial successes and the nature of the changes introduced can only be fully understood if they are seen in the larger context of Prussia's social history. The principal reason for Frederick William's decision to reform the *Régie* was the widespread opposition from different social groups. This resistance had already been increasing during the reign of Frederick. However, despite occasional complaints about *Régie* officers, Frederick had continued to support the administration and the objectives for which it had been created. By contrast, Frederick William's government was based more on a compromise with the estates and much less oriented towards economic and administrative reform. The new king was not only less able but also less willing to resist the increasing opposition to the *Régie*. This opposition manifested itself in different forms, among them popular uprisings, an increased volume of smuggling, complaints of individual taxpayers, grievances of corporations, cities and other representatives of social and local groups and the opposition and obstructionism of the General Direktorium. However, the different forms of resistance had a common origin in the lack of legitimacy of the *Régie*. This problem was associated with social and intellectual developments mainly in three areas: the escalation of the conflict between Crown and estates over taxation, an emerging bourgeois public sphere and a rising sentiment of national identity.

The creation of the *Régie* was a further step in a long-standing conflict between Crown and estates over fiscal privilege, the right to tax and administer taxation. The introduction of the *Régie* completed a process in which the role of the estates in the administration of the excise was progressively reduced. With the *Régie*, Prussia had for the first time an excise administration which established a direct relationship between taxpayer and Crown. On the one hand, this was a substantial success for the Crown. The ability of the Crown to raise tax revenue had increased significantly. On the other hand, the new situation was also problematic. The participation of the estates in the fiscal administration had been a mechanism which bestowed a form of approval on taxation and thus ensured a degree of fiscal legitimacy. The structure of the *Régie*, in turn, did not include any mechanism to create legitimacy. It rested exclusively on royal authority. This was not a coincidence; the original purpose of the *Régie* was to implement fiscal change without consent, but this quality also contributed to the end of the institution.

A second aspect of increasing opposition to the *Régie* was the social conflict associated with protests against government interference with production, commerce and consumption and with the rejection of intrusions into private houses by representatives of the state. Economic activities and private houses were increasingly considered to be part of a private sphere by an early modern corporatist bourgeois class which began to emerge in the cities. Conflicts developed where continuous administrative contact existed between government and this emerging private sphere. The administration of taxes was the most important area of contact between private and political sphere. The tax state is based on the clear distinction of the political and economic spheres, but taxation is at the same time the single most important mechanism through which the two spheres are connected. Conflicts are inevitable in particular in periods when the state increases the volume and breadth of taxation. The case of the *Régie* illustrates the ways in which an early modern fiscal administration interfered with economic activities such as the production, transportation, exchange and consumption of goods in many instances. The opposition of many city dwellers, small manufacturers and merchants against the *Régie* was motivated by the rejection of interference with their business affairs. A characteristic example was a conflict which resulted from a provision in the declaration patent by which the production of the lowest qualities of beer was banned. This rule was emphatically rejected because in many cities a part of the salary of journeymen was paid with a fixed amount of beer. An abolition of the lowest quality of beer would therefore have resulted in a considerable increase in labour costs for many manufacturers. The rule interfered with the production process by regulating the quality of a produce and altering the conditions of employment. One of the less flattering nicknames for the *Régie* officials was coined in this context: the officials were called *rats de cave* because of their frequent controls of brewery cellars. Also in many other cases, the *Régie* set quality standards, banned certain qualities of goods or regulated trade. The widespread indignation about these interventions manifested itself as an impressive amount of complaints and lawsuits by corporations, cities and individuals.

Intrusions of the *Régie* in the intimate situation of the bourgeois home were rejected with similar resentment. In order to enforce the coffee monopoly, *Régie* officers also searched private homes for smuggled coffee. The indignation about this practice is vividly expressed in a painting by the merchant-turned-painter Louis Katzenstein in which two *Régie* officers in uniform harass a group of women who are peacefully gathered for coffee and cakes in a bourgeois home. This activity afforded the *Régisseurs* yet another popular nickname: *Kaffeeriecher* or 'coffee smellers'. Anger about the violation of the most intimate spheres was also expressed by the philosopher Arthur Schopenhauer's mother, the daughter of a senator from Danzig: 'a type of hoop skirts which was in fashion at the time and which had very large inside pockets of which the content was hard to see from outside was the primary subject of the suspicion of the French riff-raff'. From these complaints speaks the full indignation of a person who, before the arrival of the *Régie*, would certainly only have been subject to a very lax search, in particular at the gates of the city where her father was a senator. These and other complaints illustrate to what extent many inhabitants of the cities perceived the operations of the *Régie* as lacking legitimacy.[29]

A third development which resulted in opposition to the *Régie* is expressed in the letters of the philosopher Johann Georg Hamann (1730–88), nicknamed the 'Magus of the North'. In order to make a living, he worked as a translator for the *Régie* in East Prussia where he had obtained a position with the help of Immanuel Kant. Much of his hatred for the institution that he served came from the fact that it was dominated by foreigners. In one of his letters to Frederick II, he complained about a French employee of the *Régie*, calling him a 'parvenu ... who my fatherland has seen arriving in the rags of a beggar and leaving with all the luxury of a marquis'. Hamann did not complain about the fiscal administration in general but specifically attacked the employment of foreigners. It is not clear whether Hamann saw his 'fatherland' as his native East Prussia, Prussia or whether he identified himself as German in one form or another. However, a clear notion of Prussian unity and a rejection of everything non-Prussian emerges clearly from Beguelin's critique of the *Régie*: 'It seemed as if *all Prussian subjects* had secretly sworn eternal enmity against the "Régie" and its directors.' He may have exaggerated in his description of an imagined 'oath on the Rütli' in which the inhabitants of the Prussian provinces united as Prussians in the face of oppressive foreign tax collectors. However, a substantial part of the lack of legitimacy of the *Régie* resulted from an opposition to the 'collection of the excise by foreigners who could never be nationalized'. The concept of the 'nation' remains vague in this context and the subsequent experience of French occupation during the Napoleonic Wars served as a catalyst for nationalistic sentiments on an infinitely greater scale. However, the *Régie* not only furthered the development of a unified Prussian state on the administrative level but also gave rise to a manifestation of rudimentary nationalist sentiments in Prussia in the late eighteenth century. These sentiments were expressed negatively as a rejection of foreign interference without positively defining the nation, which was understood to be the object of loyalty. However, even if this remained largely a nationalism without a nation, it contributed considerably to undermining the legitimacy of the *Régie*.[30]

The opposition to the *Régie* to which these social developments contributed was often voiced in a closed administrative environment, for example when the General Direktorium refused the execution of Frederick's plans for fiscal reform in 1765, or in the context of the tariff and revision commissions. This was not least due to the secrecy which surrounded early modern state finances. However, in the course of the conflict, public debates became increasingly important. In part, this was inevitable: communication between taxpayer and administration had been an integral part of fiscal administration. In the case of the *Régie*, the monarch and new administration went beyond the strictly necessary from the beginning and communicated directly with the public. The edict tried to convince the taxpayers that the new tariffs promoted economic development, distributed the tax burden more justly and protected consumers in many ways against fraud. In an early example of 'consumer politics', the declaration patent sought the support of consumers for measures which were opposed by many manufacturers and merchants. The declaration patent reflects in part Frederick's attempts to set his government in the context of Enlightenment thought. At the same time, the patent was an attempt to create legitimacy through direct communication with the taxpayers in the absence of political institutions which could ensure support for taxation. This attempt also corresponded with the administrative effects of the proposed fiscal reform which established a direct connection between taxpayer and central government.[31]

In light of the opposition to fiscal reform, the monarch and *Régie* encouraged communication with the *publicum*. However, the reaction was not what Frederick had hoped for. Cities and corporations complained against the new administration and severe measures had to be used in order to suppress public uprisings. Unfortunately, the sources are silent about the social composition of these early violent protests. During the following two decades, public critique and protest against the *Régie* became a habitual part of political communication mainly in the educated and bourgeois milieu of the cities. However, the hostility was not limited to Hamann, Schopenhauer and the like. The many nicknames which were used to express popular contempt for the *Régie* officers suggest that complaints about their work were part of everyday conversation among the population. Parallel to this development, the lack of legitimacy of the *Régie* resulted in escalating levels of public violence. Smuggling became more frequent and smugglers used increasingly aggressive tactics against *Régie* officers. The state reacted with severe punishment. In 1784, it became mandatory punishment for whoever killed a *Régie* officer to be broken on the wheel. The sentence was to be executed publicly in the city where the officer had operated. The escalation of public violence undermined the legitimacy of the *Régie* further, and Beguelin describes how the victims of exemplary punishment became the 'martyrs' of popular protest.[32]

In this situation, Frederick William established the *Revisions Kommission* in order to reform the *Régie*. The lines between the administrative work of the commission and publicly voiced opposition were blurred. The public controversy intensified from the time when the commission was established because a reform of the administration became probable. The commission invited proposals for fiscal reform, and some of the most important actors expressed their views in the context of the commission and publicly. Among the most prolific contributors to the public debate were Mirabeau and de Launay. They were used to a culture of public communication about fiscal matters which had started to develop in France in the 1760s and contributed to the first debate of this kind in Prussia where the matters of finance had been 'covered by the deepest secrecy'. A language of protest subsequently developed. It included frequent complaints about 'vexations' or *plackereyen* against commerce and privacy. The reform edict of Frederick William followed the demands voiced in the debate not only in substance but also adopted the language of bourgeois protest. The edict promised to put an end to 'vexations', 'nasty formalities' and the 'abuse of citizens'. In contrast to the type of economic reasoning that Frederick had proposed in the 1766 edict, his successor promised to bring prosperity through a fairer treatment of 'merchants, waggoners and mariners' who had been driven away from Prussia by 'time-consuming circuitousness and formalities, unnecessary searches of their cargo, rude encounters and frequent costly processes and inequitable fines'. The controversy about fiscal matters in general did not end with the edict of 1787. The issue remained important in public debate, and courts and administrations continued to deal with lawsuits against single *Régie* officers. One of the longest court cases, which involved various complaints about alleged wrongdoings between 1766 and 1786 by the provincial director of Kurmark, Nicolaus L'Oeillot de Mars, was only completely settled in 1810.[33]

The importance of public debate in the context of the abolition of the *Régie* was a significant social development for Prussia, which illustrates the increasing relevance of public debates in the Prussian polity. The only other occasion in which a public debate had a remotely similar impact was the controversy between the physicist Samuel König and the president of the Prussian academy of science, Pierre de Maupertuis, over the discovery of the physical 'principle of least action'. Frederick II continued to support Maupertuis against the unfounded accusations of plagiarism, but the public debate damaged the president of the academy so much that it contributed to his resignation in 1753. Both occasions were manifestations of an emerging public sphere in Prussia which reflect concerns with privacy but also other social and intellectual developments. As a result, public debate manifested itself in a way that could no longer be ignored. The increasing importance of such debates was the result of the underlying social developments and conflicts in Prussia. However, it is noteworthy that in the case of the König affair and in the case of the *Régie* French publicists had an important role in the debates: Voltaire led public criticism against Maupertuis in 1752, and Mirabeau was the most vocal opponent of the French administrators of the *Régie* in 1786. In both cases, the presence of publicists who were also part of the more vivid environment of public debate in France contributed to the stimulation of similar developments in Prussia.

Conclusions

If Prussia really was 'the most modern state in Europe in 1786', as Schmoller points out, this was in no small part a result of the developments associated with the *Régie*. The modern period is defined, among other developments, by the rise of the tax state and industrialization. Both processes were in the Prussian case inseparably connected with the changes introduced by the *Régie*. Not all of the changes made between 1766 and 1786 survived the change on the Prussian throne, but some of the more important reforms remained in place and prepared in many ways Prussia's social and economic development in the early nineteenth century. Most importantly, the case of the *Régie* illustrates that the fundamental fiscal transformations of Prussia in the second half of the eighteenth century can only be fully understood if they are seen in a transnational context and in the wider context of Prussia's social history. Transfers of ideas and individuals from France were crucial for the creation and evolution of the *Régie*, but the developments that led to the end of the *Régie* only come fully into focus if they are understood as a part of social change in Prussia. Above all, the *Régie* was an outstanding but not unique example of the interconnectedness of the development of the tax state in Europe. After the end of the *Régie* in 1786, the next important wave of fiscal reorganization in which transnational transfers would significantly influence the development of the Prussian tax state was little more than two decades away.

Notes

*Earlier versions of this essay were presented at the conferences 'Historical Perspectives on Tax Law and Policy', UCLA School of Law, 18 July 2005 and 'Transfers of Ideas about Taxation', Centre for Research in the Arts, Social Sciences and Humanities, CRASSH, University of Cambridge, 17 Sept. 2005. I would like to thank the commentators, Charlotte Crane and Chris Clark, and the participants of both conferences for their insightful comments. The essay was completed during a Fellowship at the Centre for the Study of Human Settlement and Historical Change, National University of Ireland, Galway. I am grateful for the support of the Irish Research Council for the Humanities and Social Sciences.

1 Where not otherwise indicated, all archival material is from Geheimes Staatsarchiv Preußischer Kulturbesitz (GStAPK), Berlin Dahlem, II. Hauptabteilung (HA II). The sources disagree on the number of French advisers. Indications range between 200 and 500. The number of 350 is a well-founded estimate of Walther Schultz, *Geschichte der preussischen Regieverwaltung von 1766 bis 1786* (Leipzig, 1888), p. 46. For an assessment of the *Régie* in the context of Prussia's financial history, see Gustav Schmoller, 'Einführung der französischen Regie durch Friedrich den Grossen 1766', in *Sitzungsberichte der Königliche Preussischen Akademie der Wissenschaften zu Berlin*, 1 (1888), pp. 63–79, p. 79.

2 For the importance of French immigrants for the economic development of Prussia, see among others: Sabine Beneke et al., *Die Hugenotten* (Berlin, 2006). Stefi Jersch-Wenzel, *Juden und 'Franzosen' in der Wirtschaft des Raumes Berlin/Brandenburg* (Berlin, 1978). Hermann Kellenbenz, *Deutsche Wirtschaftsgeschichte* (2 vols, Munich, 1977), pp. 340–8; Wilhelm Treue, *Wirtschafts- und Technikgeschichte Preussens* (Berlin, 1984), pp. 51–6. For the joint development of fiscal administration and national state, see: Rudolf Braun, 'Taxation, sociopolitical structure and state-building: Great Britain and Brandenburg-Prussia', in Charles Tilly (ed.), *The formation of national states in Western Europe* (Princeton, 1975), pp. 243–326. Hans-Peter Ullmann, *Der deutsche Steuerstaat* (Munich, 2005). For the approach of the Historical School, see in particular 'Einleitung' and 'Historischer Standpunkt' in Schultze, *Regieverwaltung*, pp. v–vii, 3–8; Gustav Schmoller, 'Die Epochen der preußischen Finanzpolitik', *Jahrbuch für Gesetzgebung, Verwaltung und Volkswirtschaft im Deutschen Reich* (1877), pp. 33–114; idem, 'Einführung der französischen Regie', pp. 63–79.

3 The excise in East Prussia was only administered by the *Régie* from 1773 and the new administration was never fully introduced in Westphalia. The provincial estates organized the tax collection and paid a fixed annual sum to the Crown. Chris Clark, *Iron kingdom. The rise and downfall of Prussia, 1600–1947* (London, 2006).

4 Some of the most important contributions to the very lively debate about cultural transfers between Germany and France are Michel Espagne and Michael Werner,

'Deutsch-Französischer Kulturtransfer im 18. und 19. Jahrhundert', *Francia*, 13 (1985), pp. 502–10; Michel Espagne und Mathias Middell, *Von der Elbe bis an die Seine: Kulturtransfers zwischen Frankreich und Sachsen im 18. und 19. Jahrhundert* (Leipzig, 1993); Michel Espagne, *Les transferts culturels franco-allemands* (Paris, 1999); Michel Espagne (ed.), *L'horizon anthropologique des transferts culturels* (Paris, 2004).

5 Except where otherwise stated, all translations are by the author. Gabriel-Honoré de Riquetti, Comte de Mirabeau, *De la monarchie Prussienne* (4 vols, London, 1788), IV, p. 207.

6 The Seven Years War cost Prussia at least 125 million thaler, more than 17 times the whole budget of 1740 (Ullmann, *Steuerstaat*, p. 20). Another heavy blow to French and British finances was dealt by the War of American Independence, 1775–83.

7 Adolph Wagner, 'Three extracts on public finance', in Richard Musgrave and Alan Peacock (eds), *Classics in the theory of public finance* (London, 1994 edn), pp. 1–15, p. 8. Further discussions of the historical context of expanding state activity are in Jan Glete, *War and the State in Early Modern Europe* (London, 2002). Eli Heckscher, *Merkantilismus* (2 vols, Jena, 1932), I, pp. 252–73. Wilhelm Treue, 'Das Verhältnis von Fürst, Staat und Unternehmer in der Zeit des Merkantilismus', *Vierteljahrschrift für Sozial- und Wirtschaftsgeschichte*, 44 (1957), pp. 26–56. Richard Bonney and W. M. Ormrod, 'Introduction', in idem (eds), *Crisis, revolutions and self sustained growth* (Stamford, 1999), pp. 1–22. Voltaire, 'Dictionnaire philosophique' (Entry: 'Impôt'), in idem, *Œuvres complètes de Voltaire*, Louis Moland (ed.) (52 vols, Paris, 1877–85), XIX, p. 452. Wolfram Fischer and Adelheid Simsch, 'Industrialisierung in Preussen. Eine staatliche Veranstaltung?', in Werner Süß (ed.), *Übergänge – Zeitgeschichte zwischen Utopie und Machbarkeit* (Berlin, 1989), pp. 107, 114. Ullmann, *Steuerstaat*, p. 20.

8 Mirabeau, *De la monarchie*, p. 52. Cited in G. Chaussinand-Nogaret, *The French nobility in the eighteenth century* (Cambridge, 1985), p. 51.

9 Vauban, *Projet d'une dixme royale* (n.p., 1707). Boisguilbert, *Testament politique de monsieur de Vauban* (2 vols, n.p., n.d.). Boisguilbert, *La France ruinée sous le règne de Louis XIV* (Cologne, 1696). Abbé de Saint-Pierre, *Mémoire pour l'établissement de la taille proportionnelle* (n.p., 1717). Voltaire, 'Lettre à l'occasion de l'impôt du vingtième', in idem, *Œuvres*, XXXIII, pp. 305–12. Fritz Mann, *Über Steuerpolitische Ideale* (Jena, 1935), p. 131. 'Receuil de mémoires sur la réforme et le rétablissment des finances (1715–1717)', Bibliothèque Nationale (BN), Paris, Ms Fr. 7765. 'Projets et mémoires sur les revenues de l'Etat (1715–1717)' Ms Fr. 7767, BN.

10 On the importance of privilege in the fiscal system of the *Ancien Régime*, see C.B.A. Behrens, 'Nobles, privileges, and taxes in France at the end of the Ancien Régime', *Economic History Review*, 15 (1963), pp. 451–75. Ernest Labrousse, *La crise de l'économie française à la fin de l'ancien régime et au début de la Révolution* (Paris, 1944). Kwass, *Privilege and the politics of taxation*, pp. 311–23.

11 'Généalogie des Fermiers Généraux', BN, NA 20533, MF 12790. Heinrich von Beguelin, *Accise und Zollverfassung in den Preußischen Staaten* (Berlin, 1797), p. 134. Kwass, *Privilege*, pp. 185, 165.

12 Mirabeau, *De la monarchie*, VI, p. 403. Schultze, *Regieverwaltung*, pp. 25–7. Heinrich von Beguelin, *Historisch kritische Darstellung der Akzise- und Zollverfassung in den preußischen Staaten* (Berlin, 1797), p. 111.

13 Schmoller, 'Epochen der preußischen Finanzpolitik', p. 61. Christoph Tenzel, *Entdeckte Goldgrube der Akzise* (Zerbst, 1685), pp. 1–11. Similar arguments can be found with other authors of the seventeenth and eighteenth centuries, Josiah Child, *A new discourse of trade* (London, n.d.), p. 5. Nathaniel Gould, *An essay on the publick debts of*

the kingdom (London, 1726), pp. 55–7. Thomas Hobbes, *Leviathan* (Amsterdam, 1670), p. 162. Montesquieu, *De l'esprit des lois* (Paris, 1755), XIII, ch. 14. Gottfried von Thile, *Nachricht von der Churmärkischen Contributions und Schoß Einrichtung* (Halle, 1768), pp. 11–15. Mirabeau, *De la monarchie*, p. 67. William Petty, *Treatise of taxes and contribution* (London, 1662), p. 94. For an overview over Prussian administration, see Gustav Schmoller, *Preußische Verfassungs-, Verwaltungs- und Finanzgeschichte* (Berlin, 1921), pp. 45–105, 133–53.

14 'Notizen über das Österreichische Accise und Zollwesen', Gen. Akzise/Zolldept., A Titel IV, no. 1. Frederick II, King of Prussia, *Oeuvres* (29 vols, Berlin, 1856), XIX, p. 398. For the importance of France for German princes, see Timothy Blanning, *The culture of power and power of culture* (Oxford, 2002).

15 'Acta betr. die Geheimen Finanz Räthe und ehemaligen accise Régisseure Herrn v. Roux und Hainchelin, 1767–1803', Gen. Akzise/Zolldept., A Titel X, no. 1. 'Cabinetsorders und Dokumente aus Akten des Generalakzise und Zolldepartments', Gen. Akzise/Zolldept., A Titel XIV, Sect. 1, no. 1c. 'Cabinetsorders Bd. I, 1766–1784', Gen. Akzise/Zolldept., A Titel XIV, Sect. 1b. 'Acta betreffend die der General Accise und Zoll-Administration von der königl. Majestät erteilte und allerhöchstselbst revidierte Instruction, dazu die in Verfolg derselben erlassenen Verfügungen. 1767', Gen. Akzise/Zolldept. A, Tit. 1, Sect 2, no. 1. 'Handel mit Frankreich, Etablierung von Franzosen in Preussen. 1769, Etatsminister v.d. Horst, De la Haye de Launay', HA I, Rep. 96, Nr. 424 D. Beguelin, *Akzise- und Zollverfassung*, pp. 122, 154–64. Jean-Claude Waquet, 'Les Fermes Générales dans l'Europe des lumières: le cas Toscan', *Mélanges de l'École Française de Rome*, 89 (1977), pp. 983–1027. Christine Lebeau, *Aristocrates et grand commis à la cour de Vienne* (Paris, 1996).

16 Marc Antoine de Lahaye de Launay, *Justification due système d'économie politique et financière de Frederic II, roi de Prusse pour servir de réfutation à tout ce que M. le Comte de Mirabeau a hazardé à ce sujet dans son ouvrage de la Monarchie Prussienne* (n.p., n.d.), p. 10. Schultze, *Regieverwaltung*, p. 18. Mann, *Steuerpolitische Ideale*, p. 44.

17 De Launay, *Justification*, pp. 100, 9. Colin Jones, *The great nation* (London, 2002), pp. 266, 554.

18 Beguelin, *Akzise und Zollverfassung*, p. 135.

19 For a detailed discussion of the changes, see Schultze, *Regieverwaltung*.

20 'Vorläufiges Declarationspatent wegen einer für sämtliche Königlich Preussische Provinzien, wo bishero die Accise eingeführt gewesen, vom 1ten Junii 1766 an, allergnädigst gut gefunden neuen Einrichtung des Accise- und Zoll-Sachen. De dato Berlin, den 14ten April 1766', *Novum Corpus Constitutionum Prussico-Brandenburgensium Preacipue Marchicarum* (12 vols, Berlin, 1771), VI, pp. 294–307, p. 294. Mirabeau, *De la monarchie*, p. 146. 'Seiner Königlichen Majestät in Preussen revidirter und mittelst allergnädigster Cabinets-Ordre vom 14ten März 1769. approbirter Accise-Tarif für die Städte des Herzogthums Vor- und Hinter-Pommern', *Novum Corpus*, IV, pp. 5397–532. De Launay, *Justification*, p. 72, 107. 'Actes concernant la formation des nouveaux tarifs d'Accises, 1768–1772', Gen. Akzise/Zolldept., A Titel XV, Sekt. 1, no. 1. 'Cabinetsorders, Erlasse, Immediatberichte', Gen. Akzise/Zolldept., A Titel XIV, Sect. 1 b. Many objections against the new tariff were also raised at the provincial level. See 'Acta wegen Anfertigung eines neuen Accise Tarifs von Preussen und Lithauen, 1768–1770', Gen. Akzise/Zolldept., A Titel XV, Sect. 3, no. 4. 'Acta wegen der Anfertigung des neuen Accise Tarifs von Pommern. 1768–1769', Gen. Akzise/Zolldept., A Titel XV, Sect. 3, no. 7. 'Acta betr. den neuen Pomm. Accise Tariff und die draus ergangene Resolut. De ano 1749', General Direktorium Pommern Materien General Accise, Nr. 20b. The administration of the excise prior to the *Régie* is described vividly in Schmoller, *Preußische Verfassungs-,*

Verwaltungs- und Finanzgeschichte, p. 150. For previous attempts of Frederick to improve the administrative efficiency, see for example 'Seiner königl. Majestät in Preussen Allergnädigster neu approbirtes Reglement und Verfassung des ganzen Accise Wesen der Vor- und Hinterpommerschen Städten. De Dato Berlin, den 28. Febr. 1749', General Direktorium, Pommern Materien General Accise, no. 20a.

21 Since the volume of files documenting conflicts and complaints is very large. In this context only some examples from East Prussia can be cited. Call numbers are BI Titel X, no. 1–9: 'Acta gen.: wegen der Accise Freiheit. 1719–1780', 'Acta die Accise Freiheit des Landadels betreffend. 1772–1799', 'Acta die Accise Freiheit auf den Communion Wein betr. 1773–1796', 'Acta gen. wegen der Accise Freiheit der Hospitäler, Zuchthäuser und Klöster und Kirchen. 1773–1815', 'Acta die von der Admiralität zu Königsberg nachgesagten Accise Freiheit auf ihren Consumptiblien betr. 1756–1809'. For the operations of the courts of the *Régie* see, for example, the files of the court in Halberstadt. Call numbers Gen. Akzise/Zolldept., B IX Titel X, no. 1–3: 'Acta des Halberstädtischen *Pronvincial* Régie Gerichts, 1767–1804', 'Objets généraux concernant le contentieux. 3 Bde 1772–1795', 'Acta betreffend den Schleichhandel mit verbotenen und hochimpostierten Waaren. Generalia. 1773–1794'. For the instructions of Frederick, see 'Vorläufiges Declarationspatent', p. 305.

22 Schultze, *Preußische Regieverwaltung*, p. 186. 'Actes concernant la formation des nouveaux tariffs d'Accises, 1768–1772', Gen. Akzise/Zolldept., A Titel XV, Sekt. 1, no. 1. For the relevance of the Historical School in the transfer of fiscal ideas in the nineteenth century, see the essays by Holger Nehring and Andreas Thier in this volume.

23 'Vorläufiges Declarationspatent', p. 294. De Launay, *Justification*, pp. 58, 57. 'Revidirter ... Accise-Tarif', pp. 5397–532.

24 Acta betr das der Splittgerberischen Fabriken erteilte Privilegium exclusivum zur Einrichtung einer Zucker Raffinerie in Bromberg'. Gen. Akzise/Zolldept., BII Tit. XXVIII, no. 3.

25 Delaunay, *Justification*, p. 72.

26 Delaunay, *Justification*, pp. 78, 60. 'Acta betr. Das der Splittgerberischen Fabriken erteilte Privilegium exclusivum zur Errichtung einer Zucker Raffinerie in Bromberg', Gen. Akzise/Zolldept., BII Titel XXVIII, Nr. 3. Delaunay, *Justification*, p. 72. Fischer/ Simsch, 'Industrialisierung in Preussen'. De Launay, *Justification*, p. 74. 'Acta betr. Die den Seiden Fabrikanten auf ihre außerhalb Landes debitierten Saiden Waaren bewilligten Bonificationen. 1768–1782', Gen. Akzise/Zolldept., A Titel XXV, Sect. 11, no. 1. 'Acta betreffend die Verbindung des 4. und 5. Departements des General Direktoriums mit der General Accise und Zolladministration zu einem Departement mit dem Namen: General Fabriken und Comerzial- wie auch Accise und Zoll Departement, 1786–1803', Gen. Akzise/Zolldept., A Titel I, Section 2, no. 2.

27 Johann Preuss (ed.), *Urkundenbuch zur Geschichte Friedrichs des Großen* (5 vols, Berlin, 1832–34), III, p. 10. Delaunay, *Justification*, p. 36. 'Vorläufiges Declarationspatent', p. 301.

28 Schultze, *Preußische Regieverwaltung*, p. 166.

29 Habermas, *Strukturwandel*, pp. 24, 83. Schultze, *Preußische Regieverfassung*, p. 222. 'Actes concernant la formation des nouveaux tarifs d'Accises, 1768–1772', Gen. Akzise/Zolldept., A Titel XV, Sekt. 1, no. 1. Beguelin, *Akzise und Zollverfassung*, pp. 127, 170. For complaints and lawsuits on the local level, see, for example, the files for East Prussia: 'Acate betr. Die von einem Gebraude Bier zu ziehende Anzahl Tonnen Courant oder Tafelbier und Versteuerung derselben, 1766–1794', BI Titel XI, no. 6. 'Acta gen. Die zu Entscheidung und Bestrafung der Accise Verbrechen

angeordneten Behörden und die dazu eingegangenen Verordnungen betr. Bd. I 1767–1776. Bd. II 1777–1786', BI Titel XXXII, no. 1. 'Acta gen. betr. Die zur Verhütung der Defraudationen und Contraventionen getroffenen Maßregeln, 1771–1798', BI Titel XXXII, no. 2. Louis Katzenstein, *Die Kaffeeriecher des Alten Fritz*, painting 1892. Cited in Bernt Engelmann, *Preußen* (Munich, 1979), p. 123.

30 Anselm Kiefer, 'Vorrede', in idem (ed.), *Weisheits-Sprüche und Witzreden aus Johann Georg Hamann's und Immanuel Kant's sämtlicher Schriften* (Amberg, 1828), p. 2. Johann Georg Hamann to Frederick II, king of Prussia, 1 Jan. 1783, in Walther Ziesemer und Arthur Henkel (eds), *Johann Georg Hamann Briefwechsel* (7 vols, Frankfurt, 1957), V, p. 1. Beguelin, *Akzise und Zollverfassung*, pp. 118, 161. My emphasis.

31 'Vorläufiges Declarationspatent', pp. 294ff.

32 Beguelin, *Akzise und Zollverfassung*, pp. 127, 118. 'Königliche Kabinetts Order wie die Contrebandiers bestraft werden sollen. De Dato Potsdam, 23 März 1784', *Novum Corpus*, VIII, pp. 2821–2, p. 2821.

33 'Acta auffassend die Inspektion für die Accise und Zoll Revisions Commission und die von derselben abgehaltenen Konferenz Protocolle. 1786–87', Gen. Akzise/Zolldept., A Titel I, Section 3, no. 1. 'Acte die bezügl. der Accise Revisions Commission erforderlich gewordenen Officanten, darunter bei Ausarbeitung der neuen Tarife und die ihnen dafür bewilligten Diäten und Gratificationen betreffend. 1786–1787', Gen. Akzise/Zolldept., A Titel I Section 3, no. 2. 'Acta die von der Accise Revision Commission betreffs Ihrer Operationen eingegangenen Nachfrange, Extrakte, Akten pp und deren Rückgabe betreffend Vorschläge', Gen. Akzise/Zolldept., A Titel I, Sect. 3, no. 3. Mirabeau, *De la monarchie*, pp. 2, 142. Beguelin, *Akzise und Zollverfassung*, p. 147. 'Accise Tarif für Berlin und sämmtliche Chur- und Neumärkischen Städte. De Dato Berlin den 20. Februar 1787', *Novum Corpus*, VIII, pp. 321–775, p. 255. 'Acta betreffend den Provinzial accise und Zoll Director Loeillot zu Cuestrin. 1780–1799', Abt. 24, Gen. Akzise/Zolldept. B V, Titel 1, no. 1. For the genealogy and ennoblement of the L'Oeillot family, see documents in the Heroldamt, GStAPK, HA I, 176, VI, L, nos. 60 and 441.

4
The Napoleonic Empire in Italy: the Transfer of Tax Ideas and Political Legitimacy, 1802–14

Alexander Grab

On 20 April 1814, a large and agitated crowd gathered outside the Senate building in Milan, the capital of the Napoleonic Kingdom of Italy. Two weeks earlier, on 6 April, Napoleon had abdicated as the French emperor. Now, opponents of the Napoleonic government in Milan were plotting an uprising, hoping to use the crowd to overthrow the regime. The anti-French atmosphere was palpable. The throng broke into the Senate, which was in session, demolishing the interior and forcing the senators to flee. The crowd was then incited to proceed to San Fedele, where the house of Giuseppe Prina, the hated finance minister, was located. Once inside the house, the angry mob looted it, beat up Prina, and threw him out of the window. The battered body of the poor finance minister continued to be hit and stabbed in the street until he perished.[1] Soon, the Austrians entered Milan and the Kingdom of Italy expired. Prina's murder symbolized the end of the Napoleonic regime in northern Italy, which had lost its legitimacy in good part due to the heavy taxes it had imposed and the efficiency with which it collected them.

It is a commonplace among Napoleonic historians that exploiting the financial resources of his satellite states (*pays conquis*) and annexed territories (*pays réunis*) was one of the two most important interests of Napoleon in those occupied lands, the second being drafting soldiers to his *Grande Armée*. French revenues were insufficient to pay for his military campaigns. Particularly after 1806, Napoleon based his fiscal policy on the principle that 'war should support war'.[2] Naturally, the more resources the French ruler extracted from the conquered territories, the less he needed to secure from France, thus reducing the internal opposition to his taxation policies. According to one estimate, during 1804–14, occupied Europe paid half of Napoleon's military expenses.[3] Aside from taxes and requisitions, the French emperor also forced satellite states to maintain costly national armies, which he then integrated into the *Grande Armée*, and to pay for the upkeep of French armies stationed on their soil. In sum, without the massive financial support from the occupied lands, Napoleon would have been unable to sustain and expand his empire.

Northern Italy constituted a highly important source of revenues for Napoleon. The Lombard plains possessed highly developed agriculture, while other areas, including the Veneto and the Papal Legations of Bologna and Ferrara, also had a solid potential for economic growth once they underwent reforms. Aside from conscription, the financial problem was the most challenging for the Napoleonic authorities of the Republic and Kingdom of Italy (1802–14). Finances constituted a pivotal element in their relations with France, involving issues of state power and legitimacy, administrative efficiency, political and economic interests, and social justice. Ideas for new tax policies, the core of public finances, were transferred into the northern Italian state from two sources: imperial France itself and pre-revolutionary Austrian Lombardy. As with other areas of Napoleonic reforms, the emperor ordered the implementation of French tax policies in Italy. This export of tax ideas and policies was motivated by Napoleon's conviction that the French system was more efficient and superior to local structures and hence would bring in higher revenues. Moreover, introducing the French system into his occupied lands and satellite states aimed at unifying and centralizing the French Empire, thereby consolidating Napoleonic rule. Here, it must be emphasized that the Republic and Kingdom of Italy constituted one of the most transformed Napoleonic satellite states.[4] This was due to the relatively long duration of French domination in northern Italy and the cooperation of the local elites. As for Austrian Lombardy, it served as a source of tax concepts and reforms for Prina, Napoleon's faithful finance minister, who restored a number of Lombard taxes that had been established successfully by the Austrian Enlightened Absolutists Maria Teresa and Joseph II.

This chapter will focus on the tax system in the Republic and Kingdom of Italy, the transfer of new tax ideas into the new state, and the similarities with the French and the Austrian Lombard systems. It will analyse the Napoleonic fiscal demands, tax revenues, the reform programmes launched by the government and how efficiently it implemented them, the impact of the tax policies on Italian society and state's power and legitimacy, and the response of the population to these policies. It will also show how finances affected the relationship between Napoleonic France and its Italian satellite state.

Napoleonic state-building in Italy

In April 1796, Napoleon launched his first Italian campaign, defeating the Austrians and establishing French hegemony in northern Italy. In June 1797 he created the Cisalpine Republic, the longest and most significant Italian 'Sister Republic', which lasted until April 1799. In January 1802, Napoleon replaced the Second Cisalpine Republic with the Italian Republic, becoming its president. In March 1805, following his coronation as emperor, Napoleon transformed that Republic into the Kingdom of Italy (*Regno d'Italia*) with him as the king and his stepson, Eugène de Beauharnais, as his viceroy in Milan.

The Kingdom, which lasted to 1814, consisted of regions formerly part of the Austrian Empire, Piedmont, the Duchy of Modena, the Venetian Republic, and the Papal State, and at its peak covered an area of 35,000 square miles with a population of 6.7 million inhabitants. The administration of the Republic/Kingdom was centralized and uniform and was modelled on the French example.

Napoleon considered northern Italy, above all Lombardy, a rich country capable of sustaining any financial burden he imposed, and seemed unconcerned with its impact on the population. In 1806, he wrote Eugène, 'You have the most prosperous finances in the world.'[5] In January 1810, despite a growing deficit, Napoleon declared that 'the Kingdom of Italy is rich and possesses several important resources'.[6] This optimistic picture of Italian finances explains Napoleon's inability to accept the deterioration of fiscal conditions in the Kingdom's last years. The emperor extracted from northern Italy increasing contributions to support his military campaigns and ordered the establishment of a costly Italian army. To fulfil those demands the Italian authorities increased existing taxes and established new ones. They reformed the financial administration, including tax collection, aiming to make it more uniform and efficient. In launching those reforms, the government borrowed ideas from Napoleonic France and Austrian Lombardy. The implementation of those innovations transformed the financial administration into one of the most well managed in Napoleonic Europe. At the same time, however, the heavier fiscal pressure alienated the population, thereby hurting the state's legitimacy and undermining political stability. Indeed, the financial policy in northern Italy serves as a good example of the Napoleonic regime's Janus face of subordination and exploitation combined with innovation and progress.[7] The new financial administration was based largely on the French model.[8]

This is not surprising since the main Napoleonic accomplishment 'belongs in the domain of financial administration; it was a more rigorous application of networks already existing or taken from an altogether classical arsenal'.[9] As in France, two separate ministries, treasury and finance, ran the fiscal administration. The Treasury received and administered the tax revenues and other types of income and made the payments. The treasury minister received reports about all those activities. No payment could be made without his signature.[10]

The finance minister, the more significant of the two, was in charge of assuring the collection of direct and indirect taxes and revenues from customs and national property.[11] The main architect behind the financial policy in the Republic/Kingdom of Italy was the finance minister Giuseppe Prina (1766–1814).[12] Prina served as finance minister during the entire 12 years of the Republic/Kingdom. A native of the city of Novara, Prina had served in the Piedmontese administration in the 1790s. In April 1802, Napoleon appointed him as the minister of finance of the Republic of Italy. Prina demonstrated total devotion to Napoleon, making every effort to satisfy his fiscal needs. His main goals were to increase state income and balance the budget. Through inexhaustible work and many reforms, Prina modernized the financial system, making it more efficient, uniform and remunerative. The emperor expressed his estimate of Prina's work in his letters to Eugène: 'There is no person who is more essential than the finance minister; he is a hard worker who knows his field.'[13] In his zeal to fulfil Napoleon's fiscal needs, however, Prina imposed an increasing burden on the population, provoking much dissatisfaction. In harmony with the French system and Napoleon's objectives, Prina exerted major efforts to create a central financial administration designed to increase state revenues, consolidate the state's power, and undermine the power of the regional elites who had controlled and manipulated the fiscal systems under the Old Regime. He was determined to create an efficient bureaucracy, loyal to the state and chosen on the basis of merit, that would routinize tax collection, eliminate fiscal privileges and reduce administrative costs. Prina stressed the political benefits of financial standardization: 'unifying the different systems of finance of the various provinces that compose the Republic, will strengthen the moral union of its diverse population'.[14]

Upon the formation of the Kingdom, Prina reorganized his ministry, aiming at centralizing the financial machinery and making it more effective. Creating new direct and indirect taxes and the annexation of new territories to the Kingdom required a restructuring of financial organization. Prina wished to introduce a greater degree of specialization in financial management. Prina also aimed at gaining complete control over property tax, which he had shared with the interior minister under the Republic. On 7 June 1805, the government placed the administration of the *censo* under the Finance Ministry, appointing Ambrogio Birago, an experienced official, to head its management. Then, on 28 June 1805, the authorities formed seven separate departments, *direzioni nazionali*, all under the authority of the finance minister: customs; salt, tobacco, powder, and consumption duties; national property and consolidated duties; *censo* and direct taxes; lottery; mints; post office.[15] With his reform, Prina constructed a hierarchical machinery consisting of qualified and loyal officials and designed to increase his control over the financial system, combat law violations, and ultimately increase state revenues and provide Napoleon with accurate and detailed annual budgets.

The two most important *direzioni* were those of *censo* and indirect imposts. The former consisted of a *direttore generale* and four *direttori* each running a different area, including the cadastre and the exaction of property, personal and professionals' taxes. Each department had a *direzione del censo* and each district had a *cancelliere del censo*.[16] Once the cadastre began in 1807, the *cancellieri* supervised its progress, looked after the maps and registrations, and made estimate corrections. They kept lists of taxpayers and provided the tax collectors with vital information.

The *direzione generale* of monopolies and consumption fees consisted of a *direttore generale* and four administrators, one for each of the taxed articles: salt, tobacco, powder and consumption duties. They managed the production, transport, sale and tariffs, and fought against law violations. The large size of the staff employed by the Finance Ministry indicates the increasing number of its functions and rising specialization. The finance minister had 245 employees and employed 5198 throughout the state.[17] In 1811, 415 people worked on the cadastre.

The success of the financial system depended on efficient tax collection. Prina invested much effort to improve and make it more rigorous and placed tax collectors under tight scrutiny. On 26 March 1804, the authorities restructured direct tax collection, modelling it on the French system.[18] Power in that area was removed from local government and placed in the hands of the central authorities. Key officials were communal tax collectors, *ricevitori comunali*, the counterpart of the French communal *percepteurs*. They were required to sign a three-year renewable contract and to place a security deposit, the equivalent of the *cautionnement* in France. They were forbidden from suspending the collection except in case of war, flood or plague. Collectors could not be related to the local officials or be public functionaries themselves. They were selected through an auction; the winner was the one who asked for the lowest compensation. Late taxpayers paid a fine, which the collectors kept. After 15 days of delay, they were authorized to confiscate the indebted taxpayer's property and sell it to cover the unpaid tax. Communal collectors were obliged to transfer the taxes to departmental collectors, the counterpart of the French *receveur général*, whether they raised them or not. The prefect constituted the ultimate authority in assuring that all the rules were followed. At the end of the year, collectors had to present all their accounts to the communal council. At the end of their three-year term, they had to submit their accounts to the finance minister. Many of these norms applied to departmental collectors who were state employees. They had to deliver the taxes that they received from the communal collectors to the Ministry of Treasury within five days.

For the purpose of collecting indirect taxes, the Republic was divided into 22 financial districts: 12 *regolatorie* and 10 *delegazioni di finanza*. The former collected taxes in 12 departments while the *delegati* did the same in 10 major cities. The government employed 2351 subordinates to carry out that task. In June 1805, the authorities transformed these offices, labelling them *intendenti*, and placed them under the *direzione generale* of salt, tobacco, powder and consumption fees.[19] The number of *intendenti* rose to 27 when the Kingdom expanded. They were assisted by the Guardia di Finanza, created in June 1804 and numbering more than 2000 men. However, the more efficient tax collection also posed problems of political legitimacy for the authorities. Most taxpayers were not used to such an effective and accurate tax system and this augmented their resentment of the Napoleonic regime and led to opposition, as we shall see. Although the government planned to have a collector in every *comune*, this proved difficult. The prefects of the departments of Adige, Bacchiglione and Passariano reported that in many remote mountainous *comuni* nobody applied for that position.[20] Prina lamented that 'the lack of a collector (in every *comune*) produces great delays in the payments of these taxes, causing very serious damage to public service'.[21] He went on to list the departments where many *comuni* lacked a collector: Passariano, about 100 *comuni*; Adriatico, 6; Tagliamento, 32; and Reno, 21. He urged the local officials to do their best to find a collector for every *comune*. The problem persisted, however, and the authorities finally decreed that wherever a collector could not be found, the prefect would appoint a temporary one for one year.[22]

Public expenditure

A major motivation behind the expansion and centralization of the financial bureaucracy was to increase public revenues and the ability to pay for the growing military expenses and other state needs. Public expenses were divided among seven ministries: war and navy, interior, finance, treasury, justice, foreign relations and religion. Two other substantial expenses included payments for the French army in Italy, and servicing the public debt.[23] Table 4.1 shows public expenses under the Republic (1804) and the Kingdom (1807, 1811).

Public expenditure doubled during the years 1802–11 from 70.6 to 142.4 million lire. Much of the rise stemmed from an escalation in military costs, by far the most important item in the budget. They paid for both the French troops stationed in Italy (*l'armée d'Italie*) and the conscripted Italian army.[24]

The combined payments for the French troops in Italy and the Italian army constituted well over half of the budget. Military costs, along with the annual expenses of the viceroy's court (civil list), amounted to more than 60 per cent of the budget. After deducting the annual expenses of servicing the public debt (10–15 per cent), only 25–30 per cent remained for the other six ministries. The Interior Ministry's budget constituted 11–15 per cent of the state's expenditure. It covered salaries of state officials, public education, health, prisons, subsidies to the arts, manufacturing and trade, welfare, national festivities, and

Table 4.1 Budget allocations (in millions of lire), 1804–11

	1804	*1807*	*1811*
War and the upkeep of the French army	52.0	70.0	84.7
Interior	10.5	15.3	16.6
Finance	24.8	2.0	3.1
Treasury	0.16	0.6	2.0
Justice	1.2	6.0	7.6
Foreign relations	1.4	1.0	0.8
Religion	0.13	0.2	0.2
Public debt	–	15.6	21.0
Total	90.19	110.7	136.0

Source: *Conto dell'amministrazione delle finanze del Regno d'Italia degli anni* 1804, 1807, 1811.

maintenance and expansion of transportation infrastructure. The ministries of Treasury and Finances paid primarily for salaries and office expenditures. The budget of the Justice Ministry increased considerably under the Kingdom, owing to the introduction of *Code Napoléon* and the expansion of the judiciary system. The budget of the Foreign Ministry paid for salaries and other costs, like trips, post and couriers of the diplomatic delegations in various cities, most notably Paris, and for the Foreign Ministry in Milan. The budget of the Ministry of Religion, the smallest one, consisted of bureaucratic expenses and officials' salaries.

Taxation policies in Napoleonic Italy

Direct taxes

Revenues of the Republic and Kingdom of Italy consisted of taxes, sale of national properties, customs and lottery. Yet taxes constituted the main source of state income. To respond to Napoleon's rising fiscal pressure and augment public revenues, state government reformed the tax system, increasing existing taxes and creating new ones. Prina drew the idea for many of the new taxes from the experience of Lombardy when it had been governed by the Habsburg rulers before the arrival of the French armies. His efforts to increase state revenues were greatly helped by the Kingdom's territorial expansion during 1806–10, and the addition of tens of thousands of new taxpayers. Prina transferred the new taxes and tax collection methods into these lands, including the Veneto, parts of the Papal State, and South Tyrol, aiming to integrate them into the Kingdom of Italy and increasing tax revenues.

Taxes were divided into two main groups, direct and indirect. Direct taxes consisted of land tax, personal tax, and tax on free professionals, artisans and merchants.

Land tax was the most important source of revenues, constituting more than one-third of the state's income. Property tax, *la contribution foncière*, had existed in France since 1791 while its counterpart, *l'imposta fondiaria*, was established in Austrian Lombardy in 1760. The Italian authorities set up an annual land tax rate, ordering landowners to pay a fixed amount of *denari* for every *scudo* of property value. In 1812, the total land value stood at 297,080,366 *scudi*. Prina tried hard to keep the land tax at a relatively modest level. At times, however, he had to impose a surtax (*sovrimposta*) to satisfy Napoleon's military needs. In 1805 and 1806 he raised land tax from 40 to 60 and 61 *denari*.[25] In 1808, he lowered it to 48, where it stayed for the remainder of the Napoleonic years. Prina's pro-landowner policy is striking since state expenses increased progressively and prices of agricultural products were rising after 1806, meaning that landowners paid proportionately lower taxes.[26] This policy was motivated by his desire to secure the support of landowners, the most important social base of the regime. Moreover, it reflected the fact that Napoleon pursued the same land tax policy in France where the weight of the *contribution foncière* was lowered from 240 million francs in 1791 to 208 million in 1810.[27] As in France, rallying the landowning class to the regime aimed at strengthening the state's power and political legitimacy. The rise in the number of taxpayers from the new territories, and frequent increases in indirect taxes, a policy that hurt the lower classes, enabled Prina to maintain moderate levels of land tax. However, while Prina reduced the land tax, the government imposed new payments on the departments and the *comuni*, which forced them to increase local property taxes. In short, the burden on landowners was higher than the national land tax indicated (see Table 4.2).

It is difficult to estimate precisely what percentage of their income property owners paid in land tax. The contemporary Milanese economist Giuseppe Pecchio estimated that it ranged between one-third and one-quarter or even less. He insisted, however, that 'the total load, although heavy, was not exorbitant', as can be proved by agricultural prosperity and the small number of persons in arrears.[28] Indeed, in most years, at least 90 per cent of land tax was paid on time. Out of a total of 258.6 million lire owed in land tax during 1805–9, landowners had paid all but 3 million (1.16 per cent) by 1 October 1811.[29]

The most serious flaw in the land tax system was the lack of a uniform land evaluation. While the Lombard departments possessed the celebrated Theresian cadastre (*catasto*),[30] other departments possessed either no survey or had old and unreliable ones. Differences in tax assessment caused great inequalities among taxpayers. The interior minister complained of 'enormous disparities of treatment' between taxpayers in the departments of Mella and Serio.[31] Officials in the departments of Mella, Rubicone and Serio reported on irregularities in land evaluation, and discontented taxpayers.[32]

The six Veneto departments, annexed to the Kingdom in 1806, posed grave problems in particular, endangering the state's legitimacy and undermining its support in the new departments. Shortly after their annexation, the authorities imposed a property tax of 12.25 million lire on the Veneto.[33] In March 1808, the government established a provisional *estimo* for the entire region, amounting to 90,898,442 *scudi*, dividing it among the various departments.[34]

Table 4.2 Gross income from land tax, 1801–12

Year	*National*	*Departmental*	*Communal*	*Total*
1801	50,771,644	5,230,806	–	56,002,451
1802	37,027,445	5,276,180	–	42,303,626
1805	45,323,501	8,344,501	6,086,348	59,753,875
1808	49,098,440	1,238,819	7,392,868	57,010,201
1810	50,981,846	1,568,624	8,472,621	61,023,092
1812	51,120,347	5,235,069	11,166,628	67,522,041

Source: *Conto*, 1804, 1805, 1808, 1810, 1812.

Those reforms aroused great dissatisfaction among landowners, who viewed the new *estimo* as excessive. In the department of Adriatico property owners complained that their tax surpassed their income.[35] In Tagliamento 'many proprietors disappear because of their inability to satisfy a tax poorly applied to them'.[36] In Bachiglione officials concluded that the *estimo* needed to be corrected, and reported that growers extirpated mulberry trees to reduce their property's value.[37] Vociferous challenges against the land tax estimate in the department of Passariano forced the authorities to reduce it by 5.4 million lire.[38]

A standardized property survey was needed to eliminate those problems. The main model for Prina was the successful Theresian cadastre, *catasto*, which entered into effect in Lombardy in 1760. The finance minister strongly supported a uniform land assessment, believing that it would increase the amount of taxable land.[39] Eugène concurred, stressing the advantages of such a reform: 'This operation is very essential; there is no doubt that it will augment the profits of the Treasury and at the same time establish just equality among tax payers.'[40] Moreover, by launching a cadastre, the state would strengthen its control over the tax system and hence its political power. Yet, during the Republic the landed classes succeeded in blocking any change, fearing higher taxes and loss of their ability to manipulate the system. Prina summed up that opposition: 'The cadastre has as enemies entire departments which know that they contribute less than what they have to.'[41]

With the formation of the Kingdom, the need to rationalize the property tax grew more urgent. Launching a uniform property survey controlled by the central government was part of the efforts of the authorities to integrate the different provinces into a strong, unified state. Besides, compiling a cadastre clearly aimed at instituting a more precise and remunerative fiscal system capable of better satisfying the state's rising costs. Napoleon viewed the cadastre as a sanction of the right of private property that was the centrepiece of his Civil Code and mentioned that reform in his coronation speech in May 1805.[42]

On 12 January 1807, the emperor ordered the initiation of a land survey in the Kingdom.[43] On 13 April, the government published measurement and mapping rules.[44] This coincided with land assessments in France (15 September 1807) and the Kingdom of Holland (20 January 1807).[45] In the Kingdom of Italy, each department was divided into surveyed *comuni*, and for each *comune* a map was drawn where proprietors' plots were marked. Surveyors had to prepare a register (*sommarione*), specifying the landowner's name, size, quality of the property, and the cultivated product. The state, departments and *comuni* shared the expenses of this operation.[46]

Under Prina's supervision this operation progressed smoothly. He insisted that the cadastre replaced 'centuries of confusion and complaints' with order and was the only method that could 'create the bases of a reasonable equality among tax payers'.[47] In 1811, 415 assessors were surveying property in 15 departments. By the end of 1812, Prina informed Napoleon that close to

50 per cent of the total state's area (namely 40,781,352 *pertiche* out of 83,826,712) had been assessed.[48] Since five departments (Agogna, Alto Po, Lario, Mincio and Olona), with a total area of 15,824,898 *pertiche*, had completed accurate land surveys under previous regimes, it meant that by 1812 only 27,202,462 *pertiche* remained unassessed. Prina expected to complete the entire enterprise by 1816 or 1817. While the Napoleonic regime never concluded the land survey, it constituted a very significant reform that increased tax revenues. Moreover, it established uniformity and equality among taxpayers, strengthened the central government and helped to undermine the traditional autonomy of the local elites who had controlled the old system.

The two remaining direct taxes, personal tax and the tax on free professionals, merchants and artisans, serve as good examples of Prina's transfer of tax ideas into the new state. Both originated from Austrian Lombardy. A version of the latter, known as the *patente*, also existed in France. Prina re-established them during the Kingdom years in response to the growing Napoleonic fiscal pressure. Under the Habsburgs, personal tax amounted to seven lire and was paid by the male population aged 14 to 60. The income was equally divided between state and *comuni*. The revolutionary authorities had abolished the half that went to the state in 1796 and the portion of the *comuni* in 1801. In July 1802, Prina reintroduced the quota allocated to the local expenses for unwalled towns, *comuni aperti*. In December 1805, he re-established the state's portion.[49] Only the rural population, which lived in the *comuni aperti*, paid personal tax. While the state exacted its entire quota, the *comuni* usually collected less than their share in order to alleviate the tax burden on the lower classes. In 1807, the average personal tax reached 4.62 per taxpayer, rising to 5.10 lire in 1811.

Personal tax constituted a major burden on the poor country population, serving as a concrete example of the increasing tax load on the lower classes under Napoleon. Maintaining personal tax as a permanent imposition after 1806 aimed at offsetting the reduction of land tax. Collection of the hated personal tax met with some opposition. Local officials were under pressure not to comply with the new tax and many failed to complete the taxpayers' rolls. Prina complained that while the rural population rose, the number of taxpayers fell. Many people failed to pay the tax on time. In 1809 and 1810, only 70 and 83 per cent, respectively, paid the tax by the due date. To combat those tax evasions, Prina issued a comprehensive *Regolamento* aimed at tightening the tax management.[50] In 1812, Prina reported that tax rolls were 'more exact'. Annual revenues from personal tax posted gains from 3.2 million lire in 1806 to 5.1 million, largely due to territorial expansion.

The third direct levy fell primarily on the bourgeoisie, made up of free professionals, merchants and artisans. In Austrian Lombardy such a tax (*tassa mercimoniale*) had affected only merchants and artisans. Revenues were divided between the state and *comuni*. This tax was revoked during the Revolutionary Triennium (1796–99), and although the Cisalpine Republic later proclaimed a tax on merchants, it was never implemented.

The Napoleonic demands forced Prina to resurrect that tax (December 1805). He ordered professionals, merchants and artisans to contribute 1,250,000 lire to help pay for Napoleon's extraordinary imposition of 15 million lire.[51] In 1807, the government turned it into a permanent tax.[52] The state received three-quarters of the tax and the *comuni* got the rest. Local administrators had to compile tax rolls of those who practised trades and professions. Prina believed that a gradual tax rate would encourage compliance by taxpayers. The authorities divided the merchants and professionals into various tax brackets, depending on their occupation and location. Residents in larger cities paid higher taxes than those in small towns. Professionals and merchants in Milan paid the highest tax.

Revenues from that tax rose from 1.5 to 2.3 million lire during 1806–12, primarily due to the Kingdom's enlargement. A decline in revenues in 1810–11 prompted a frustrated Prina to blame the municipal authorities for granting tax exemptions and placing many taxpayers in low tax brackets.[53] A more important reason for the drop, which continued in 1812, was a slump in economic and commercial activity provoked by the constraints of the Continental System. In an effort to reverse the fall of revenues, state authorities decided to clamp down, and in June 1811 ordered municipal officials to appoint special inspectors to compile the tax rolls.[54] Those inspectors were authorized to visit taxpayers' homes to verify their tax classifications. Professionals and merchants also needed to have a licence. This was one more example of the growing Napoleonic pressure over citizens' lives. Not surprisingly, taxpayers loathed and complained about those intrusive rules.[55]

Indirect taxes

The authorities imposed indirect taxes on a long list of consumer goods. Some of them, most notably the monopolies on salt and tobacco, originated in Austrian Lombardy. Indirect taxes were very remunerative, comprising about 50 per cent of the annual state income. The Italian government gradually increased them to offset any reduction in land tax, thereby aggravating the fiscal burden on the poor. Significantly, this policy reflected the Napoleonic tax policies in imperial France.

The salt *gabelle* represented the most profitable indirect tax. Its revenues were second only to property tax. Moreover, it was also a secure source of revenue since salt was a basic necessity. Many European states held the monopoly over the *gabelle* for several centuries. In Lombardy the salt monopoly originated in 1395 and persisted under the Spanish and Austrian rule.

The Cisalpinian government upheld the *gabelle*, unlike Revolutionary France which had abolished this hated tax in 1791.[56] However, plagued by increasing military costs, Napoleon reinstated the *gabelle* in France in 1806. Prina was aware of its significance and invested great efforts in strengthening state regulations and management. In January 1803, the government affirmed the salt monopoly and prohibited the sale of salt except with permission.[57] Salt could be bought only at state stores, and shipping more than 15 *libbre* required a licence. Salt mines in Cervia and Istria and imports satisfied the population's needs, which exceeded 1 million *quintali* in 1806.[58] Mine owners had to sell their salt to the authorities at a fixed price. The government increased salt prices often to augment state revenues. A family of five, with an annual average consumption of 15 *libbre* per person, spent 7.5 lire more in 1811 than in 1804.[59] Aldini commented that the price of salt was raised to a very high level and urged Napoleon to reduce it.[60]

Price augmentation hurt primarily the lower classes and increased their hostility to the Napoleonic regime. Price hikes caused some decline in consumption and spurred violations of salt regulations, including smuggling and thefts from salt mines. During uprisings in 1809, brigands seized much salt and distributed or sold it for a low price.[61] The government responded by placing armed guards in salt mines and forbidding salt production from sea water, which was hard to monitor, however. Despite those violations, income from salt more than doubled during 1802–11, rising from 11.5 to 25.4 million lire. After deducting costs of transport, refining and salaries, the net income reached 21 million lire in 1811.

State monopoly of tobacco had also existed in *ancien régime* Italy and was a lucrative enterprise, owing to the widespread use of tobacco and the fact that a *libbra* of tobacco sold for three times its original cost.[62] Initially, the Cisalpinian government liberalized the tobacco system, but then restored state monopoly.[63] Prina was aware of tobacco's fiscal value and the widespread frauds, smuggling in particular, that plagued its trade and hurt state revenues. He tightened state control over tobacco cultivation and retail sale, requiring licences to grow, sell and transport tobacco.[64] In February 1804, the authorities reaffirmed the state's monopoly and established harsher penalties. Much of the raw tobacco was imported and worked in seven state factories. Like salt, the government raised tobacco prices several times to augment state income.[65]

Costlier prices lowered tobacco consumption and increased smuggling, especially from Ticino canton, where growers cultivated it freely. The authorities confiscated smuggled tobacco, seizing a record level of 42.104 *libbre* in 1810.[66] Fraud in tobacco cultivation was widespread as well, prompting the authorities to clamp down on growers. The government also improved tobacco quality and increased the number of tobacco brands to spread consumption, thereby raising its revenues. Price rise, stricter rules and the expansion of the state resulted in the doubling of gross income from 5.4 to 11.8 million lire between 1802 and 1812.[67] Expenses, including the price of tobacco leaves, transport and administration, amounted to 3.1 million lire in 1812, leaving a net income of 8.7 million. Indeed, it is quite possible that the high revenues secured in Italy helped convince Napoleon to restore the state monopoly over purchase, production and sale of tobacco in France in 1810. In other words, here was a case of transfer of a tax idea from a satellite state to imperial France.

Consumption duties (*dazi di consumo*) constituted another important set of indirect taxes. They consisted of two types: (1) duties on goods such as wine, flour, meat, oil and hay imported to walled cities (*octroi*); (2) annual licence fees paid by vendors of bread, meat, wine and liquor, in small unwalled *comuni* without toll gates.

Urban *octroi* existed in pre-Revolutionary France. The Directory introduced them in late 1798. It imposed duties on tobacco, playing cards, carriages, and gold and silver ware. Consumption duties had existed in Austrian Lombardy, where the authorities divided the major cities into three categories based on their size: (1) Milan; (2) Mantua; (3) Cremona, Pavia and Lodi. In 1801, the government of the Second Cisalpine Republic replaced those tariffs with a single duty in all cities.[68] The system continued in the Republic of Italy, but widespread abuses and ineffective enforcement of the *octroi* led to a decline in state revenues. Prina instructed officials to employ rigorous measures against law violators, while Melzi ordered municipal officials to repair city walls and close gates properly to prevent smuggling.[69] The authorities divided the state's 26 cities into five classes based on size of population and imposed on each group a different tariff.[70] Imported goods to Milan, the richest city, were charged the highest fee. The tariff on a *quintale* of wine was 18 *soldi* in Milan and only 8 in a fifth-class city. While revenues increased in 1806, violations and tax evasions persisted and the authorities responded with stricter regulations and stiffer penalties. They ordered that taxpayers receive an official receipt confirming the tax payment, which they then presented to a municipal officer.[71] Grain and flour had to be brought in and out of mills through a single entrance, while animals arrived at city slaughterhouses through designated gates. Abuses continued, however, forcing the authorities to issue more provisions in 1813.[72]

The *octroi* brought the state much more income than the annual licences in rural unwalled towns. In 1807, for example, a person in a large city paid an average of 18.15 lire while an inhabitant of a small open town paid less than 1 lira.[73] Prina believed that the rural population was capable of paying more and revised the tax system in open *comuni*. In March 1809, the government increased the licence fees on millers, bakers, butchers and innkeepers and imposed new duties on flour, wine, animals for slaughter, and liquor sold in those towns.[74] A month later the authorities issued 89 cumbersome rules aimed at regulating consumer tax payments.[75] Particularly aggravating was a new milling fee and 24 new provisions designed to regulate milling. The new impositions and, in particular, the milling tax, provoked a major rural uprising in July 1809, the most widespread in the Kingdom's history, resulting in 2000 dead, mostly peasants.[76] The insurrection forced Prina to suspend the milling fee.

Revenues from consumption duties steadily increased. Gross income in large cities more than doubled from 7.5 to 15.4 million lire, and tripled in unwalled *comuni* from 2.8 to 7 million lire during 1802–12. Moreover, as a percentage of total state income, they increased from 8.5 to about 16 per cent. The rise

Table 4.3 Land tax, personal tax and indirect taxes, 1804–11

Year	*Land tax*	*Personal tax and indirect taxes*
1804	35.1 (34.6%)	32.8 (32.3%)
1808	48.8 (39.4%)	46.3 (37.3%)
1810	50.6 (37.6%)	53.1 (39.4%)
1811	50.9 (37.0%)	55.0 (40.9%)

Sources: *Conto*, 1804, 1808, 1810, 1811.

in tax rates, the increase in the number of taxpayers, the extension of taxation to products previously exempt, and the tightening of police measures all explain this rise in revenues.

In fact, this increase provides additional proof of the authorities' inclination to augment indirect taxes and increase the burden on the lower classes, thereby arousing their resentment and opposition to the regime. Indeed, when adding up state revenues of personal tax, salt and tobacco monopolies, and the consumption fees, all of which aggravated the conditions of the poor, we can see (Table 4.3) that they rose both in absolute terms and as a percentage of the state's income. Property tax, on the other hand, rose in absolute amounts, but after 1808 declined as a percentage in the state budget.

Aside from the three monopolies and the consumption duties, the government drew income from indirect taxes imposed on legal documents, newspapers and licences, as well as a variety of other fees. The authorities largely created or extended this group of five taxes under the Kingdom in response to Napoleon's growing fiscal pressure. Some of those taxes had existed in Austrian Lombardy and the Italian authorities preserved them. To make them more remunerative and their collection more effective, Prina modelled their regulations on the French system during the Kingdom years.

Conclusion

How successful was Prina in achieving his financial goals? He succeeded in increasing state revenues and satisfying Napoleon's needs. During 1802–12, state income rose from 81 to 141.1 million lire, a 74 per cent increase. The rising revenues enabled the government to meet the expanding military expenses and to pay close to 300 million lire for the upkeep of the French army in Italy, the development of infrastructure, and servicing the public debt.

The territorial expansion of the Kingdom and the rise in the number of taxpayers constituted an important reason for the augmentation of state revenues. Even more important in accomplishing this goal, however, was Prina's hard work and efficiency. The finance minister was the ultimate example of a dedicated bureaucrat utterly loyal to the Napoleonic state. Prina initiated many tax reforms, appointed and supervised state functionaries, collected considerable data, and sent accurate detailed budget reports to Paris. Indeed, thanks to his efforts, the government could count on a growing number of capable and loyal officials. The division of the various financial branches into separate *direzioni*, each in charge of a particular area, increased administrators' efficiency and expertise. The heads of the *direzioni generali* received a constant flow of information from their representatives in the departments, which Prina used when compiling the annual budget he sent to Paris.[77]

The core of the financial system was the tax system Prina implemented. He increased existing taxes and introduced new imposts. Those new taxes were based on ideas and programmes that had existed in France and Austrian Lombardy. Rather than being a tax innovator, the finance minister borrowed ideas and policies, transferred them into the Napoleonic state, and applied them effectively. It was in harmony with the wishes of the emperor, who believed that northern Italy was wealthy and capable of sustaining a growing tax burden. A good case in point of an effective enforcement was the property tax, the most important source of state revenue. In proclaiming the new land survey in 1807, Prina used the Theresian model. The Kingdom's cadastre began at the same time that Napoleon launched a cadastre in France. It progressed smoothly, placing the various provinces under a unified, precise and reliable property assessment. It eliminated abuses, past inequalities and exemptions. Naturally, the government was in charge of the assessment process. Property tax remained in effect after the fall of Napoleon, and the Austrian government completed the cadastre. Personal tax, the tax on merchants and professionals, salt, tobacco and consumption duties also constituted good examples of effective transfer of tax ideas and policies by the Italian finance minister.

Moreover, Prina was successful in bureaucratizing tax collection, placing it under state control. The government fixed tax rates, regulated deadlines, established the rules of tax collection and ordered tax collectors to rapidly transfer taxes to the national treasury. Yearly collection costs amounted to a mere 8.5 per cent of the total amount raised, which compared favourably with other countries, especially France.[78] Direct tax collection was more cost efficient than indirect tax, amounting to a mere 1.4 and 2.4 per cent of the sum raised in 1808 and 1812, respectively. Moreover, each year the authorities were able to collect about 90 per cent of the taxes by the end of the fiscal year, and to raise most of the outstanding revenues within a year. Out of 347 million lire owed for 1804–6, only 4.1 million (1.3 per cent) remained uncollected by 1 January 1808.[79]

These figures notwithstanding, it must be emphasized that Prina's policies did face opposition and his tax policies did not yield even results throughout the state. In fact, popular resentment of the new tax policies and the efficiency of their application posed a threat to the legitimacy of the Napoleonic state. Tax collection in the Veneto and the Marche, which were annexed later to the Kingdom, was less effective than in the older departments. Property owners in the Veneto vociferously protested about the *estimo*. On the other hand, property tax collection in Lombardy, which had had an accurate assessment since the Austrian period, progressed without difficulties. Mountainous departments were not as accessible to tax collectors as departments in the plain. Many *comuni* in the departments of Passariano, Tagliamento and Reno lacked a tax collector. Collection of personal tax in the *comuni aperti* faced opposition, and salt and tobacco were smuggled, thereby hurting state income. Those actions came primarily from the lower echelons of society who were the most hurt by the formation of personal tax and the increase of indirect imposts.

Moreover, the rising pressure by Napoleon augmented the fiscal difficulties of the Italian authorities during the last years of the French rule. In August 1808, Prina complained that the financial situation posed a 'major burden' and warned that more serious problems would arise in 1809.[80] He spelled out the economic and financial problems the Kingdom was facing: difficulties in selling national property, scarcity of coins, a decline in customs revenues and silk exports, and ministers being late in paying for supplies.

By 1809, the accumulated deficit of the previous years amounted to 7.4 million lire.[81] In 1810, the budget could be balanced only through the sale of 8.3 million lire worth of bonds. In 1811, the deficit amounted to 5 million. In December 1812, Melzi reported to Eugène that several departments and many *comuni* were unable to cover their expenses.[82] Prina insisted that 'every tax has been pushed to the highest level, and that the ordinary resources can barely suffice for the current expenses'.[83] In 1812, state expenditures rose to 149.4 million lire with a deficit of 4 million. Eugène appealed to Napoleon to reduce his demands, 'The present situation of the treasury of your Kingdom of Italy necessitates, Sire, that Your Majesty comes to its aid through some extraordinary means', and proposed that the emperor reduce the 30 million lire annual payment for the French army in Italy.[84] Napoleon refused to make any concessions. In 1813, Prina proposed to cover a deficit of 21 million lire by increasing land tax and granting special import licences.[85] The finance minister concluded his report with a gloomy statement: 'the situation of the finances in Italy is not what Your Majesty would desire'. In the same year the government resorted to desperate steps to increase state revenues; in August, it increased land tax, and in November it required the wealthiest property owners and merchants to lend the government 3 million lire. It also issued two sets of government bonds worth 24 million lire.[86]

Yet those measures were to no avail and the Treasury was near bankruptcy. Melzi wrote to Eugène that the bonds' value was constantly falling,[87] probably due to lack of buyers. The Kingdom was no longer able to sustain tax increases without threatening social and political stability. The growing fiscal pressure on the population increased discontent and hostility towards the Napoleonic state and the finance minister, in particular. Most viewed Prina's devotion to Napoleon as servility to the emperor, and he was identified as the embodiment of a merciless fiscal system of French oppression. The desperate measures of

1813 alienated the propertied classes. They were furious at the rise of departmental and especially communal taxes and resented the loss of their fiscal privileges and ability to manipulate the system. The lower classes accused Prina of raising indirect taxes and introducing the hated personal tax. In practice, everybody resented the growing effectiveness of the state in collecting taxes.

Meanwhile, the Austrians invaded the Kingdom, forcing Eugène's troops to retreat towards Milan. The anti-French atmosphere became more intense and unrest in Milan was growing. On 20 April 1814, Melzi wrote to Eugène about an increasing 'fermentation' and 'profound and universal hatred against the French' in the capital.[88] The anti-French climate culminated when a Milanese crowd killed Prina, the most hated representative of the Napoleonic regime. This uprising and Prina's death marked the end of the Napoleonic regime in northern Italy. On 26 April Eugène bade farewell to the people of the Kingdom of Italy and left with his wife for Bavaria.[89] Shortly thereafter, the Austrians completed the occupation of the Kingdom and restored their rule in Lombardy-Veneto.

Notes

1 John Rath, *The fall of the kingdom of Italy* (1814) (New York, 1975, a reprint), pp. 98–120.
2 Louis Bergeron, *France under Napoleon* (Princeton, 1981), p. 40.
3 D.M.G. Sutherland, *France 1789–1815. Revolution and counterrevolution* (New York, Oxford, 1986), p. 413.
4 Carlo Zaghi, *L'Italia di Napoleone dalla Cisalpina al Regno* (Turin, 1987), pp. 293–650; Alexander Grab, 'From the French Revolution to Napoleon', in John Davis (ed.), *Italy in the nineteenth century* (Oxford, 2000), pp. 34–41.
5 *Correspondance de Napoléon I publié par ordre de l'empereur Napoléon III* (Paris, 1863), 25 April 1806, vol. 12, p. 307.
6 Melchiore Roberti, *Milano capitale napoleonica. La formzaione di uno stato moderno 1796–1814* (Milan, 1946–47), vol. 2, p. 372, n. 2.
7 Alexander Grab, *Napoleon and the transformation of Europe* (London, 2003), pp. 19–33.
8 On the French financial system, Jacques Godechot, *Les Institutions de la France sous la Révolution et l'empire* (Paris, 1968), pp. 638–55.
9 Bergeron, *France*, p. 38.
10 Roberti, *Milano capitale*, vol. 2, pp. 185–6.
11 *Bollettino delle leggi* (henceforth *Bdl*), 25 May 1802, p. 95.
12 Albert Pingaud, *Les hommes d'état de la république italienne 1802–1805* (Paris, 1914), pp. 94–106; Luigi Ceria, *Leccidio del Prina e gli ultimi giorni del Regno d'Italia* (Milan, 1937); Alexander Grab, 'Giuseppe Prina and the politics of finance in the Kingdom of Italy', in *The consortium on revolutionary Europe 1750–1850* (Florida State University, 2002), pp. 360–6.
13 *Correspondance*, 7 June 1805, vol. 10, p. 490; 5 August 1805, vol. 11, p. 64.
14 Roberti, *Milano capitale*, vol. 2, p. 343.
15 *Bdl*, 1805, pp. 347–55; Roberti, *Milano capitale*, vol. 2, pp. 383–91.

16 *Bdl*, 8 June 1805, p. 144.
17 Archivio di stato di Milano (henceforth ASM), *Aldini, cartella* (henceforth *c.*) 89, two documents entitled, 'Ruolo del Ministero delle fiananze' and 'Riassunto del numero e de' soldi impiegati nel Ministero delle finanze e nelle diverse amministrazioni da esso dipendenti'.
18 ASM, *Censo, parte moderna* (henceforth, *p.m.*) *c.* 496; *Bdl*, 1804, pp. 149–60. On the French system, Bergeron, *France*, pp. 47, 50; Godechot, *Les institutions*, pp. 640–1.
19 *Bdl*, 1805, pp. 344–6.
20 ASM, *Censo, p.m. c.* 497, letter by Bono, the Consigliere de Stato Direttore Generale dell'amministrazione de' comuni, to interior minister, 3 January 1810.
21 ASM, *Censo, p.m. c.* 497, letter 28 September 1811.
22 *Bdl*, 23 December 1811, pp. 1214–20.
23 Budget data, expenses and revenues, can be found in annual budget reports entitled, *Conto dell'amministrazione delle finanze del Regno d'Italia*, sent by Prina to Napoleon during 1802–1814. They are located in the Bibliotecca Braidense, segn. 8.16.F. 1–7.
24 On the Italian army, see Franco Della Peruta, *L'esercito e societa nell'Italia napoleonica* (Milan, 1988); Alexander Grab, 'Army, state and society: conscription and desertion in Napoleonic Italy (1802–1814)', *The Journal of Modern History*, 67 (March 1995), pp. 25–54.
25 *Bdl*, 8 September 1805, pp. 481–2; 15 December 1805, pp. 614–15.
26 Pecchio, *Saggio storico sull'amministrazione finanziaria dell'ex-Regno d'Italia dal 1802 al 1814* (London, 1830), p. 7.
27 Godechot, *Les institutions*, p. 643.
28 Pecchio, *Saggio storico*, p. 10.
29 *Conto*, 1812, pp. 2–3.
30 On the Lombard *catasto*, see Carlo Capra, 'Il Settecento', in Carlo Capra-Domenico Sella, *Il Ducato di Milano dal 1535 al 1796* (Turin, 1984), pp. 310–16; Daniel Klang, *Tax reform in eighteenth-century Lombardy* (Boulder, New York, 1977), pp. 338–50.
31 ASM, *Censo, p.m. c.* 132, 25 February 1804.
32 ASM, *Censo, p.m. c.* 128, 131, 132.
33 *Bdl*, 1806, pp. 761–2.
34 *Bdl*, 12 March 1808, pp. 201–4.
35 ASM, *Censo, p.m. c.* 125, letter by prefect of Adriatico, 7 August 1811.
36 ASM, *Censo, p.m. c.* 127, letter, 9 September 1811.
37 ASM, *Censo, p.m. c.* 127, letter, 2 October 1812.
38 *Bdl*, 23 August 1811, p. 848.
39 ASM, *Aldini, c.* 97, Prina to Eugène, 15 July 1806.
40 ASM, *Aldini, c.* 97, letter to Napoleon, 24 October 1807.
41 ASM, *Aldini, c.* 97, letter to Napoleon, 15 July 1806.
42 Roberti, *Milano capitale*, vol. 2, p. 503.
43 *Bdl*, 1807, p. 25.
44 Ibid., pp. 193–203.
45 On the French land survey, see Marcel Marion, *Histoire financière de la France depuis 1715. 1797–1818. La fin de la révolution, le consulat et l'empire la liberation du territoire* (New York, 1925), vol. IV, pp. 307–12; in the Kingdom of Holland, Roger Kain and Elizabeth Baigent, *The cadastral map in the service of the state. A history of property mapping* (Chicago and London, 1992), pp. 225–9, 32–6.
46 *Bdl*, 1807, p. 200.
47 *Conto*, 1807, p. 13.

48 *Conto*, 1812, p. 15.
49 *Bdl*, 15 December 1805, p. 616.
50 ASM, *Censo, p.m. c.* 929, decree 23 May 1809.
51 *Bdl*, 15 December 1805, pp. 614–19; 11 April 1806, pp. 299–303.
52 *Bdl*, 20 January 1807, pp. 81–94; 22 June 1807, pp. 317–41.
53 *Conto*, 1811, p. 46.
54 *Bdl*, 13 June 1811, pp. 621–37.
55 Pecchio, *Saggio storico*, p. 25.
56 Godechot, *Les institutions*, p. 645.
57 *Bdl*, 18 January 1803, pp. 12–14.
58 *Conto*, 1807, p. 37.
59 Pecchio, *Saggio storico*, pp. 50–1.
60 ASM, *Aldini, c.* 9, 27 March 1809.
61 Alexander Grab, 'State power, brigandage and rural resistance in Napoleonic Italy', *European History Quarterly*, 25 (January 1995), p. 57.
62 Bruno Caizzi, *Industria, commercio e banca in Lombardia nel XVIII secolo* (Milan, 1968), p. 265.
63 *Raccolta degli ordini* (ed. Veladini), 20 July 1798, vol. V, pp. 209–10.
64 *Foglio officiale della Repubblica italiana*, 14, 20, 21 July 1802, pp. 134–6, 141–2, 145–8; *Bdl*, 13 July 1802, pp. 140–1, 4 October 1802, pp. 386–7.
65 *Bdl*, 18 September 1805, pp. 488–9; 5 September 1806, pp. 917–21; *Conto*, 1808, p. 57; *Conto*, 1809, p. 53.
66 *Conto*, 1811, p. 60.
67 *Conto*, 1804 and 1812, pp. 13 and 63.
68 Pecchio, *Saggio storico*, p. 41.
69 *Foglio officiale*, 14 July 1802, pp. 136–9; 23 June 1804, pp. 86–7.
70 Pecchio, *Saggio storico*, p. 41.
71 *Bdl*, 4 May 1807, pp. 241–50.
72 *Bdl*, 6 August 1813, pp. 423–30.
73 *Conto*, 1807, pp. 60–1.
74 *Bdl*, 27 March 1809, pp. 92–3.
75 *Bdl*, 19 April 1809, pp. 137–60.
76 Melzi d'Eril, *I carteggi di Francesco Melzi d'Eril duca di Lodi Il Regno d'Italia* (Milan, 1965), p. 93; Grab, 'State power, brigandage', pp. 39–70.
77 This can be seen in the annual *Conti* Prina sent to Paris during 1804–12.
78 Pecchio, *Saggio storico*, p. 93.
79 ASM, *Aldini, c.* 98, Aldini's report, 8 September 1808.
80 ASM, *Aldini, c.* 98, letter to Napoleon, 11 August 1808.
81 *Conto*, 1810, pp. 1, 4–5.
82 Melzi, *I carteggi, Il Regno d'Italia*, pp. 310–11.
83 ASM, *Aldini, c.* 103, Aldini to Napoleon, 19 April 1812.
84 ASM, *Aldini, c.* 103, 17 April 1812.
85 ASM, *Aldini, c.* 103, 21 December 1812.
86 Melzi, *I carteggi, Il Regno d'Italia*, 25 October 1813, p. 434.
87 Ibid.
88 Ibid. p. 551.
89 Rath, *The fall*, pp. 124–5.

Part II
Federal Polities

5
The Transfer of Ideas about Taxation in a Federal State: the Example of the German Empire, 1875–1914*

Andreas Thier

A fundamental change of tax policy took place in Germany after the foundation of the second German Empire in 1871. The income tax was established in nearly all German states as the dominant part of the tax system (for the first time in Saxony in 1874) often in combination with a wealth tax.[1] At the same time, elements of a wealth tax were also introduced at the level of the central state. In 1913, a bill was passed in the Reichstag, the German diet, which is often considered the first step towards an imperial income tax.[2] Prior to the foundation of the German Empire, tax policies in the German states had been characterized by a mixture of object taxes (especially in the southern states) and personal taxes (as in Prussia and the other northern states).[3] A coherent income tax order, however, had existed in none of the German states. After the foundation of the German Empire, a process of convergence among the German states and between the state and central levels began to take shape.[4]

Viewed from the perspective of constitutional history, this development seems surprising. The Constitution of the Second German Empire (1871) clearly separated the tax legislation powers of the individual states and the central state.[5] The German states received the power to levy direct taxes, while the Empire itself was only permitted to establish indirect taxes and customs duties. But in spite of this decentralization of tax powers, all tax legislators used their power in similar ways. This suggests that a process of circulation and interpretation of concepts, a transfer of ideas about taxation, took place within the federal system of the German Empire.

The meaning of 'transfer', in particular 'legal transfer', is much debated in the discourses of legal history and comparative law, not to mention the discussions in the field of comparative history.[6] Alan Watson has described 'transfer' as a phenomenon of 'legal transplants', a sort of borrowing of legal institutions and rules from a certain legal context and their transplantation to another.[7] Despite some criticism, Watson's concept has become influential.[8] In other areas of legal scholarship, legal transfer is rather considered as a fact of rule-making processes in different communicative contexts.[9]

The concept of 'transplant' leaves out some aspects, however, which are linked to the effects of external elements on a specific discourse. In some cases, conceptual elements, such as the idea of the parliamentary monarchy in its English manifestation, might affect other political discourses without being implemented and might function merely as a point of reference (as can be seen in the German discussion about the specific structures of the German constitutional monarchy).[10] Even though 'transplantation' does not take place in such cases, the presence of those external conceptual elements as yardsticks in the lawmaking discourse is evident. 'Transfer of ideas' is, therefore, not necessarily linked to the acceptance of ideas.

This essay argues that there are some indications for such transfers of ideas in different legislative discourses about taxation in the German Empire. The tax legislation processes at the levels of the central state and individual states were influenced by taxation concepts which sometimes emerged beyond the institutional boundaries. This chapter follows the transfer of ideas in three key areas: first, debates among economists in the late 1870s and their importance for the circulation and transfer of taxation concepts; second, the question whether and to what extent governments, parliaments and political parties were actors in processes of the transfer of ideas; third, this chapter examines if and to what extent fiscal needs and the phenomenon of tax competition influenced the transfer of taxation concepts in Germany. The economists provided the framework for transfer processes, but they did not participate in the legislative debates directly. Transfers within and among governments were, by contrast, much more dynamic. The institutional framework of a federal state supported the transfer of conceptions on taxation. Fiscal needs were another stimulus for the transfer of taxation concepts between individual states.

Economics, tax legislation and the transfer of ideas about taxation in imperial Germany

In 1872/73, the Association for Social Policy (Verein für Socialpolitik) was founded.[11] This association gave German economists, such as Gustav von Schmoller, Lujo Brentano and Adolph Wagner, a forum for their social-reform proposals, including suggestions for tax reform.[12] The Association for Social Policy was more than a purely academic circle. This becomes clear when considering the list of contributors for a great inquiry into the aims and means of a tax reform, which was debated at the assembly meeting in 1875 and addressed the question of establishing an income tax in particular.[13] There were not only reports by academic economists like Adolf Held, Erwin Nasse or Friedrich Neumann, but also by political and administrative practitioners like Count Wilko of Wintzingerode and the secretary of the Saxonian chamber of commerce, Walter Gensel.[14]

Even though the contributors to the association's inquiry disagreed about details, the majority pleaded for establishing an income tax with a tax-free minimum and a progressive scale.[15] They also suggested a general wealth tax or a special tax on capital gains and the revenues by landed property. Conversely, they criticized the system of indirect taxes and customs as an unjust burden on the poorer groups of society. The association's general assembly adopted these proposals, and a final resolution of the meeting demanded that 'a general income tax with a progressive tariff scale in its lower levels combined with a general wealth tax be established as a main direct tax'.[16] It took only one year before Adolph Wagner, perhaps the best-known German economist of his time, began to formulate a complex concept for the reorganization of the tax law.[17] Like the Association for Social Policy, Wagner argued for a general income tax with a progressive tariff as the main tax for the state. Great wealth was to be burdened with an estate duty, while consumer taxes would only have a supporting function. Concepts such as Wagner's and the demands of the Association for Social Policy came to be very influential in academic discussions. In 1881, Gustav Schmoller diagnosed that 'there [was] more and more, stronger and stronger demand [...] for a correct and greater progression of the [tax] tariff' and for a distinction in tax law between incomes by wealth and by personal labour.[18]

At the time, there existed a broad *academic* consensus throughout the Empire on the parameters for the basic structures of taxation. From this point of view, the academic community of economists and their associations as well as periodicals, such as *Finanzarchiv*, could be seen as transfer mechanisms for ideas about taxation in the German federal system.[19] Moreover, some economists also acted as politicians and the transfer of their ideas about taxation found support through these channels. Together with Adolf Stöcker, Adolph Wagner founded the anti-Semitic Christian Social Party in 1879. Later, from 1882 to 1885, he served as a member of the Prussian House of Commons for the German Conservative Party.[20]

The question arises, however, how we can evaluate the political influence of such activities. Some historians and legal scholars have argued that the tax legislation in the German Empire depended on concepts voiced by economists. Reginald Hansen, for example, has pointed out that the tax policy in late nineteenth-century Germany was in effect the product of Gustav Schmoller's and Adolph Wagner's ideas.[21] There is, however, little evidence for academic influence on the whole of German tax legislation. The tax legislations in the German middle states (such as Bavaria, Baden and even Saxony) still await their historians.[22] We have slightly more information on Prussia and the Reich.[23] While Adolph Wagner, as a member of the Prussian parliament during the early 1880s, tried to win support for his concepts in a series of speeches, he failed even in his own faction. No one in the Prussian House of Commons followed his radical demands for a strong wealth-tax burden or his plea for a tax-financed form of state socialism.[24]

We also lack concrete evidence for academic influences on the governmental drafting of tax bills. The bills were prepared by government officials and civil servants, who worked, in most cases, without any professional support from outside. This can be demonstrated by the history of tax reform bills, which were drafted by order of the finance minister Bitter from 1879 to 1881.[25] In only one of the preparatory reports, a 'Memorandum concerning the reform of the direct taxes in Prussia', written by Theodor Eilers in 1880, can we find a direct reception (and a critical survey) of the views of the academic economists.[26] It was quite typical in this context that Eilers stated that there was 'no room [...] for exhaustive theoretical analyses'.[27] Nevertheless, tax reform concepts, such as the ones used by Eilers and his colleagues, resembled at least in part the ideas of the academic economists: for example, they favoured a progressive tariff, or sometimes demanded the obligation for self-declaration.[28] In most cases, the Prussian administrative experts acted on their own account and without major academic input. The autonomy of the high-level officials, particularly in the Ministry of Finance, was almost proverbial. Bismarck called the Ministry of Finance sarcastically 'the republic of the senior civil servants'.[29]

Even when this situation began to change slightly during the era of Johannes Miquel, perhaps the most influential Prussian minister of finance, direct contacts between economists and ministry officials remained an exception.[30] Miquel asked some economists for their opinion about his concept of a wealth tax.[31] But the reports of economists such as Schmoller, Cohn or Wagner had only marginal influence on Miquel's tax bills.[32] The Prussian tax reforms were based on concepts which were formed in part by the Prussian parliament, in part by Miquel himself and in only a small part by Wagner and Nasse. At its core, the Prussian tax reform, like the finance reforms at the level of the Empire after the turn of the century, was a political compromise between the interests of the landed property in the Prussian east and the bourgeois industrial interests of the western provinces.[33]

While academic discussions had little direct impact on politics, the journal *Finanzarchiv* became important for detailed reports on the tax reforms in the individual German states by leading German economists.[34] The economists thus informed the political public, decision makers in government and parliaments as well as foreign observers about the problems, details and outcomes of the tax legislation.[35] In one case, during the run-up to the finance reform bills of 1909, German economists acted as communicators for governmental concepts of taxation.[36] Sponsored by the Economic Bureau at the Imperial Office of the Exchequer (Reichsschatzamt), a number of well-known economists like Wagner or Schmoller and administrative officials (especially from the Prussian Ministry of Finance) published articles in favour of the planned imperial estate duty.[37] Governmental ideas about taxation were thus transferred into the public domain. Moreover, an increasing number of statistical analyses of tax laws was published from the late 1870s onwards.[38] These studies made it possible to evaluate the fiscal consequences of tax legislations in the individual German states. These data might have been an important factor for framing subsequent debates on tax legislation, as they stressed the advantages of an income tax based on self-declaration and a progressive tariff.

Economists acted as both producers and communicators of ideas about taxation. The network structure of their scientific community allowed them to circulate different taxation concepts throughout the Empire.[39] Their direct influence on tax legislation remained quite weak, however, especially when compared with the importance of civil jurisprudence in codification processes in Germany over the course of the nineteenth century.[40] In this area governmental commissions were set up, and professors of civil law played an important and sometimes dominant role, with Bernhard Windscheid's participation in the first commission for the drafting of the German Civil Code being the most remarkable.[41] Playing such a dominant role in lawmaking remained a dream for Adolph Wagner and his colleagues.

The role of governments, parliaments and political parties

The constitutions of the individual German states divided legislative power between parliaments, first chambers, such as the Prussian House of Lords (Herrenhaus), and the Crown, represented by its ministry.[42] The same was true for the constitution of the German Empire, where the Bundesrat (the assembly for the governments of the member states) and the Reichstag (the federal diet) shared the legislative power. The legislative implementation of ideas about taxation was primarily a task and a challenge for the governments.[43] In the political practice of these constitutions, bills drafted by parliamentary bodies were highly exceptional. Almost every tax law in nineteenth-century Germany was based on its origins as a governmental bill, although these bills were always subject to parliamentary amendments. It was characteristic of this practice when a Prussian parliamentarian spoke about 'the difficulties, which a tax bill features, which the royal government has not proposed'.[44]

Even though governments like the Prussian State Ministry were the most important actors in the tax legislation process, their importance for the transfer of taxation concepts is quite difficult to evaluate. Of course, during the whole history of the German Empire the governments of the individual states cooperated in the field of tax legislation. Institutionally, they came together in the Bundesrat, which formed the constitutional organ for the representation of the individual states, and shared legislative power with the Reichstag.[45] But the Bundesrat was not really a place for the exchange of ideas about taxation. In constitutional practice, Prussia dominated here, mainly because of the large number of votes assigned to it.[46] If conflicts arose between the members of the Bundesrat, they were mostly concerned with the financial interests of the states. In particular, individual states feared a 'control of the direct taxes in the individual states by the Empire and [...] a mediatization of the individual states', as the Prussian finance minister Rheinbaben remarked in

1903, when the project of an imperial estate duty was discussed at a conference of state finance ministers.[47]

Nevertheless, there is some evidence for a transfer of ideas from the level of the individual states to the level of the Empire, particularly in the period before the turn of the century. This was particularly true for Prussia. The Prussian state was closely connected to the imperial government. The German chancellor was usually also Prussian prime minister and always head of the Prussian Foreign Office (as he had to have control over the Prussian votes in the Bundesrat). The topics of the Bundesrat meetings were, therefore, also debated in the Prussian State Ministry.[48] Since 1896, the heads of the imperial administration boards, the *Reichsstaatssekretäre*, were invited to the meetings of the Prussian State Ministry, if a draft bill was discussed which had been prepared in an imperial office.[49] Thus, especially after the turn of the century, a few draft proposals concerning imperial tax legislation and prepared by the Reich secretary of the exchequer, circulated within the Prussian State Ministry in order to be discussed afterwards.[50] The Great Imperial Tax Reform of 1909 was intensively debated between the Prussian finance minister on the one hand and the imperial state secretary, also a member of the Prussian State Ministry, on the other.[51]

The transfer of ideas between Prussia and the Reich cannot be analysed from an institutional perspective alone, however. Bismarck had tried to promote the concept of a 'federal tax reform' since the 1870s.[52] The main purpose of the reform was to shift the tax burden from direct to indirect taxation. As indirect taxes could be levied only by the Empire, Bismarck sought to increase imperial taxes and to decrease the direct taxes of the individual states, especially those of Prussia. Even though the poor state of imperial finances of the 1870s made new revenues for the Reich necessary, the perspective of the individual states dominated in Bismarck's reform plan.[53] Until 1879, the Empire was mainly financed by the so-called matricular contributions (*Matrikularbeiträge*) of the individual states. Against this background, it was a crucial point for Bismarck, that, as a result of a future tax reform, 'the empire pays [to the individual states] [. . .] instead of demanding [payment by them]'.[54] Bismarck failed in his attempts at reform. Even though the matricular contributions were decreased and finally even changed to some kind of matricular payments *from* the Reich level *to* the individual states, the tax systems in Prussia and the other states remained unchanged. The arrangements in the individual states gave the imperial administration more autonomy, however. The central government was now able to focus on the needs and problems of the imperial fiscal structures. Moreover, the permanent fiscal crisis of the Empire after the turn of the century, caused by rising military expenditures, created a situation of political pressure towards new imperial taxes.[55]

It was due to this situation that the governments of the individual states came up with proposals for imperial taxation whose structures were derived from tax systems of the individual states. In 1903, for example, the Bavarian

Ministry of Finance proposed an imperial estate duty.[56] This sort of tax had played an important role in the Bavarian tax system for a long time.[57] Its concept was now transferred to the level of the central state. Similar processes took place in other areas. Between 1906 and 1913, the imperial tax legislation appropriated more and more elements of a wealth tax system.[58] Before, wealth taxes had been established only at the state level, especially in Prussia.[59] This development towards an imperial wealth tax came close to breaching the constitutional division of tax legislation powers between the Empire and the individual states. Nevertheless, the governments of the individual states had to accept this transfer of wealth taxation elements on the imperial level. Otherwise, they would have had to face an enormous increase of the matricular contributions, which no one would have wanted to incur.

These developments could be described as a *vertical transfer* of ideas about taxation. But were there also *horizontal transfers* of tax legislation concepts? Given the state of research, it is impossible to offer more than a few preliminary thoughts on this question, although there is some evidence that horizontal transfers did take place. The Württemberg Ministry of Finance appears to have studied the tax reform processes in Baden and Saxony in 1883.[60] In the parliamentary materials of tax bills, like those of Prussia, references to taxation concepts in other states can occasionally be found.[61] However, such references do not say anything about a transfer of the ideas. It is more likely that in this case, the example of other states served as a political argument and a reference in the legislation process. For the case of Prussia in the years between 1871 and 1893 such arguments had little impact. It might be stated, therefore, that horizontal transfers of ideas about taxation were exceptional phenomena.

It is even more difficult to assess the impact of vertical transfers on debates within parliaments and political parties. As has been shown above, some members of the Prussian House of Commons were at the same time members of the Reichstag.[62] Thus, especially during the Bismarck era, problems of the Prussian tax policy came to be debated in the Reichstag, while the Prussian House of Commons became the place for parliamentary discussion about the tax policy of the Empire.[63] Such links gave strong support for the transfer of taxation concepts between both parliaments. In fact, during the early 1880s, both houses of parliament came to act nearly in unison against Bismarck's tax reform plans.

Such parliamentary actions were based primarily on coordination between the political parties. The precise importance of such coordination for the transfer of taxation concepts is difficult to gauge, however. The political parties of the Empire were – with the exception of the Centre Party – institutional representatives of segmented economic and social interests.[64] They were often closely connected to specific geographical regions. The German Conservative Party, for example, had its most important base in the eastern provinces of Prussia, while the National Liberal Party in Prussia represented the bourgeoisie of the western Prussian provinces.[65] Nevertheless, the political parties came to acquire increasingly centralized structures and thus to act like channels for the spread of taxation concepts in all regions of the Empire.[66] The conservative parties and factions in both the Reichstag and the Prussian House of Commons, for example, demanded a high fiscal burden of moveable capital.[67]

It is a question for further research as to how this obvious transfer of taxation concepts worked in the political arena. In the case of left-wing liberals and socialists, it seems that political concepts were implemented in a hierarchical manner by political leaders such as Eugen Richter and August Bebel.[68] In the case of parties with a lower grade of organization, regional interests might have been more important. For example, during the parliamentary drafting of the Prussian *Ergänzungssteuer* (a wealth tax) in 1892/93, the liberal wing of the National Liberal Party and a group of Centre Party delegates tried to halt the bill. In another case, the impact of specific regional interests was even stronger. During the debates about the suspension of the land tax exemption in Prussia 1892/93, representatives from Schleswig-Holstein fought against this project, even though their factions, the Free Conservative and the German Conservative parties, supported the bill.[69] Similar phenomena could also be found on the level of the Empire. During the reform of the imperial finance system in 1909, the National Liberal faction in the Reichstag split into supporters of an estate duty and proponents of a higher tax burden on mobile capital.[70] In this case, the integrative power of the discourse within the National Liberal faction was not strong enough to moderate the transfer of taxation concepts, which had evolved from the different social and cultural environments of the National Liberal Party.

Transfer of taxation concepts, fiscal needs and tax competition

Fiscal needs have always been a strong argument to evaluate and adopt new taxation concepts. This has implications for the transfer of ideas about taxation. A fiscally successful taxation concept is often adopted by other states. This phenomenon can be observed in the case of the Prussian income tax legislation of 1891. In 15 years following the Prussian law, nearly all major German states adopted the essential parts of the Prussian system and in particular the principle of self-declaration and the income taxation of corporations.[71] Fiscal needs seemed to stimulate the transfer of taxation concepts within a federal organized state.

Another possible factor for the transfer of taxation concepts might have been tax competition within the federal German Reich.[72] Historians and economists currently debate whether German states and municipalities were locked in a competition between their tax regimes.[73] Mark Spoerer has pointed out with regard to the state level that tax competition at an institutional level was unlikely, although he has also shown that competition for wealthy taxpayers existed in some Prussian regions.[74] Competitors probably also made use of each others' taxation concepts.[75] The available sources do not allow a precise statement on this matter. A possible starting point for further analysis, in particular for the Prussian example, might be the files of the middle sections of the state administration, the *Regierungen*. These authorities sanctioned the tax regulations of all municipalities in their district.[76] It is possible that the municipal bodies justified their decisions concerning the local taxation regimes by arguments which referred to (possible) tax competition.

Concluding remarks: legal transfers in a federal state

The German Empire represents a special case of legal transfer situations. In contrast to constellations of possible transfers between nation states with autonomous mechanisms of lawmaking, institutions for the participation of the individual states like the Bundesrat exist in federal states and create institutional interfaces between different legislative discourses. This chapter has shown that these interfaces stimulated the circulation of taxation concepts between the central state and the individual states in the German Empire. It seems that the vertical transfer of ideas about taxation was quite intensive. The situation might be similar to the constellation of legal transfer phenomena in modern supranational organizations and their member states, such as the European Union.[77]

Horizontal transfer is, however, more difficult to prove, even though there are strong indications for the adoption of the Prussian income taxation concept in the German states in the period after 1891. Here, the possible transfer of taxation concepts may have been facilitated by the economists and their reports, perhaps also by the political parties. Yet, as in the case of legal transfers between nation states, more empirical research is needed.

Notes

*I would like to thank Holger Nehring and Florian Schui for their numerous helpful comments on this chapter. I am also indebted to Peter Becker for his comments on my talk at the conference and for his helpful suggestions for this essay.

1 Joe Metzger and Ulrike Weingarten, *Einkommensteuer und Einkommensteuerverwaltung in Deutschland: ein historischer und verwaltungswissenschaftlicher Überblick* (Opladen, 1989), pp. 40–57; Hans-Peter Ullmann, *Der deutsche Steuerstaat. Geschichte der öffentlichen Finanzen* (Munich, 2005), pp. 72–80.

2 'Gesetz über einen einmaligen außerordentlichen Wehrbeitrag', 3 July 1913, *Reichsgesetzblatt* 1913, p. 505. For the history of its origins, cf. Rudolf Kroboth, *Die Finanzpolitik des Deutschen Reiches während der Reichskanzlerschaft Bethmann Hollwegs und die Geld- und Kapitalmarktverhältnisse (1909–1913/14)* (Frankfurt/Main, Berne, New York, 1986), pp. 189–318.

3 For a survey, see A. Siebert, 'Die Entwicklung der direkten Besteuerung in den süddeutschen Bundesstaaten im letzten Jahrhundert', *Zeitschrift für die gesamte*

Staatswissenschaft, 68 (1912), pp. 1–52 (on Baden, Württemberg and Bavaria). For the developments in Baden, see Rosemarie Siegert, *Steuerpolitik und Gesellschaft. Vergleichende Untersuchungen zu Preußen und Baden 1815–1848* (Berlin, 2001), pp. 93–103, 183–238; on Württemberg, cf. Eckart Schremmer, 'Zusammenhänge zwischen Katastersteuersystem, Wirtschaftswachstum und Wirtschaftsstruktur im 19. Jahrhundert: Das Beispiel Württemberg, 1821–1877/1903', in Ingomar Bog (ed.), *Wirtschaftliche und soziale Strukturen im Wandel. Festschrift Wilhelm Abel* (Hanover, 1974), pp. 679–706. More generally, cf. idem, *Steuern und Staatsfinanzen während der Industrialisierung Europas. England, Frankreich, Preußen und das Deutsche Reich 1800 bis 1914* (Berlin, 1994), pp. 111–13, 123–50; Erwin von Beckerath, *Die preussische Klassensteuer und die Geschichte ihrer Reform bis 1851* (Berlin, 1912, reprint Bad Feilnbach, 1990), pp. 88–91; Mark Spoerer, *Steuerlast, Steuerinzidenz und Steuerwettbewerb. Verteilungswirkungen der Besteuerung in Preußen und Württemberg (1815–1913)* (Berlin, 2004), pp. 47–60.

4 Max von Heckel, *Die Fortschritte der direkten Besteuerung in den deutschen Staaten 1880–1905* (Leipzig, 1904).

5 For the following, see Art. 4 no. 2 and Art. 35 section 1 of the Constitution of the German Empire: 'Gesetz, betreffend die Verfassung des Deutschen Reiches', 16 April 1871, *Reichsgesetzblatt* 1871, p. 64. For an analysis of the German Constitution and its problems: Thomas Nipperdey, *Deutsche Geschichte 1866–1918*, vol. 2: *Machtstaat vor der Demokratie* (Munich, 1995), pp. 85–109.

6 For a short survey, see Margrit Seckelmann, 'Im Labor. Beobachtungen zum Rechtstransfer anhand des Europäischen Verfassungsvertrages', *Rg – Rechtsgeschichte* 8 (2006), pp. 70–83 and David Kennedy, 'The methods and the politics', in Pierre Legrand and Roderick Munday (eds), *Comparative legal studies: traditions and transitions* (Cambridge, 2003), pp. 345–433 for a sceptical approach to this debate. For a historical perspective, cf. Christiane Eisenberg, 'Kulturtransfer als historischer Prozess: ein Beitrag zur Komparatistik', in Hartmut Kaelble and Jürgen Schriewer (eds), *Vergleich und Transfer. Komparatistik in den Sozial-, Geschichts- und Kulturwissenschaften* (Frankfurt/Main, 2003), pp. 399–417.

7 Alan Watson, *Legal transplants. An approach to comparative law* (Athens, Ohio, and London, 1993).

8 Cf. William Ewald, 'Comparative jurisprudence (II): the logic of legal transplants', *The American Journal of Comparative Law*, 43 (1995), pp. 489–510; Daniel Berkowitz, Katharina Pistor and Jean-Francois Richard, 'Economic development, legality, and the transplant effect', *European Economic Review*, 47 (2003), pp. 165–95. For a very severe criticism, see Pierre Legrand, 'The impossibility of legal transplants', *Maastricht Journal of European and Comparative Law*, 4 (1997), pp. 111–24.

9 David Nelken, 'Comparatists and transferability', in Pierre Legrand and Roderick Munday (eds), *Comparative legal studies: traditions and transitions* (Cambridge, 2003), pp. 437–66, 459–66; Gunther Teubner, 'Rechtsirritationen: Zur Koevolution von Rechtsnormen und Produktionsregimes', in Günter Dux and Frank Welz (eds), *Moral und Recht im Diskurs der Moderne. Zur Legitimation gesellschaftlicher Ordnung* (Theorie des sozialen und kulturellen Wandels, vol. 2) (Opladen, 2001), pp. 351–81; Marie Theres Fögen and Gunther Teubner, 'Rechtstransfer', *Rg – Rechtsgeschichte*, 7 (2005), pp. 38–45, here pp. 41–5.

10 Christoph Schönberger, *Das Parlament im Anstaltsstaat. Zur Theorie parlamentarischer Repräsentation in der Staatsrechtslehre des Kaiserreichs (1871–1918)* (Frankfurt/Main, 1997), pp. 291–4.

11 Erik Grimmer-Solem, *The rise of historical economics and social reform in Germany 1864–1894* (Oxford, 2003), pp. 67–71 and 171–86; Dieter Lindenlaub,

Richtungskämpfe im Verein für Sozialpolitik. Wissenschaft und Sozialpolitik im Kaiserreich vornehmlich vom Beginn des 'Neuen Kurses' bis zum Ausbruch des Ersten Weltkrieges (1890–1914) (2 vols), Wiesbaden, 1967), I, pp. 1–43.

12 Rüdiger vom Bruch, 'Gustav Schmoller', in Notker Hammerstein (ed.), *Deutsche Geschichtswissenschaft um 1900* (Stuttgart, 1988), pp. 219–38; James J. Sheehan, *The career of Lujo Brentano: a study of liberalism and social reform in imperial Germany* (Chicago and London, 1966); Volker Müller, *Staatstätigkeit in den Staatstheorien des 19. Jahrhunderts* (Studien zur Sozialwissenschaft, vol. 108) (Opladen, 1991), pp. 376–78. Karl Häuser, 'Adolph Wagner – Leben und Werk', in *Vademecum zu einem Klassiker der Finanzwissenschaft* (Düsseldorf, 1991), pp. 39–55.

13 'Materialien zu einer Reichseinkommenssteuer IV: Aus den Gutachten des Vereins für Socialpolitik', *Annalen des Deutschen Reiches* 1874, col. 979–84; *Verhandlungen der dritten Generalversammlung des Vereins für Socialpolitik am 10., 11. und 12. Oktober* (Schriften des Vereins für Socialpolitik, vol. 11) (Leipzig, 1875), pp. 15–70 (debates on the 10 Oct. 1875). For the reports, see *Die Personalbesteuerung. Gutachten auf Veranlassung der Eisenacher Versammlung zur Besprechung der socialen Frage* (Schriften des Vereins für Socialpolitik, vol. 3) (Berlin, 1873); Friedrich J. Neumann, *Die progressive Einkommensteuer im Staats- und Gemeindehaushalt. Gutachten über die Personalbesteuerung* (Schriften des Vereins für Socialpolitik, vol. 8) (Leipzig, 1874).

14 Gerhard Stavenhagen, 'Held, Adolf', in *Neue Deutsche Biographie*, vol. 8 (Berlin, 1969), pp. 461–2; Georg von Below, 'Nasse', in *Allgemeine Deutsche Biographie*, vol. 55 (Leipzig, 1910), pp. 844–8; Wilhelm Kosch, 'Eugen Kuri', in *Biographisches Staatshandbuch*, vol. 2 (Berne, Munich, 1963), p. 915; 'Gensel, Walter (Julius)', in *Deutsche Biographische Enzyklopädie* (Munich, 2004); Bernhard Mann, Martin Doerry, Cornelia Rauh and Thomas Kühne (eds), *Biographisches Handbuch für das preussische Abgeordnetenhaus 1867–1918* (Düsseldorf, 1988), no. 2560.

15 For the following, see Andreas Thier, *Steuergesetzgebung und Verfassung. Staatssteuerreformen in Preußen 1871–1893* (Frankfurt/Main, 1999), pp. 280–90.

16 *Verhandlungen der dritten Generalversammlung des Vereins für Socialpolitik*, pp. 68–9.

17 For the following, see Thier, *Steuergesetzgebung*, pp. 295–9. Recently also Wagner's concept for a major reform of private law has been investigated by Katharina Hoppe, *Eigentum, Erbrecht und Vertragsrecht: die Reformvorstellungen des Nationalökonomen Adolph Wagner (1835–1917)* (Berlin, 2003).

18 Gustav Schmoller, 'Theorie und Praxis der deutschen Steuerreform in Reich, Staat und Gemeinde', *Jahrbuch für Gesetzgebung, Verwaltung und Volkswirthschaft*, new ser. 5 (1881), pp. 421–87, here p. 438.

19 *Finanzarchiv. Zeitschrift für das gesamte Finanzwesen* (Tübingen, 1884–1931, old series). For a short survey, see Grimmer-Solem, *Rise of Historical Economics*, pp. 83ff.

20 Uwe Puschner, 'Stoecker, Adolf', in *Biographisch-bibliographisches Kirchenlexikon X* (Hamm, 1995), coll. 1507–11; Hans Fenske, *Deutsche Parteiengeschichte* (Paderborn, 1994), pp. 140–1; Mann et al., *Biographisches Handbuch*, no. 2417.

21 Reginald Hansen, *Die praktischen Konsequenzen des Methodenstreits. Eine Aufarbeitung der Einkommensbesteuerung* (Berlin, 1996), pp. 203–28.

22 For Mecklenburg, see Gerald Rosenberg, *Finanzen und Finanzverfassung in den beiden Grossherzogtümern Mecklenburg von 1850 bis 1914* (Münster, 1999), pp. 927–62 and pp. 1119–43.

23 For Prussia, see Andreas Thier, 'Die Gesetzgebungsverfassung der deutschen konstitutionellen Monarchie als bewegliches System: Preußische Steuergesetzgebung 1879–1893', in Bärbel Holtz and Hartwin Spenkuch (eds), *Preußens Weg in die politische Moderne: Verfassung – Verwaltung – politische Kultur zwischen Reform und*

Reformblockade (Berlin, 2001), pp. 285–320. For the Empire, see Peter-Christian Witt, *Die Finanzpolitik des Deutschen Reiches von 1903 bis 1913, eine Studie zur Innenpolitik des Wilhelminischen Deutschlands* (Lübeck and Hamburg, 1970).

24 Thier, *Steuergesetzgebung*, pp. 369–71.

25 For further details, cf. Thier, *Steuergesetzgebung*, pp. 306–19.

26 *Denkschrift, betreffend die Reform der direkten Steuern in Preußen* (6 June 1880), in Geheimes Staatsarchiv Preussischer Kulturbesitz (hereafter cited as GStA PK), I. HA Rep. 151 HB, no. 1681, fol. 77^{r}–159^{r}. For the biography of Eilers, see Hartwin Spenkuch, *Die Protokolle des Preußischen Staatsministeriums 1817–1934/38*, vol. 7: *8. Januar 1879 bis 19. März 1890* (Hildesheim, 1999), p. 375.

27 Eilers, *Denkschrift*, fol. 90^{r}.

28 For another reform concept of a Prussian high-level official cf., for example, Marot, *Vorläufige Denkschrift betreffend Reform der Einkommensteuer* (12 Sept. 1879), in GStA PK, I. HA Rep. 151 HB, no. 1681, fol. 3^{r}–21^{v}; Eilers, *Denkschrift*, fol. 116^{r}–121^{v}; Burghart, *Bemerkungen zu der vorl. Denkschrift betr. Reform der direkten Steuern* (concerning Marot's memorandum [earlier in this note]), in GStA PK, I. HA Rep. 151 HB, no. 1681, fol. 22^{r}–24^{v}, 24^{v}.

29 See Otto v. Bismarck, letter to Wilhelm I, 1 July 1879, in idem, *Die gesammelten Werke (Friedrichsruher Ausgabe)*, vol. 6c: *Politische Schriften*, Werner Frauendienst (ed.) (Berlin, 1935), no. 161, pp. 150–2, 151: Finance Ministry as *Republik der Ministerialräthe*.

30 Hans Herzfeld, *Johannes von Miquel. Sein Anteil am Ausbau des Deutschen Reiches bis zur Jahrhundertwende*, vol. 2: *Konservative Wendung und staatsmännisches Wirken* (Detmold, 1938).

31 Johannes Miquel to Adolph Wagner, Gustav Schmoller, Gustav Cohn, Harzburg, 24 Aug. 1892/26 Aug. 1892, in GStA PK, I. HA Rep. 151 HB, no. 1724, fol. 211^{r}.

32 Gustav Schmoller, letter to Miquel, Berlin 26 Sept. 1892, in GStA PK, I. HA Rep. 151 HB, no. 1724, fol. 249^{r}–250^{r}; Gustav Cohn, letter to Miquel, Göttingen 8 Sept. 1892, GStA PK, I. HA Rep. 151 HB, no. 1724, fol. 215^{r}–218^{v}. For a biographical sketch, see Walter Braeuer, 'Cohn, Gustav', in *Neue Deutsche Biographie*, vol. 3 (Berlin, 1957), pp. 315–16; Adolph Wagner, *Bemerkungen zu dem Gesetzentwurf eines Ergänzungssteuergesetzes* (sent to Miquel 24. 9. 1891), in GStA PK, I. HA Rep. 151 HB, no. 1724, fol. 220^{r}–226^{r} (the letter, mentioned before ibid., fol. 219^{r}).

33 Thier, *Steuergesetzgebung*, pp. 432–623; Witt, *Finanzpolitik*, pp. 219–23.

34 Cf., for example, Adolph Wagner, 'Die Reform der direkten Staatsbesteuerung in Preussen im Jahre 1891: Erster Artikel', *Finanzarchiv*, old series 8 (1891), pp. 551–810; 'Zweiter Artikel', *Finanzarchiv*, old ser. 11 (1894), pp. 1–76; Georg Schanz, 'Die direkten Steuern Hessens und deren neueste Reform', *Finanzarchiv*, old series 2 (1885), pp. 235–529; idem, 'Die Novelle zum sächsischen Einkommensteuergesetz vom 2. Juli 1878. Vom 10. März 1894', *Finanzarchiv*, old ser. 12 (1895), pp. 281–313; idem, 'Die sächsische Steuerreform vom Jahre 1902', *Finanzarchiv*, old ser. 20 (1903), pp. 234–55; for a biographical survey, see Christian Waldhoff, 'Schanz, Georg von', in *Neue Deutsche Biographie*, vol. 22 (Berlin, 2005), pp. 559–60.

35 See Holger Nehring's contribution in this volume.

36 For the following see Witt, *Finanzpolitik*, pp. 219–26.

37 Rudolf Morsey, *Die öffentlichen Aufgaben und die Gliederung der Kompetenzen zwischen Norddeutschem Bund, Reich und Bundesstaaten (1867–1914)*, in Kurt G. A. Jeserich, Hans Pohl and Georg-Christoph von Unruh (eds), *Deutsche Verwaltungsgeschichte* (6 vols) (Stuttgart, 1984), III, pp. 128–86, at pp. 156–8.

38 For a survey on the development of statistical research in the field of economics during the late nineteenth and early twentieth centuries, see Grimmer-Solem,

The rise of historical economics, pp. 62–7 and J. Adam Tooze, *Statistics and the German state, 1900–1945: the making of modern economic knowledge* (Cambridge, 2001).

39 For a survey from the perspective of the Historical School, see Grimmer-Solem, *The rise of historical economics*, pp. 67–86.

40 Bernd Mertens, *Gesetzgebungskunst im Zeitalter der Kodifikationen. Theorie und Praxis der Gesetzgebungstechnik aus historisch-vergleichender Sicht* (Tübingen, 2004), pp. 109–22.

41 For a biographical survey, see Jan Schröder, 'Bernhard Windscheid (1817–1892)', in Gerd Kleinheyer and idem (eds), *Deutsche und Europäische Juristen aus neun Jahrhunderten*, 4th edn (Heidelberg, 1996), pp. 442–6. For his role in the drafting of the German Civil Code, see Werner Schubert, 'Windscheid und das Bereicherungsrecht des 1. Entwurfs des BGB', *Zeitschrift für Rechtsgeschichte, Romanistische Abteilung*, 92 (1975), pp. 186–233, especially pp. 219–23.

42 For a survey of the situation in the Prussian monarchy, see Thier, *Steuergesetzgebung*, pp. 75–89 (with special emphasis on the role of the ministry, ibid., pp. 77–80); for an analysis of the Prussian Constitution in general, Hans Boldt, 'Die preußische Verfassung vom 31. Januar 1850. Probleme ihrer Interpretation', in Hans-Jürgen Puhle and Hans-Ulrich Wehler (eds), *Preußen im Rückblick* (Göttingen, 1980), pp. 224–46.

43 For further discussion of this argument, see Thier, 'Gesetzgebungsverfassung', pp. 307–8, 312, 319–20.

44 Wilhelm von Rauchhaupt, *Stenographische Berichte des preussischen Hauses der Abgeordneten, 16th legislative periode, 2nd session, 1887, Verhandlungen II, 53rd meeting (12. 5. 1887)*, pp. 1205–10, 1210.

45 Walther Peter Fuchs, 'Bundesstaaten und Reich: Der Bundesrat', in Otto Pflanze and Elisabeth Müller-Luckner (eds), *Innenpolitische Probleme des Bismarck-Reiches* (Munich and Vienna, 1983), pp. 239–56; Hans Boldt, 'Der Föderalismus im deutschen Kaiserreich als Verfassungsproblem', in Helmut Rumpler (ed.), *Innere Staatsbildung und gesellschaftliche Modernisierung in Österreich und Deutschland 1867/71 bis 1914 – Historikergespräch Österreich Bundesrepublik 1989* (Vienna and Munich, 1991), pp. 31–40.

46 For an analysis of the hegemonial position of Prussia in the constitutional framework of the German Empire, see Kersten Rosenau, *Hegemonie und Dualismus: Preußens staatsrechtliche Stellung im Deutschen Reich* (Regensburg, 1986), pp. 10–117.

47 Reinhold Zilch, 'Rheinbaben, Georg Freiherr von', in *Neue Deutsche Biographie*, vol. 21 (Berlin, 2003), pp. 487–8; Witt, *Finanzpolitik*, pp. 82–4, quote p. 84.

48 Spenkuch, *Protokolle*, vol. 7, pp. 12–13; *Die Protokolle des Preußischen Staatsministeriums 1817–1934/38*, vol. 8/I: *21. März 1890 bis 9. Oktober 1900*, ed. idem (Hildesheim, 2003), pp. 17–20.

49 Minutes of the meeting of the State Ministry, 11. Nov. 1896, in GStA PK, I. HA Rep. 90a , B III 2b no. 6, vol. 126, fol. 102^{r}–126^{v}, 132^{r}–133^{r}; for a digest, see Spenkuch, *Protokolle*, vol. 8/I, no. 257, pp. 245 et seq., here p. 246.

50 Cf. the legislation in 1905/6: Witt, *Finanzpolitik*, pp. 105–14. For a digest of the crucial State Ministry meeting 9/10 June 1905, cf. *Die Protokolle des Preußischen Staatsministeriums 1817–1934/38*, vol. 9: *23. Oktober 1900 bis 13. Juli 1909*, ed. Reinhold Zilch (Hildesheim, 2001), no. 114, pp. 154f.

51 Witt, *Finanzpolitik*, pp. 208–16; digest of the meetings of the State Ministry, 12./14. 6. 1908 (minutes in GStA PK, I. HA Rep. 90a, B III 2b no. 6, vol. 156, 213^{r}–234^{v} and 236^{r}–260^{r}) in Zilch, *Protokolle*, vol. 9, nos. 190, 191, pp. 215–16.

52 Thier, *Steuergesetzgebung*, p. 129 and pp. 132–76.

53 Karl Hofmann, speech at the meeting of the individual states ministers of finance, 5 Aug. 1878, minutes in GStA PK, I. HA Rep. 151 HB, no. 1679, fol. 133r.
54 Bismarck, letter to Camphausen, 31 Dec. 1877, in Bismarck, *Werke*, no. 105, pp. 97–8, here p. 97.
55 For a survey, see Kroboth, *Finanzpolitik*, pp. 29–33, 116.
56 Witt, *Finanzpolitik*, p. 83.
57 Georg von Schanz, 'Das bayerische Ertragsteuersystem und seine Entwicklung', *Finanzarchiv*, 17 (1900), pp. 556–85.
58 For further details, cf. Kroboth, *Finanzpolitik* and Witt, *Finanzpolitik*.
59 Thier, *Steuergesetzgebung*, pp. 593–623.
60 Cf. Metzger, and Weingarten, *Einkommensteuer*, p. 62.
61 Cf., for example, the bill for the taxation of alcohol in *Stenographische Berichte des preussischen Hauses der Abgeordneten, 15th legislative period, 1st session, 1882/83, Anlagen I*, no. 25, pp. 108–31, 117. For the use of foreign taxation concepts by members of the Prussian parliament, see *Stenographische Berichte des preussischen Hauses der Abgeordneten, 17th legislative period, 5th session, 1892/93, Anlagen V*, pp. 2308–62, here p. 2336 (and as appendix, ibid., pp. 2369–83).
62 Mann et al., *Biographisches Handbuch*, pp. 456–60.
63 Thier, *Steuergesetzgebung*, pp. 328–44.
64 See M. Rainer Lepsius, 'Parteiensystem und Sozialstruktur. Zum Problem der Demokratisierung der deutschen Gesellschaft', in idem, *Demokratie in Deutschland. Soziologisch–historische Konstellationsanalysen. Ausgewählte Aufsätze* (Göttingen, 1993), pp. 25–50.
65 Fenske, *Deutsche Parteiengeschichte*, pp. 112–19, 137–9.
66 See for a survey Nipperdey, *Deutsche Geschichte 1866–1918*, vol. 2, pp. 514–21.
67 For examples of such demands see Witt, *Finanzpolitik*, pp. 127, 267; Kroboth, *Finanzpolitik*, pp. 207–8; Thier, *Steuergesetzgebung*, pp. 397, 458.
68 Andreas Thier, 'Richter, Eugen', in *Neue Deutsche Biographie*, vol. 21 (Berlin, 2003), pp. 526–8; Francis L. Carsten, *August Bebel und die Organisation der Massen* (Berlin, 1991).
69 Thier, *Steuergesetzgebung*, pp. 616–19, 587–9.
70 Kroboth, *Finanzpolitik*, pp. 35–7.
71 Jürgen Ketterle, *Die Einkommensteuer in Deutschland. Modernisierung und Anpassung einer direkten Steuer von 1890/91 bis 1920* (Cologne, 1994), pp. 75–201, who emphasizes the impact of the Prussian concepts.
72 Cf. Frances Lynch's chapter in this volume for more recent examples.
73 Mark Hallerberg, 'Tax competition in Wilhelmine Germany and its implications for the European Union', *World Politics*, 48, no. 3 (April 1996), pp. 324–57.
74 Spoerer, *Steuerlast*, pp. 185–92.
75 For the phenomenon of the transfer of administrative knowledge on the level of the local communities in the first third of the twentieth century in general, see Wilfried Rudloff, 'Das Wissen der kommunalen Sozialverwaltung in Deutschland: Diffusion, Formen und Konflikte 1900–1933', *Jahrbuch für europäische Verwaltungsgeschichte*, 15 (2003), pp. 59–83.
76 Wolfgang Rüfner, 'Preussen', in Kurt G. A. Jeserich, Hans Pohl and Georg-Christoph von Unruh (eds), *Deutsche Verwaltungsgeschichte* (6 vols) (Stuttgart, 1984), III, pp. 678–714, here p. 689; for the development of the state supervision in Prussia, see also Berthold Grzywatz, *Stadt, Bürgertum und Staat im 19. Jahrhundert. Selbstverwaltung, Partizipation und Repräsentation in Berlin und Preußen 1806 bis 1918* (Berlin, 2003), pp. 146–7, 375–6, 583–4.
77 For a case study in this field, cf. Seckelmann, 'Im Labor'.

6

The Paradoxes of State-Building: Transnational Expertise and the Income Tax Debates in the United States and Germany, *c.*1880–1914*

Holger Nehring

In 1906, the British author H. G. Wells observed that 'first and chiefly, I have to convey what seems to me to be the most significant and pregnant thing of all ... I think it is best indicated by saying that the typical American has "no sense of the state"'.[1] By contrast, the Germans had quite a different reputation at the time. In his 1887 study *The Railroads*, Charles Francis Adams, Jr stated: 'The inclination of the German mind, especially the North German, is bureaucratic [...] With us, in America, it is just the opposite [...].'[2] These contemporary assessments notwithstanding, the debates about the introduction of a federal income tax in the German Reich and the United States had strikingly similar features: in both countries, the introduction of the income tax was highly contested, and the perception that a federal income tax might lead to an all-powerful federal government defined the positions of critics in both countries. There is also a striking chronological parallel: both countries first introduced some kind of federal income tax in 1913. Both federal polities also faced the same dual challenge posed by the growth of expenditure for naval armaments and the growing demands for state intervention in order to create 'welfare' for all and solve the 'social question'.

This chapter examines the transfer of ideas about income taxation from Germany to the United States, focusing on the Progressive Era in the USA and the Wilhelmine Period in Germany. The aim of this chapter is to use connective history to cast a different light onto American and German history and to shift the 'vanishing point' of each country's history away from contemporary perceptions.[3] Clearly, the income tax debates in both countries not only pertained to state-building, but also revolved around other issues, such as progressive political aims and party-political allegiances.[4] There were also crucial connections to the political systems, due to the implications income taxes had for the role of parliaments on a state and federal level.[5] Yet, the concern with state strength united the debates in both countries.

Given the seemingly different concepts of state and civil society in Germany and the United States, historians have usually regarded these two political systems as quite distinct, which would make the transfer of ideas about taxation rather unlikely. When historians, such as Daniel Rodgers in his impressive book *Atlantic Crossings*, have examined the connections, they have neglected taxation and have focused on the expenditure side, such as social welfare policies.[6]

Against this backdrop, this chapter suggests that a connective look at the income tax not only enhances our understanding of transatlantic history. It also shows that the American federal state in the Progressive Era played a far greater role, more akin to the allegedly strong German one, than many observers have realized. Throughout, the perspective suggested here combines attention to structural factors with highlighting the importance of mutual observation that was mediated by experts. This also means finding a way to bring together the entanglements of federal and member-state politics *and* transnational influences. State-building did not just happen from above. There was a complex web of interactions, particularly within both countries' federal systems, but also with actors outside the governments and even outside each country. This created a process during which the observation of the other was essentially an assessment of one's own position in the world. It was this mutual observation as self-observation which drove the debates about a federal income tax in both countries.

By emphasizing the importance of *perceptions* of statehood, this chapter develops further recent work on the Progressive Era which emphasizes that the roots and early development of the American income tax had more to do with placating revenue demands and a sophisticated form of conservatism than with economic equity.[7] Such studies have abandoned perspectives that progressive grass-roots pressure led to the passing of income tax laws on the state and federal levels and have instead emphasized the paradoxes of state-building: progressive legislation in the field of social welfare came with the strengthening of the federal state's power over individual lives.[8] Conversely, research on German financial history has pointed to the weakness of the federal financial base.[9]

The debates about income taxation in both countries are, therefore, classic cases for the paradoxes of state-building in the modern period: transnational links and progressive ideals did not weaken the state's 'container'. Rather, the debates about income tax were deeply embedded in the states' competition with other states for power and wealth and thus led to the strengthening of federal state structures. This chapter first explores the economic, political and social conditions which made these changes feasible. It then considers the transfer of ideas and its implications in more detail.[10]

Structural preconditions and constraints for the transfer of ideas

In order to appreciate the transfer of ideas between Germany and the United States fully it is necessary to give an outline of the structural factors which established a resonance for these ideas in the general public and the institutional constraints which hindered a direct application. The ground for the introduction of the most recent federal income tax regime in the United States was prepared by the Republican administrations under Theodore Roosevelt and William Taft for the introduction of a federal income tax after a failed first attempt in 1894[11]; in particular, Roosevelt's concept of government chimed well with some of the progressives' demands. The Democratic Wilson administration introduced the income tax as an emergency measure, but thus paved the way for further expansion during the First World War, which proved to be crucial for the introduction of the tax.[12] The 1913 legislation in the USA, formed after the failed attempt of 1894, had a very high exemption level ($3000 in 1913 for corporate and individual incomes at 1 per cent; $4000 for married couples; surtax rates that peaked at 6 per cent for incomes over $20,000). The Act established a 'normal' rate of 1 per cent on both individual and corporate incomes, with a high exemption ($3000 for single taxpayers). This excluded virtually all middle-class Americans from the tax. There was a graduated surtax of up to 6 per cent, but this did not come into play for incomes under $20,000. In the first few years of the tax, only 2 per cent of all American households contributed, and contemporaries regarded it as a wealth tax.[13] After their introduction in 1913, federal income taxes were repealed several times, as the Supreme Court ruled them unconstitutional. Only during Roosevelt's New Deal did a longer-lasting introduction of income taxation emerge.[14]

In Germany, the income tax was also introduced under the label of an emergency measure by the government under Chancellor Theobald von Bethmann Hollweg. The income tax, which was introduced as an interim *Wehrbeitrag* (a kind of armament contribution) to cover the military budget in 1913, went up to a maximum rate of 8 per cent. But there were still other more important taxes and rates for German taxpayers.[15] In Germany, the war threw federal finances into disarray, and a solid federal tax base was only created under Matthias Erzberger's reforms in the 1920s.[16]

Although the level of taxation was, by today's standards, small, and although duties and excise continued to dominate federal revenue, the introduction of federal taxation on income was an important break with previous traditions and was perceived as such, despite predecessors in times of war in both countries.[17] In 1880, in the USA, customs duties and the excise taxes on alcohol and tobacco made up nearly 90 per cent of all federal government receipts. By 1930, these two types of taxes accounted for less than 25 per cent of government revenues, and the income tax amounted to about 60 per cent of federal government receipts.[18] Lawrence Friedman has accordingly called the income tax the 'opening wedge for a major transformation of American society'.[19] By the end of the twentieth century, the progressive income tax had become the central pillar of American public finance, accounting for almost 55 per cent of federal revenue and around 40 per cent of state-level receipts.[20] This was also true for Germany.[21]

These wide-ranging reforms came as a response to a crisis in federal state finance in both countries at the end of the nineteenth and the beginning of the twentieth century. Party-political factors also played a crucial role.[22] Financial reform thus became one of the main domestic political topics in both countries in the decade before 1914.

The increasing problems with these arrangements in quickly industrializing and urbanizing economies led to increasing perceptions of financial crisis in both countries, which put greater pressure on local, state and federal governments.[23] This made calls for financial reforms more effective. To illustrate the crisis in Reich finance: gross expenditure grew significantly: in 1890, it was at 1044 million marks, in 1900, 1094 million marks, in 1901, 2691 million marks, and in 1913, 3418 million marks (in current prices). This meant that Reich expenditure as part of the gross domestic product rose from 4.5 per cent in 1872/80 to 5.4 per cent in 1901/13.[24]

Like the German Reich, the American federal government became increasingly active at home and abroad. Both the Spanish-American War at the end of the nineteenth century, which brought the entry of the US onto the world stage, and the expansion of the navy to counter the Japanese bid for supremacy in the Far East brought about a need for more federal revenue.[25] By 1900, the Department of Army and Navy constituted the single largest category of federal spending, amounting to almost 40 per cent of total expenditure. These issues combined with the increasing concentration of wealth during this period, diagnosed by many social experts at the time, to encourage politicians to look for alternative solutions. Especially the panic of 1893, which triggered the ensuing depression, exacerbated the visibility of growing poverty and class conflict.[26] The economic crisis of 1907, following in the wake of the 1906 San Francisco earthquake, underlined this case.[27] The economic contraction during the mid-1890s brought with it an unemployment rate of about 20 per cent of the workforce and a huge bank and business failure rate, only surpassed by the Great Depression during the 1930s.[28] It was the perception of these conditions that ultimately led to the weakening of the opposition to federal income tax legislation and the achievement of a consensus across the political parties.[29]

Experts and the transfer of ideas

Experts who acted in state or federal tax commissions played a crucial role in framing the problem perception. And most experts who advocated a federal income tax participated in a transatlantic transfer of ideas. It was their expertise and their participation in transnational networks which made the introduction of an income tax feasible. Here, the transfer of ideas was primarily observation, rather than personal interaction or any mechanical diffusion.[30] Although the experts participated in international conferences and transnational networks, their educational background and their common interests proved to be the most important factors which allowed for the observation. This observation had mainly one direction: from Europe and especially Germany to the United States.

The direct influence of German Historical Economy on American scholars is difficult to gauge. There are strong indications, however, that American scholars were influenced by the ideas of their colleagues across the Atlantic. They marketed ideas of a new kind of liberalism, akin to that of the German *Kathedersozialisten* such as Gustav Schmoller and Adolph Wagner, which had a very affirmative view of the state's role in economy and society and which paid particular attention to the historical specificities of economic development.This transfer of ideas from Germany to the USA led to the transformation of American liberalism away from its nineteenth-century emphasis on individual liberties towards a more progressive conception which stressed an active role for state involvement.[31] Protective labour legislation, the rise of antitrust laws, food and drug regulation, and the expansion of women's suffrage were all part and parcel of this reorganization.[32] This observation of the German academic scene by American scholars was only possible because they perceived their own literature on finance as 'shabby in the extreme'.[33]

The German-trained tax reformers became government advisors, or were at least used by the state and federal governments for propaganda purposes. They were part of a larger cohort of academics who sought to dismantle the orthodox theories of laissez-faire. They expressed their identity through professional bodies, first through the American Economic Association, founded in 1895, and claimed that their knowledge was apolitical and objective and thus legitimized their interventions.[34]

Henry Carter Adams in Wisconsin,[35] Carl C. Plehn in California,[36] as well as Richard T. Ely and Edwin R. A. Seligman in New York, played key roles.[37] Ely had studied at Heidelberg with Karl Knies to complete his doctorate and brought the German seminar model of teaching back to Johns Hopkins University, where he began his teaching career.[38] Edwin Seligman had family ties in Germany and studied with the historical economist Adolph Wagner.[39] Likewise, Adams had studied at universities in Heidelberg and Berlin.[40] While more recent research has pointed out that this Historical School was more divided than scholars have assumed so far,[41] what matters in our context is that the American tax reformers adopted their scepticism towards laissez-faire economics and towards formal rules for economic reasoning. Throughout this period, the American scholars were engaged in intensive exchanges of letters and ideas, and shared articles and reviews, with their German counterparts.[42]

The reformers highlighted the importance of historical change and the dynamic development of economic norms.[43] It was this assumption which led them to demand a more positive role for the state. By adopting this almost metaphysical idea of statehood out of historical necessity, the American economists, paradoxically, denied that they had merely adopted a German model. They claimed that it was a manifestation of the Zeitgeist, rather than of ideas linked to any particular country.[44]

As in Germany,[45] the main explicit argument for income taxation in the United States was primarily one about political and distributive justice, and it is this argument on which most historians have concentrated so far: these economists introduced the notion of the ability to pay into American discussions on public finance, often pointing to sociological research on poverty.[46] They used the language of ethical duties and social solidarity less to clarify their philosophical position, but with possible political constituencies in mind.[47]

While engaging with the ideas by their German counterparts, the economists responded to a variety of factors which they observed in American society and economy: these had primarily to do with the concentration of wealth and corporate power, cycles of economic crisis as well as the increasing prevalence of intangible wealth in the form of stocks and bonds. Even opponents of the income tax regretted that the tariff policies led to increasing prices for consumer goods, and were unstable and inflexible when responding to the changing economic situation.[48] Thus, the application of economic thinking akin to that of the German Historical School was only possible because of the changed character of the economic cycle: rather than seeing the economy as an organic whole which developed in and of itself, they regarded it as an entity which could be influenced.[49] Writing in the wake of the 1893 panic, during the last recession of the nineteenth century, the Chicago labour economist Robert Hoxie observed that 'the customs revenue system, through inherent inflexibility and instability, is incapable of serving as an adequate source of revenue in times of emergency'.[50] Especially Ely did not come to the issue of public finance through an abstract engagement with public finance issues, but through his work as an expert for the Baltimore and Maryland tax commissions in the mid-1880s.[51]

Seligman, by contrast, supplied a more theoretical critique of property taxes – property taxes were not exceptional to American conditions, he argued, and because they were not unique, they were susceptible to historical change. More importantly, he argued that the property tax was flawed because property was no longer the criterion of 'faculty', or taxpaying ability. For him, the introduction of income taxes had to do with the goals of alleviating the lower-earning families from the burden of indirect consumption taxes and with levying taxes on the richer echelons of society through the introduction of property taxes and income taxes (albeit still with a rather moderate progression).[52]

The context for Seligman's demand was the discussions about the wealth of large corporations in the United States during the Progressive Era. A tax regime based around the property tax was unable to tap the wealth of large corporations; only an income tax regime could achieve this and do away with some of what Seligman regarded as the regrettable social consequences of the current arrangements. Reformers such as Seligman called for the 'ethical agency' of state power and saw the income tax as a means to weaken the influence of business on politics.[53]

While the German-inspired social reformers argued in favour of income taxation, traditional liberals and conservatives were opposed to it. They feared the intrusion into private life which was connected to the introduction of income taxes. Legal measures had a special part to play in allowing this intrusion finally to happen: they played the role of unifying the structurally diverse and tenuously connected elements of the American state.[54] Accordingly, Seligman argued against conservative critics of the Sixteenth Amendment, which allowed for a federal income tax: 'Let us not make a fetish of "self-government", and let us not oppose central authority in those cases where self-government means retrogression rather than progress.'[55] In Germany, with the Civic Code (*Bürgerliches Gesetzbuch*), ratified in 1900, this can be dated quite precisely.[56]

But transfer not only took the form of observation between Germany and the United States. Transfers of ideas also happened within the American federal system.[57] Most of the American tax reformers' careers started in the states. The American progressive movement was particularly strong in Wisconsin,[58] but spread out from there, either through national progressive associations or more specialized bodies such as the National Tax Association.

Like in Germany, the American states had already introduced income tax regimes to generate more revenue to cope with increasing infrastructural and social welfare demands. Throughout the nineteenth century, the general property tax dominated state and local revenues. Over time, however, structural changes in the economy eroded the ability of property tax to provide sufficient revenue. New forms of intangible wealth, such as bonds and stocks, became increasingly prevalent.[59]

These developments in the states removed some of the practical and legal hurdles for the introduction of similar kinds of taxes on the federal level. The comment by the English observer Sydney Brooks in the *North American Review* is revealing in this respect. He noted that this was 'an auspicious sign that even in America things move and the dead hand is not omnipotent'.[60] Since at the least the 1890s, the climate within state legislatures towards progressive taxation had grown increasingly favourable. In 1890, for example, only six states maintained inheritance taxes, by 1903, 27 of the 46 states used inheritance taxation in some form and by 1913, 35 of the now 48 states had enacted similar proposals.[61]

Interestingly, there was no clear socio-economic pattern to the distribution of American states with income tax regimes. They spread across the sea boards, the North, the South and the Midwest. By 1913, only six states had income tax laws in effect: Massachusetts, the Carolinas, Virginia, Oklahoma and Wisconsin, which introduced the tax in 1911.[62] And the state tax systems diverged rather than converged during this period.[63] Yet, what is important in this context is that the state courts were unwilling to distinguish between the progressive inheritance taxes and income taxes on the one hand and other forms of non-progressive taxation on the other. The Wisconsin Supreme Court, for example, ruled in *State ex. Rel. Bolens* v. *Frear* of 1912 that the income tax was constitutional.[64]

We can see that the transfer here consisted not merely in the passing on of discrete packages of ideas. Rather, ideas were mediated, both through ideas and through institutions, in a process of 'social learning'.[65] This happened in the period between the 1890s and the 1900s when tax reformers' voices became increasingly influential in the national debates. During this period, alternative revenue, such as customs duties and excise, or non-progressive taxes on property, became increasingly unpopular.

These arguments had previously remained unheeded, as tariffs had assumed the cornerstone of political debate between Democrats and Republicans up to the 1880s and 1890s; even the Populist movement for an income tax that might replace some of the tariff revenues and simultaneously assault monopoly power did not increase the demand for expert knowledge which was necessary to enact these measures productively.[66]

The erosion of party politics and patronage and their replacement by a more competitive political process further contributed to the rise of a fiscal, regulatory and administrative American state.[67] The perceived crisis, a favourable political climate as well as the rationalization of knowledge at that time made this emergence of discussions about income tax ideas possible.

States and citizens – transnational reconfigurations

The *implicit*, yet fundamental thread which ran through the American reformers' thinking was Seligman's and Ely's criticism on administrative grounds of the property tax. They had come to these conclusions through a scholarly engagement with German ideas of statehood, and thus participated in a transnational discussion on the reconfiguration of statehood and citizenship during this period. For them, the property tax was a levy which could not be effectively collected because it could not reach the increasing forms of intangible or invisible wealth, such as bonds, stocks and mortgages: 'it put a premium on dishonesty and debauches the public conscience'.[68] This highlights the fundamental point which undergirded discussions in both countries: different perceptions of the role the federal state had to play in the lives of its citizens. Both the USA and Germany were part of a transatlantic development. We can see here how the development of administrative capacities by the federal states and the observation of ideas interacted with each other in shaping the debate.

Income taxation meant that states did not demand payment of a flat share of certain visible incomes (such as the model developed in revolutionary France). Rather, they sought a transparent system that would be used to determine what the person received as income, how it was spent and what share the state could reasonably claim. It was this aspect of tax reform, and not the sheer weight of the tax, that became the focus of public opposition in the United States and in Germany. It threatened to expose the citizen before an inquisitorial state.

The controversy about privacy was reflected in one of the paradoxes of nineteenth-century tax regimes as they moved incrementally from a tacit recognition of the 'individual' to a definition of 'personality'. Historically, the introduction of progressive taxation legislation meant a different relationship between states and citizens.[69] The tax regime of revolutionary France was meant to ignore the legal ascription of the taxpayer by focusing on properties and income.[70] This deliberate policy of avoiding legal estate overlapped with another: the explicit recognition of the autonomy of the individual, which barred the Treasury from investigating the private life of the payer. Hence, external indicators were adopted in the following years by European countries and by the USA – the system allowed assessment of the properties from the outside, but it did not allow government inspectors to enter the properties. Technically, taxes were levied on things, not on people, so that the individual of fiscal policy was constructed negatively, in terms of its immunities.

Paradoxically, however, this meant that tax offices – both on the federal level and on the state level – acquired more information than ever about personal economic activity, including ownership and income from property.[71] Beginning with the Prussian income tax of 1891 in particular, the data relating to economic activity were now attached to persons and merged into a comprehensive profile of what contemporaries called the 'economic personality' or the 'visible personality'. The payer, rather than incomes and properties, now became the subject of taxation.[72] Borrowed from psychiatry, the term 'personality' implied an entity that was complex, composed of expenditures and incomes.[73] Most importantly, the personality was visible and open to scrutiny from the outside; indeed, it was constructed according to official categories which had been developed by governmental officials in coordination with social experts and lawmakers. The lobbying for similar tax regimes in the United States meant that these features of information gathering had to be improved on the federal level in the USA as well, so that, in essence, the advocacy of income taxation went hand in hand with efforts to strengthen the federal administrative apparatus and the role experts and knowledge production played within it. To be sure, the tax rates were still relatively low at the time and the exemption limits were quite large, especially in the United States.[74]

Nevertheless, the creation of the legal and constitutional basis for income tax regimes in both Germany and the United States were the first steps towards a system which relied on a more inquisitive state as outlined above. The *Wall Street Journal*, opposed to the income tax, thus warned of these arrangements by mentioning the French experience. It suggested that no one was safe from the pervasive reach of an income tax.[75] In short, the introduction of federal income tax regimes in both countries marked the visible beginning of what

Peter Holquist has termed the 'governmental state'.[76] This state was less interested in managing the population legitimately and righteously, but effectively and economically. In these states, the production of knowledge about 'society' and the taxpayers was linked to a differentiation and specialization of the administration. Civil servants now became experts in how to deal with these problems. These developments made the transfer of ideas possible and were, at the same time, the content of that transfer.[77] Government research bureaux were one side effect of the exponential growth of government services and taxation that characterized the corporate state, causing major problems for the governments' political legitimacy and making the transparency for the budgeting process all the more necessary.[78]

There was a paradox here, however, which observers in both Germany and the United States noticed and highlighted. This paradox had to do with the importance of 'personality' for these income tax regimes. For it was precisely the promise of integration on a personal level and the quelling of social disaffection connected to it that was especially important to the authors of the reform. In this transnational debate, the tax reformers thus recast taxation as a civic process and a mark of inclusion, an 'honour' rather than a burden imposed by an alien state.[79]

Exemption from that honour meant, in fact, civic exclusion – it was this motive, more than others, that brought the labour movement in the United States finally to back the proposals for an income tax reform. In these debates, only those who paid these taxes were deemed to be proper citizens and political actors. Paradoxically, however, this argument allowed corporations to gain social standing as respectable and responsible members of the community who paid their dues. Rather than weakening corporate power, this strengthened the corporate state in the United States.[80] Large corporations in the USA which were heavily taxed under the income tax regime thus gained social prestige at a time when their activities had come heavily under fire. In the United States, this debate was connected to a general discourse about citizenship, as more recent research on the race relations in the southern United States has shown; as in the tax debates, the emphasis was on the 'best and responsible men' with the ability to pay in order to strengthen the state.[81] The slow emergence of 'social citizenship' with a 'whole range [of social rights] from the right to [a] modicum of economic welfare and security to the right to live the life of a civilized being according to the standards prevailing in society', therefore, started, rather ironically, in those sections of society which least needed it.[82] The highest earners in society were now able to claim equality with everyone else, rather than the other way around. In Germany, by contrast, the industrialists did not regard the income tax as an opportunity to prove their worth for the fatherland. Instead, they bemoaned, much more vehemently than their American counterparts, the confiscatory character of the new legislation.[83]

Hence, this connective and transnational perspective shows that progressive hopes for civic inclusion, more social justice and state-building were not really polar opposites, as Robert Stanley has argued in his *Dimensions of Law in the Service of Order* for the American case.[84] They were two sides of the same coin. One of the hallmarks of European and American fiscal reform during this time period was the tension between the individual's rights and the economic personality which was the basis of the tax collection – the individual was indivisible and to a degree private and defined by its immunities and rights; the personality was complex, divisible and open to scrutiny. In practice, the income tax regime was, therefore, the function of knowledge, information and participation, rather than mere compulsion.[85] The person was a member of the state to the extent that the person's identity or personality was formed by official parameters and reconfirmed within state practices; but much of the knowledge on which the American and the German federal states depended was supplied by the population itself. The American tax reformer Seligman formulated this quite succinctly by rejecting the view that people could expect benefits for paying taxes:

> It is now generally agreed that we pay taxes not because the state protects us, or because we get any benefits from the state, but simply because the state is part of us. The duty of supporting it is born with us. In a civilized society the state is as necessary to the individual as the air he breathes [...] We pay taxes because [...] the state is an integral part of us.[86]

Likewise, Ely claimed that taxes could not be justified based 'on the old fiction of reciprocity'. Taxes were 'not exchanges' or 'payments' for goods and services: 'The sovereign power demands contributions from citizens regardless of the value of any services which it may perform for its citizen [...] The citizen pays because he is a citizen, and it is his duty as a citizen to do so.'[87]

It was this distinction which made the contemporary debates in the United States and Germany so ambiguous: this distinction provided critics and advocates of the income tax in most countries with two competing principles for arguing their case, so that the demand for personal integration could be tempered by the insistence on individual autonomy. The arguments' ambiguous character allowed the ideas about the income tax to travel from the constitutional and only slowly democratizing German Reich to the, in contemporaries' perceptions at least, nominally democratic United States. The concept could be sold differently in both political contexts, but it entailed the same shift towards a more governmental and investigative state. This became particularly clear in the United States. Here, the Wilson administration's programme, during the First World War, of steering between socialism and unmediated capitalism focused the debate over taxation on the question of what stake society had in corporate profits. The administration thus capitalized on the class-based southern populism embodied by North Carolina's Claude Kitchin.[88] The price was an increase in corporate influence on the federal government and an increase in socio-economic rivalries.[89]

And it was the ambiguity of the concept which made the system tenable in the United States, but, in the long run, destabilized the German Empire. The American political system had high exemption levels and opportunities for social actors to appeal against the tax and was thus able to juggle the paradoxes.[90] In fact, appeals were granted several times until the introduction of a more enduring federal income tax regime under Roosevelt's New Deal in the 1930s. The German Empire, by contrast, collapsed as the language of civic inclusion used to justify the income tax and other levies during the First World War led to the escalation of contradictions between increasing demands for transparency on the one hand and the demands of the investigatory state on the other.

Conclusion

There was, therefore, no contradiction between transnational interaction and state-building. Both were inextricably connected, and the American and the German federal states were more similar than contemporary observers took them to be. 'Transfers of ideas' in this context were, therefore, not merely a diffusion of concepts from one polity to another, in an almost organic way, leading, as though steered by the forces of nature, to the adoption of similar tax regimes. Instead, the 'transfer of ideas' was a specific form of communication, which consisted primarily in observation. This observation was not mutual: Americans were more interested in the German system than vice versa.

While the adoption of specific policy measures was due to very specific political, social and economic factors in both countries, there existed an underlying theme in both countries which made this observation possible and which created the very foundations on which the income tax regimes rested. Federal state-building efforts played a crucial role in both debates, especially with regard to the issue of privacy. The history of American taxation is, in this period, not the linear and continuous story of tax resistance that has often been portrayed.[91] Arguments about fairness and social justice were used to justify the expansion of the federal state, thus giving corporations a greater role.[92]

There were, however, crucial differences as well. Developments towards a more unitary state took place far more quickly in Germany than in the USA (but, I would argue, not because of a strong-state tradition, but because of the greater problems with the specific institutions of public finance). Also, partly as a consequence, partly independently, the different structures of the political systems determined to a large degree how the measure of income taxation could be communicated to the population. This had important implications for the ways in which state-building in general and income taxation in particular were perceived. It was thus in this area of *perception* that the American and German experiences differed. While both political systems began to integrate citizens more into the fabric of the state, the success with which they achieved this differed quite markedly. The American federal government was far better at coming to terms with the paradox that an allegedly liberal measure such as the income tax resulted, in fact, in more governmental control.

In the USA, many of the arrangements came slowly and by stealth, often only felt on a local or state level. The discussions of solutions for these problems in the United States did not necessarily involve talking about state-building or the changing role of the state. As Marc Stears has recently shown for British–American progressive discussions, the points of reference for these debates were the revitalization of the community and freedom of the Constitution (in order to make change more manageable), rather than 'the state'.[93] Similar attempts to endow this new form of governmentality with liberal credentials could also be seen in Germany during this period, but they were ultimately not successful in generating legitimacy for the Reich.[94] These findings should encourage us to abandon the strong state/weak state dichotomy in favour of an approach which examines perceptions rather than state capacities as such.[95]

If we want to assess income taxation and state-building, we cannot, therefore, leave out this side of observation, perceptions and self-reflection. It was precisely these factors which made it possible for us now to highlight the differences between the German and American experiences, rather than emphasizing their connections.

Notes

*I should like to thank Elliott Brownlee, Julia Moses and Stephen Tuck for their insightful comments on an earlier draft of this chapter.

1 H. G. Wells, *The future in America. A search after realities* (London, 1906), p. 14.

2 Charles Francis Adams, Jr, *Railroads. Their origins and their problems* (New York, new edn 2005 [1887]), p. 12.

3 On the 'vanishing point', cf. Helmut Walser Smith, 'The vanishing point of German history: an essay on perspective', *History & Memory*, 17 (2005), pp. 269–95.

4 For Germany, cf. Peter-Christian Witt, *Die Finanzpolitik des Deutschen Reiches von 1903 bis 1913: Eine Studie zur Innenpolitik des Wilhelminischen Deutschland* (Lübeck and Hamburg, 1970); for the United States: John D. Buenker, *The income tax and the Progressive Era* (New York, 1985).

5 Cf. John F. Witte, *The politics and development of the federal income tax* (Madison, Wisc., 1985), p. 67; Bennett D. Baack and Edward John Ray, 'Special interests and the adoption of the income tax in the United States', *Journal of Economic History*, 45 (1985), p. 607; Peter H. Lindert, *Growing public: social spending and economic growth since the eighteenth century* (Cambridge, 2004); Christopher Howard, *The hidden welfare state: tax expenditures and social policy in the United States* (Princeton, 1997), pp. 49–50; Elizabeth Sanders, *Roots of reform: farmers, workers, and the American state, 1877–1917* (Chicago, 1999), pp. 160–72; Richard Franklin Bensel, *The political economy of American industrialization, 1877–1900* (Cambridge, 2000), pp. 159–61. For Germany, cf. Witt, *Finanzpolitik*, and Mark Hallerberg, 'The political economy of taxation in Prussia, 1871–1914', *Jahrbuch für Wirtschaftsgeschichte* (2002), pp. 11–33.

6 Cf. Daniel T. Rodgers, *Atlantic crossings: social politics in the Progressive Age* (Cambridge, Mass., 1998). For a general history of the Progressive Era, albeit without much attention to law and constitutionalism, cf. Nancy Cohen, *The reconstruction of American liberalism, 1865–1914* (Chapel Hill, 2002).

7 Cf. Robert Stanley, *Dimensions of law in the service of order: origins of the federal income tax, 1861–1913* (New York, 1993), p. 231; Albert L. Ellis, 'The Regressive Era: Progressive Era tax reform and the National Tax Association – roots of the modern American tax structure' (unpublished Ph.D. dissertation, Rice University, 1991); Morton Horwitz, *The transformation of American law, 1870–1960: the crisis of legal orthodoxy* (New York, 1992); James Weinstein, *The corporate ideal in the liberal state, 1900–1918* (Boston, 1968), pp. 140–2. More generally, Gabriel Kolko, *The triumph of conservatism: a reinterpretation of American history, 1900–1916* (New York, 1963), pp. 112, 129.

8 For an exposition of the classic view, cf. Cf. Elmer Ellis, 'Public opinion and the income tax, 1860–1900', *Mississippi Valley Historical Review*, 27 (1940), pp. 225–42; Sidney Ratner, *American taxation. Its history as a social force in democracy* (New York, 1942). Important revisionist studies include Stanley, *Dimensions of law*; Stephen Skowronek, *Building a new American state. The expansion of national administrative capacities, 1877–1920* (New York, 1982): idem and Karen Orren (eds), *The search for political development* (Cambridge, 2004); R. Rudy Higgens-Evenson, *The price of progress. Public services, taxation, and the American corporate state, 1877–1929* (Baltimore and London, 2003); Martin J. Sklar, *The corporate reconstruction of American capitalism, 1890–1916* (Cambridge, 1988); most recently James A. Henretta, 'Charles Evans Hughes and the strange death of liberal America', *Law and History Review*, 24 (2006), pp. 115–72. For a critique, cf. Robert D. Johnston, 'Re-democratizing the Progressive Era: the politics of Progressive Era historiography', *Journal of the Gilded Age and Progressive Era*, 1 (2002), pp. 68–92.

9 Cf. Niall Ferguson, 'Public finance and national security: the domestic origins of the First World War revisited', *Past and Present*, 142 (1994), pp. 141–68.

10 For a systematic analysis of these criteria, cf. F. Neumark, 'Internationale Gemeinsamkeiten und nationale Eigenarten der Finanzpolitik', *Kyklos*, 2 (1948), pp. 317–48.

11 Cf. Richard J. Joseph, *The origins of the American income tax: the revenue act of 1894 and its aftermath* (Syracuse, NY, 2004). On federal spending, cf. Theda Skocpol, *Protecting soldiers and mothers: the political origins of social policy in the United States* (Cambridge, Mass., 1992), pp. 160–2.

12 Brownlee, *Federal taxation*, p. 40.

13 Cf. *Tariff of 1913*, ch. 16, §2, 33 Stat. 144, 166, 169; 'Anti-wealth policy', *New York Times*, 2 September 1913; W. Elliott Brownlee, *Federal taxation in America. A short history* (Cambridge, 1996), p. 46; John F. Witte, *The politics and development of the federal income tax* (Madison, Wisc., 1985), p. 78.

14 Brownlee, *Federal taxation*, pp. 66–88.

15 'Gesetz über einen einmaligen außerordentlichen Wehrbeitrag/Besitzsteuergesetz vom 3. Juli 1913', *Reichsgesetzblatt*, 505–21/524–43, especially §§56ff. and 76ff. Cf. also Hans-Peter Ullmann, 'Die Bürger als Steuerzahler im Deutschen Kaiserreich', in Manfred Hettling and Paul Nolte (eds), *Nation und Gesellschaft in Deutschland. Historische Essays* (Munich, 1996), pp. 231–46, pp. 235–6. Cf. also Wilhelm Gerloff, *Finanz- und Zollpolitik des Deutschen Reiches* (n.p., 1913), p. 213.

16 Cf. Carl-Ludwig Holtfrerich, 'The modernization of the tax system in the First World War and the Great Inflation, 1914–1923', in Peter-Christian Witt (ed.), *Wealth and taxation in Central Europe: the history and sociology of public finances*

(Leamington Spa, 1987), pp. 125–35 and Hans-Peter Ullmann, *Der deutsche Steuerstaat. Geschichte der öffentlichen Finanzen* (Munich, 2005), pp. 88–114.

17 For data cf. Hans-Ulrich Wehler, *Deutsche Gesellschaftsgeschichte*, vol. 3: *Von der 'Deutschen Doppelrevolution' bis zum Beginn des Ersten Weltkrieges, 1849–1914* (Munich, 1995), pp. 637–61; US Bureau of Census, Department of Commerce, *Historical statistics of the United States, colonial times to 1970*: http://www2.census.gov/prod2/statcomp/documents/CT1970pl_o1.pdf, pp. 1106–8; John Mark Hansen, 'Taxation and the political economy of tariff', *International Organization*, 44 (1990), here pp. 527 and 529.

18 Cf. *Historical statistics of the United States*, pp. 1106–8.

19 Lawrence M. Friedman, *A history of American law* (New York, 1985), p. 567.

20 US Bureau of Census, Department of Commerce, *Statistical Abstract of the United States*, 2002, p. 314, table 464: http://www.census.gov/prod/www/statistical_abstract_04.html.

21 Cf. Eckart Schremmer, *Warum die württembergischen Ertragssteuern von 1821 und die sächsische Einkommenssteuer von 1874/8 so interessant sind* (Stuttgart and Leipzig, 2002).

22 For the US, cf. Ajay K. Mehrotra, 'Creating the modern American fiscal state: the political economy of U.S. tax policy, 1880–1930' (unpublished Ph.D. dissertation, University of Chicago, 2003); for Germany: Witt, *Finanzpolitik*.

23 Cf., for example, David P. Thelen, *The new citizenship: origins of progressivism in Wisconsin, 1885–1900* (Columbia, 1972), pp. 133–4; John B. Legler, Richard Sylla and John J. Wallis, 'U.S. city finances and the growth of government', *Journal of Economic History*, 48 (1988), pp. 347–56.

24 Cf. Ferguson, 'Public finance'.

25 Cf. William Appleman Williams, *The tragedy of American diplomacy* (Cleveland, 1959).

26 Cf. Charles Hoffmann, *The depression of the nineties: an economic history* (Westport, Conn., 1970), pp. 4, 57–8, 285–97.

27 Margaret Myers, *Financial history of the United States* (New York, 1957), pp. 245–6.

28 Cf. *Historical statistics of the United States*, p. 1115.

29 Cf. Charles V. Stewart, 'The federal income tax and the realignment of the 1890s', in Bruce A. Campbell and Richard J. Trilling (eds), *Realignment in American politics. Toward a theory* (Austin, Tex., 1980), pp. 263–87; idem, 'The formation of tax policy in America, 1893–1913' (unpublished Ph.D. dissertation, University of North Carolina at Chapel Hill, 1974); Richard F. Bensel, *Sectionalism and American political development, 1880–1980* (Madison, Wisc., 1984), pp. 60–103; Paul Wolman, *Most favored nation: the Republican revisionists and U.S. tariff policy, 1897–1912* (Chapel Hill, 1992); C. K. Yearley, *The money machines. The breakdown and reform of governmental and party finance in the north, 1860–1920* (Albany, NY, 1970), pp. 39–41.

30 Cf. from a different perspective Ajay Mehrotra, 'Envisioning the modern American fiscal state: Progressive-Era economists and the intellectual foundations of the U.S. income tax', *UCLA Law Review*, 52 (2005), pp. 1793–866. Generally cf. Axel R. Schäfer, 'German historicism, progressive social thought, and the interventionist state in the United States since the 1880s', in Mark Bevir and Frank Trentmann (eds), *Markets in historical contexts. Ideas and politics in the modern world* (Cambridge, 2004), pp. 145–69. For similar processes in Canada, cf. Eric H. Reiter, 'Imported books, imported ideas: reading European jurisprudence in nineteenth-century Quebec', *Law and History Review*, 22 (2004), pp. 445–92.

31 Cf. Morton White, *Social thought in America. The revolt against formalism* (New York, 1949); Jeff Sklansky, *The soul's economy. Market society and selfhood in*

American thought, 1820–1920 (Chapel Hill, 2002). On the transatlantic dimensions, cf. James T. Kloppenberg, *Uncertain victory: social democracy and progressivism in European and American thought, 1870–1920* (New York, 1986), p. 355.

32 Cf. Sidney Fine, *Laissez-faire and the general-welfare state* (Ann Arbor, 1956); Morton Keller, *Regulating a new economy: public policy and economic change in America, 1900–1933* (Cambridge, Mass., 1990).

33 Thus Adams's mentor at Johns Hopkins, Francis A. Walker, 'The principles of taxation', *Princeton Review*, 2 (1880), pp. 92–4.

34 Cf. Mary O. Furner, *Advocacy and objectivity. A crisis in the professionalization of American social science, 1865–1905* (Lexington, 1975); Dorothy Ross, *The origins of American social science* (Cambridge, 1991); Thomas L. Haskell, *The emergence of professional social science: the American Social Science Association and the nineteenth-century crisis of authority* (Urbana, 1977); Michael J. Lacey and Mary O. Furner, 'Social investigation, social knowledge, and the state: an introduction', in idem (eds), *The state and social investigation in Britain and the United States* (Cambridge, 1993), pp. 3–62.

35 Cf. A. W. Coats, 'Henry Carter Adams: a case study in the emergence of the social sciences in the United States, 1850–1900', *Journal of American Studies*, 2 (1968), p. 177; S. Laurence Bigelow et al., 'Henry Carter Adams', *Journal of Political Economy*, 30 (1922), pp. 201–11.

36 Cf. Mansel G. Blackford, *The politics of business in California, 1890–1920* (Columbus, Ohio, 1977).

37 Cf. Franek Rozwadowski, 'From recitation room to research seminar: Political Economy at Columbia University', in William J. Barber (ed.), *Breaking the academic mould: economists and American higher learning in the nineteenth century* (Middletown, Conn., 1982), p. 196.

38 Jurgen Herbst, *The German Historical School in American scholarship: a study in the transfer of culture* (Ithaca, 1965); Joseph Dorfman, 'The role of the German Historical School in American economic thought', *American Economic Review*, 45 (1955), p. 17.

39 Cf. Wesley C. Mitchell, 'Tribute', in *Edwin Robert Anderson Seligman, 1861–1939* (1942), p. 60; 'In Memoriam: Edwin Robert Anderson Seligman', *Political Science Quarterly*, 54 (1939), p. 480; Carl S. Shoup, 'Edwin R. A. Seligman', in David L. Sills (ed.), *International Encyclopedia of the social sciences* (New York, 1968), p. 163.

40 Rodgers, *Atlantic crossings*, pp. 96–7.

41 Cf. Erik Grimmer-Solem, *The rise of historical economics and social reform in Germany 1864–1894* (Oxford, 2003); Heath Pearson, 'Was there really a German Historical School of Economics?', *Historical Political Economy*, 31 (1999), p. 547.

42 Seligman to Gustav Schmoller, 19 April 1894: *Geheimes Staatsarchiv Preußischer Kulturbesitz*, Berlin, VI, *Hauptabteilung Familienarchive und Nachlässe*, Gustav Schmoller papers, no. 153; Irving Fisher (Yale) to Lujo Brentano, 10 January 1913: *Bundesarchiv* Koblenz, Lujo Brentano papers, NL1001/69; 'Notebooks from Classes in Berlin', 'Lecture notes taken by Edwin R. A. Seligman': Seligman papers, Butler Library, Columbia University, New York City, box 86.

43 Edwin R. A. Seligman, *The income tax: a study of the history, theory and practice of income taxation at home and abroad* (New York, 2nd edn, 1914), pp. 12–14.

44 Edwin R. A. Seligman, 'Change in the tenets of political economy with time', *Science*, 7 (1886), p. 382.

45 Cf. Witt, *Finanzpolitik*, p. 59.

46 Cf. Henry C. Adams, *The science of finance: an investigation of public expenditures and public revenues* (New York, 1898), p. 300.
47 Gina L. Keel, 'A social fiscal science: the progressive origins of federal income taxation' (unpublished Ph.D. dissertation, Brandeis University, 1998).
48 'Taxing food', *New York Times*, 1 June 1891, p. 4; Edwin R. A. Seligman, *The shifting incidence of taxation* (New York, 1899), p. 374.
49 Cf. Mary O. Furner, 'Knowing capitalism: public investigation and the labor question in the long Progressive Era', in Furner and Supple (eds), *The state and economic knowledge*, pp. 241–86.
50 Robert F. Hoxie, 'Adequacy of the customs revenue system', *Journal of Political Economy*, 3 (1894), pp. 39–71.
51 Cf. Richard T. Ely, *Ground under our feet. An autobiography* (New York, 1938), pp. 172–3; John Prentiss Poe and Richard T. Ely, *Report of the tax commission of Baltimore* (Baltimore, 1886).
52 Edwin R. A. Seligman, 'The general property tax', *Political Science Quarterly*, 5 (1890), p. 24.
53 Ely, *Ground under our feet*, p. 136. On the general context cf. Richard L. McCormick, 'The discovery that "business corrupts politics": a reappraisal of the origins of Progressivism', *American Historical Review*, 86 (1981), pp. 247–74.
54 Cf. Stanley, *Law in the service of order*.
55 Edwin R. A. Seligman, 'The income tax amendment', *Political Science Quarterly*, 25 (1910), pp. 193, 213–14.
56 Cf. Michael John, 'The peculiarities of the German state: bourgeois law and society in the Imperial Era', *Past and Present*, 119 (1988), pp. 105–31.
57 On parallels in Germany, cf. Andreas Thier's chapter in this volume.
58 Cf. W. Elliott Brownlee, *Progressivism and economic growth: the Wisconsin income tax, 1911–1929* (Port Washington, NY, 1974).
59 Cf. George C. S. Benson et al., *The American property tax: its history, administration, and economic impact* (Claremont, Calif., 1965), p. 83; Jon C. Teaford, *The rise of the states: evolution of American state government* (Baltimore, 2002), pp. 42–68; William G. Roy, *Socializing capital: the rise of the large industrial corporation in America* (Princeton, 1997), pp. 4–5. For Germany cf. Eckart Schremmer, *Steuern und Staatsfinanzen während der Industrialisierung Europas. England, Frankreich, Preußen und das Deutsche Reich 1800 bis 1914* (Berlin et al., 1994), p. 145.
60 William E. Borah, 'Income tax amendment', *North American Review*, 191 (1910), pp. 763–4. Cf. also Norris Brown, 'The income tax amendment', *Outlook*, 94 (1910), p. 215.
61 Cf. Max West, 'Recent inheritance tax statutes and decisions', *Journal of Political Economy*, 6 (1898), p. 437; Department of Commerce, Bureau of the Census (ed.), *Wealth, debt, and taxation 1913* (Washington, DC, 1915), p. 22; *Literary Digest*, 46 (1913), pp. 325–8.
62 Seligman, *The income tax. A study of the history, theory, and practice of income taxation at home and abroad* (New York, 1911), pp. 398, 415–24.
63 Cf. Higgens-Evenson, *Progress*, p. 39.
64 Cf. 134 N. W. 637 (Wisc.)
65 Cf. Hugh Heclo, *Modern social politics in Britain and Sweden* (New Haven, 1974), pp. 304–22; Mary O. Furner and Barry Supple, 'Ideas, institutions, and state in the United States and Britain: an introduction', in Furner and Sapple (eds), *The state and economic knowledge. The American and British experiences* (Cambridge, 1990), pp. 3–39, here p. 27.

66 Cf. Brownlee, *Federal taxation*, p. 41; Daniel P. Carpenter, *The forging of bureaucratic autonomy: reputations, networks and policy innovation in executive agencies, 1862–1928* (Princeton, 2001); Ajay Mehrotra, '"More mighty than the waves of the sea": toilers, tariffs, and the income tax movement, 1880–1913', *Labor History*, 45 (2004), pp. 165–98.
67 Richard L. McCormick, *The party period and public policy: American politics from the age of Jackson to the Progressive Era* (New York, 1986); Joel Silbey, *The American political nation, 1838–1893* (Stanford, 1991). Cf. however, Richard R. John, 'Farewell to the "Party Period": political economy in nineteenth century America', *Journal of Policy History*, 16 (2004), p. 117.
68 Seligman, 'Property tax', p. 24.
69 Cf. Seligman, *Income tax*, p. 35; Richard Büchner, *Die Finanzpolitik und das Bundessteuersystem der Vereinigten Staaten von Amerika von 1789 bis 1926* (Jena, 1926), p. 101. Cf., more generally, on this conflict Charles Taylor, *Sources of the self: the making of modern identity* (Cambridge, Mass., 1989), p. 185; for parallels in Russia, cf. Yanni Kotsonis, '"Face to face": the state, the individual, and the citizen in Russian taxation, 1863–1917', *Slavic Review*, 63 (2004), pp. 221–46; idem, '"No place to go": taxation and state transformation in Late Imperial and Early Soviet Russia', *Journal of Modern History*, 76 (2004), pp. 531–77, here p. 539. On similar concerns in inter-war Britain, cf. Richard Toye, 'Keynes, the Labour movement, and "How to pay for the war"', *Twentieth Century British History*, 10 (1999), pp. 255–81.
70 Cf. Gabriel Ardant, *Histoire de l'impôt*, vol. 1 (Paris, 1972).
71 Cf. the chapter by Christine Lebeau in this volume.
72 Cf. Seligman, *Income tax*, pp. 13–17.
73 Cf. John W. Meyer, 'Myths of socialization and personality', in Thomas C. Heller, Morton Sosna and David E. Wellberry (eds), *Reconstructing individualism: autonomy, individuality, and the self in Western thought* (Stanford, 1986), pp. 208–9; John L. Comaroff, 'Images of empire, contests of conscience', in Frederick Cooper and Ann Laura Stoler, (eds), *Tensions of empire. Colonial cultures in a bourgeois world* (Berkeley, 1997), pp. 170–1.
74 Cf. *Historical statistics of the United States*, pp. 106–110.
75 Quoted from *Literary Digest*, 46 (1913), p. 324.
76 Peter Holquist, '"Information is the Alpha and Omega of our work": Bolshevik surveillance in its pan-European context', *Journal of Modern History*, 69 (1997), pp. 415–50. For predecessors, cf. Marc Raeff, 'The well-ordered police state and the development of modernity in seventeenth- and eighteenth-century Europe: an attempt at a comparative approach', *American Historical Review*, 80 (1975), pp. 1221–43.
77 For a later view cf. John H. Leenhouts, 'Income taxation and its administrative requirements', in *Proceedings of the Twenty-First Annual Conference on Taxation under the Auspices of the National Tax Association* (Columbia, SC, 1929), pp. 447–77.
78 Cf. Jonathan Kahn, *Budgeting democracy. State building and citizenship in America, 1890–1928* (Ithaca, 1997) and Michael J. Lacey, 'The world of the bureaus: government and the positivist project in the late nineteenth century', in idem and Furner (eds), *State and social investigation*, pp. 127–70.
79 Higgens-Evenson, *Progress*, pp. 50, 79. On the general context, cf. Charles Steinwedel, 'Making social groups, one person at a time', in Jane Caplan and John Torpey (eds), *Documenting individual identity* (Princeton, 2001), pp. 67–82. On the power of this in a different context, cf. Alain Blum and Martine Mespulet, *L'anarchie bureaucratique: pouvoir et statistique sous Staline* (Paris, 2003).

80 Cf. also Ellis W. Hawley, 'Economic inquiry and the state in New Era America: antistatist corporatism and positive statism in an uneasy coexistence', in Furner and Supple (eds), *The state and economic knowledge*, pp. 287–324.
81 Cf. Glenda Elizabeth Gilmore, *Gender and Jim Crow: women and the politics of white supremacy in North Carolina, 1896–1920* (Chapel Hill, 1996); Alexander Keyssar, *The right to vote: the contested history of democracy in the United States* (New York, 2000).
82 On the concept of 'social citizenship', cf. T. H. Marshall, *Citizenship and social class* (Cambridge, 1950), p. 78.
83 'Industrie, Wehrbeitrag und Vermögenszuwachssteuer', *Deutsche Industrie*, 12 (June 1913), pp. 178–87; 'Steuerfragen, Industrie und Parteipolitik', *Deutsche Industrie*, 16 (August 1913), pp. 247–9.
84 Stanley, *Law in the service of order*, p. 11.
85 Cf. on the general context, Richard Franklin Bensel, *Yankee Leviathan: the origins of central state authority in America, 1859–1877* (New York, 1990) and Skowronek, *American state*.
86 Edwin R. A Seligman, *Essays in taxation* (1895), p. 72.
87 Richard T. Ely, *Taxation in American states and cities* (New York, 1888), pp. 13, 7.
88 Cf. Arthur S. Link, 'The south and the "New Freedom": an interpretation', *The American Scholar*, 20 (1950–1), pp. 314–24; George B. Tindall, *The emergence of the new south, 1913–1945* (Baton Rouge, 1967), pp. 1–60.
89 Brownlee, *Federal taxation*, p. 50.
90 Cf. W. Elliott Brownlee, 'Economists and the formation of the modern tax system in the United States: the World War I crisis', in Furner and Supple (eds), *The state and economic knowledge*, pp. 401–35; idem, 'Social investigation and policy learning in the financing of World War I', in Lacey and Furner (eds), *The state and social investigation*, pp. 323–64.
91 Cf., for example, Steven R. Weisman, *The great tax wars. Lincoln to Wilson – the fierce battle over money and power that transformed the nation* (New York, 2002).
92 Cf. for a later period Mark H. Leff, *The limits of symbolic reform. The New Deal and taxation, 1933–1939* (Cambridge, 1984).
93 Cf. Marc Stears, *Progressives, pluralists, and the problems of the state. Ideologies of reform in the United States and Britain, 1906–1926* (Oxford, 2002).
94 Cf. Young-sun Hong, 'Neither singular nor alternative: narratives of modernity and welfare in Germany, 1870–1945', *Social History*, 30 (2005), pp. 133–53, here p. 145.
95 Cf. also Franz Neumann, *Democratic and authoritarian states. Essays in political and legal theory* (Glencoe, Ill., 1957), p. 3. For other possibilities of reconceptualizing the state, cf. Peter Baldwin, 'Rethinking the state in comparative policy history', *Journal of Policy History*, 17 (2005), pp. 12–33. For a good analysis along these lines, cf. Patrick Wagner, 'Gutsherren–Bauern–Broker. Die ostelbische Agrargesellschaft in der zweiten Hälfte des neunzehnten Jahrhunderts', *Journal of Modern European History*, 2 (2004), pp. 254–78.

7

Harmonization through Competition? The Evolution of Taxation in Post-War Europe*

Frances M. B. Lynch

The period since the end of the Second World War has been marked in Western Europe by a massive expansion of the state and the gradual liberalization and integration of the European economy. This expansion of the state has rested on a greatly enlarged fiscal base. Government receipts as a proportion of gross domestic product (GDP) more than doubled between 1950 and 1990 – a scale of increase associated historically with periods of war rather than peace.[1] Yet while all European countries experienced a rise in the proportion of GDP collected by the government as tax revenue, both the proportion of GDP and the rate of increase have varied considerably. There have also been major differences in the composition of each country's revenue base.[2] Whether these differences have declined over time due to the twin pressures arising from liberalization and integration is the central question addressed in this chapter. In the first part of the chapter, we use documentary evidence, based on the records of national governments and of the supranational European institutions, to analyse the impact of trade liberalization since 1950 on ideas of indirect taxation within member states of the ECSC and EEC. For this reason the focus is on the introduction of a single tax, value added tax (VAT). In the second part, we employ statistical evidence (since the documentary evidence remains closed) to assess the impact of the more rapid liberalization of the European economy in the last two decades of the twentieth century on overall tax rates and structures within the EU. The broad sweep of taxes levied by member states thus comes into view. In spite of a wealth of published data, there has, surprisingly, been little attempt in the growing literature on tax competition to describe how taxes have developed over the post-war period.[3] The chapter assesses the role of the transfer of ideas in attempts to harmonize European tax systems. It highlights the resilience of national systems of state finance and emphasizes the role of economic processes and the communication about them among policy-makers to explain the continued divergences of national tax systems within the European Union (EU).

From the earliest stages of trade liberalization within the European Coal and Steel Community (ECSC), founded in 1951, there was concern that as tariff barriers were removed on trade in coal, iron and steel between member states, differences in members states' fiscal systems would themselves become impediments to free trade. This led to calls for the harmonization of member states' indirect taxes, and, although these calls were rejected by the High Authority of the ECSC, they did eventually lead to the replacement of member states' indirect taxes by a common system of VAT within the European Economic Community (EEC). However, in spite of persistent attempts by the European Commission to harmonize rates of VAT and move to a system whereby all taxes in the EU would be levied in the country of origin, with member states retaining a veto over all fiscal legislation, the abolition of fiscal frontiers has still not been achieved.

With the introduction of the Single European Act (SEA), signed in 1986, it was widely predicted that, in the absence of any formal harmonization of rates, the effects of increased competition, particularly in capital markets, would lead to a convergence of tax rates within the EU. Whether such tax competition would lead to greater efficiency and maximize welfare, as the American economist Charles Tiebout had argued, or simply reinforce market failure, as the German economist Hans-Werner Sinn maintained, remains a live issue.[4] One widely predicted consequence of liberalization in the SEA for government revenue was that it would provoke 'a race to the bottom' as countries competed with each other to lower taxes on the most mobile factors of production leading to higher unemployment,[5] or lower public expenditure, particularly on welfare,[6] or more efficient public services.[7] This would, in turn, lead to changes in the level and structure of a country's fiscal system and a possible convergence of fiscal systems. The accession to the EU of ten new member states in 2004, including Estonia, Latvia and Lithuania which had introduced flat rates of income tax in the mid-1990s, raised questions about the spread of these new ideas of flat taxes to existing member states. What we need to establish is whether, with the greater exchange among governments of ideas about taxation and the greater mobility of the factors of production, differences in tax rates and fiscal structures have declined over time.

The introduction of value added tax

Concerns about the impact of trade liberalization on national fiscal systems were first raised by West German steel firms in the early 1950s. Faced with the prospect of having to compete more openly with French steel firms within the ECSC, after years of operating within the protected confines of the European steel cartel, the West German steel firms pointed to the problems arising from differences in taxation in the two countries. Their particular grievance was that, according to international convention, tax rebates on exports were given for indirect taxes paid but not for direct taxes, on the grounds that only indirect taxes were reflected in the selling price. In effect, this implied that, in international trade, direct taxes were paid in the country of origin but indirect taxes were paid in the country of destination.[8] This, the German steel firms argued, meant that steel produced in a country such as France, in which the government raised relatively more of its income from indirect taxes, would be at a competitive advantage when exported. In the early 1950s, the French government raised almost 60 per cent of its revenue from indirect taxes, compared with 40 per cent in West Germany.[9]

Without accepting the substance of the steel firms' complaints, the president of the High Authority of the ECSC, Jean Monnet, decided to set up a commission of inquiry, under the Dutch Nobel laureate in economics, Jan Tinbergen,[10] to consider whether there was a case for removing fiscal borders within the ECSC and taxing all coal, iron and steel in the country of origin. Tinbergen, while at that time director of the Dutch Central Planning Bureau, had gained experience as an international adviser when working for the Economic and Financial Committee of the League of Nations in the 1930s,[11] and more importantly perhaps, was seen to be a neutral party in the Franco-German dispute. The conclusions of the Tinbergen Commission were that, in the partial customs union of the ECSC, relative prices would be distorted if only three products were taxed in the country of origin, while the rest were taxed in the country of destination.[12] In its own separate study, the High Authority of the ECSC concluded that it was the differences in the tax burden on industries, or on firms in the same industry within one country, which distorted competition, rather than differences in the tax burden between countries in the ECSC.[13]

A further potential problem for German exporters arose in 1954 when the French government replaced the French turnover tax, a cumulative tax set up in 1920 and levied on each stage of production, with a new tax on value added (VAT). Although the introduction of VAT had been under discussion in French governmental and trade union circles since the end of the Second World War, it was the recognition of the growing importance of trade to the French economy in the early 1950s which convinced the French government to adopt VAT.[14] Since VAT was not a cumulative tax, it made no distinction between domestic production and exports. Thus, when a product was exported, the amount of tax which the exporter could reclaim represented the amount paid on the last stage of production. Although it involved a lot of paperwork VAT was entirely transparent. By contrast, the cumulative or cascade tax which was common elsewhere in Europe was highly discriminatory in its incidence. First of all, it favoured firms which were integrated vertically. This was particularly true of many of the large steel firms in Germany which owned coal mines. Indeed, in the immediate post-war period, the Allies had tried to remove the tax advantage given to vertically integrated firms in Germany by taxing transactions between a parent company and its affiliates, but the law ended up applying to only a minority of cases. Not only did the cascade tax favour vertically integrated firms, but it also favoured labour-intensive firms, since, unlike the cost of capital investment, the cost of labour was not subject to the tax. This, its critics claimed, held back technical progress and distorted the prices paid by the consumer. It also distorted trade, since the amount of the tax which was refunded on export was based on the taxes paid as a good passed through an average number of different stages of production. This meant that for some exports, particularly from vertically integrated firms, more tax was refunded than had actually been paid.[15]

However, rather than upset this set of privileges and adopt VAT as the system of indirect taxation, the West German government took the opportunity, during the negotiations to set up the EEC, of insisting that all goods should be taxed in the country of origin. Their argument was that the removal of tariff barriers in the common market should be accompanied by the removal of fiscal barriers.[16] Faced with a French insistence that indirect taxes should continue to be levied in the country of destination, the Germans argued that, all things being equal, the nationals of a member state should not pay other or higher taxes in other member states than the nationals of these other member states paid in identical conditions. They went on to argue for export rebates and import duties to be eliminated gradually on trade between member states, and to be harmonized gradually by member states in their trade with third countries. However, the French minister of finance insisted that it was absolutely indispensable for France to maintain the principle that indirect taxes be paid in the country of destination, and that, given the experience of the ECSC, precise rules for export rebates and import taxes should be stipulated in the Treaty of Rome.[17] What was finally agreed under articles 95–98 of the Treaty of Rome was that transitional arrangements would be put in place to ensure that there were no abuses of fiscal frontiers until fiscal harmonization, as established under article 99, had taken place. Article 99 envisaged the replacement of all the existing forms of indirect taxation in member states by a community-wide turnover tax.[18] However, since the French refused to accept that any change to a country's taxation could be made without the consent of that country, the abolition of fiscal frontiers, so desired by the Germans, was to be agreed on unanimously. In the half century since the Treaty of Rome was signed, such unanimous agreement has proved illusory.

Thus, at France's insistence, no mention was made in the Treaty of Rome of the abolition of fiscal frontiers, nor indeed of what was meant by fiscal harmonization. All that was established was that as trade barriers were removed, fiscal barriers would remain, with taxation in the country of destination unless there was unanimous agreement to move to a community-wide turnover tax with similar rates for similar products in all member states.

It was left in the first instance to the Commission of the EEC to propose how articles 95–99 of the Treaty of Rome would be implemented.[19] In a preliminary meeting in Milan with national tax experts on 22 June 1959, there was general agreement that the cascade tax operating in all member states except France was itself a barrier to free trade.[20] Article 97 of the Treaty of Rome had allowed member states which operated a cascade tax to calculate export rebates based on an estimated average tax paid on products or groups of products. However, it was evident to all the tax experts and the members of the European Commission that those average taxes would be based on the taxes paid as a good passed through several stages of production, and would greatly benefit firms which were vertically integrated, so that these firms paid less tax as a result. Since the structure of production was different in each member state, all parties agreed that the optimum solution lay in harmonizing turnover taxes in all member states. Not only did cascade taxes, in promoting vertical integration, distort competition within a single economy, but they distorted competition between member states, and it was the fact that they did so for fiscal rather than economic reasons which led the tax experts and the Commission to agree that it was the tax systems which would have to change.[21]

Although all the member states except France operated a cascade tax, the way in which it operated differed from one country to the next. The system in Luxembourg was similar to the German one apart from the rate of tax. The Dutch system was also broadly similar to the German one apart from the fact that the Dutch tax did not cover the retail sector and the measures taken to correct the bias in favour of vertical integration were more numerous. In addition, the tax rates were higher, as were the number of products exempt from the tax altogether. The normal rate of the tax was 5 per cent, but goods such as cars which were considered to be luxuries, were taxed at 15 per cent. The systems in Belgium and Italy were considered by tax experts to be more complicated and archaic than the others.[22]

In view of the agreement reached in Milan that harmonizing taxes meant agreeing a common system of taxation, the Commission set up three working groups to consider the various options for such a common system. The choices were seen to range from imposing the common tax at the retail stage, to imposing it at the wholesale stage, or at both stages, or levying a common tax on production combined with an autonomous tax on distribution, or a common tax on value added.[23]

Each option had its critics. Indeed, since the Germans and the Italians questioned whether the cascade tax actually did encourage industrial concentrations, given that countries had legislation to counter such abuses, there was some resistance to making any change to the existing systems. The Italians in particular were concerned that, given the fragmentation of the production process in Italy and the very large number of small producers, any change in the tax system would be a nightmare to administer. One advantage of the cascade tax, which was appreciated particularly in West Germany, was that it enabled the tax rate to be kept low. To replace it with a non-cumulative tax would necessarily mean an increase in the tax rates, unless revenue were to fall, which the Germans felt would be unpopular politically. But whereas the Germans favoured a common tax with a common rate on production combined with an autonomous tax on distribution, the French objected to the infringement of national sovereignty which such a common rate would entail.

On the other hand, the Germans criticized the way in which VAT operated in France. From its inception, the French had decided to exempt investment from VAT. This, the Germans argued, favoured large firms, was potentially destabilizing to the economy on a short-term basis, and was not compatible with the principles of GATT (General Agreement on Tariffs and Trade) or the Treaty of Rome.[24]

But if the Germans ultimately wanted to abolish fiscal frontiers and to tax goods in the country of origin without altering national fiscal legislation, studies undertaken by the Benelux countries demonstrated the problems inherent in such an approach. On the one hand, as the experience of the Benelux customs union had shown, there would be problems arising from differences in indirect tax rates between countries if fiscal frontiers were abolished. On the other hand, if national legislation were harmonized, this would lead to such disturbance in national budgets and in the structure of prices that it would not be compensated for by the abolition of fiscal borders. While recognizing this problem, the working groups set up by the Commission nevertheless felt that the harmonization of fiscal legislation and indirect tax rates could be retained as a long-term objective.[25] They failed, though, to make specific recommendations to the Commission on how articles 95–99 of the Treaty of Rome could be implemented.[26]

At this stage, the Commission decided to set up a Fiscal and Financial Committee chaired by the German economist, Professor Fritz Neumark, to consider the broad question of the impact of member states' public finances on the operation of the common market. After ten days of meetings spread over two years, the Neumark Committee issued a report which in some respects was more definite in its conclusions and recommendations than the Commission's own working groups had been.[27] However, on the broad issue of the impact of taxation on competition the authors were inconclusive. Recognizing that high taxation and high public expenditure influenced prices, they argued that it was impossible to draw any firm conclusions as to the ultimate impact on competition. They did, however, consider that it was more important to harmonize turnover taxes rather than direct taxes, and were definite in recommending that cumulative taxes should not be retained within the common market. Unlike the German and Italian members of the working group, they believed that cascade taxes did encourage vertical integration, in cases in which integration would not otherwise take place, and that since it was impossible to calculate accurately the countervailing import charges or export rebates, this acted as an indirect subsidy for some firms.

On the thorny issue of whether or not fiscal barriers should be removed, the committee failed to reach any agreement, however. A majority argued that the optimum solution was to remove fiscal barriers and to tax goods in the country of origin at the production or wholesale stage. A tax at the retail stage as a major source of revenue was not seen as a practicable proposition. A majority advocated that the existing cumulative taxes should be replaced by VAT, and that a single rate of VAT should be imposed with as few exceptions as possible. On the assumption that VAT receipts would not cover all the revenue needs of member states, the committee suggested that each country should have an autonomous compensatory retail tax for its own particular needs. If rates of VAT were then standardized product by product in every member state, this would automatically lead to the abolition of fiscal frontiers.[28] Although a minority of the Neumark Committee rejected these recommendations, it was the majority view that taxation should ultimately be levied in the country of origin which fitted with the Commission's own political agenda. On receiving the Neumark Committee's report in July 1962, the Commission lost little time in preparing proposals for abolishing fiscal barriers on intra-EEC trade. By the beginning of November 1962 the Commission had drafted a proposed directive on VAT for the consideration of the Council of Ministers. As article 4 of the proposed directive stated, 'The Commission was to examine how and when the harmonization of turnover taxes should reach its final objective, which was the abolition of fiscal barriers on the entire EEC trade. The Council was to take a decision on this before the end of the transitional period.'[29]

The Committee of Permanent Representatives to the European Economic Community (Coreper), on receiving the Commission's proposed directive, considered that, given its importance, the Council of Ministers should have the chance to debate it before deciding whether to pass it to the Assembly and the Economic and Social Committee for their consideration. Within Coreper, Belgium and Luxembourg were in favour of replacing the cumulative tax system with one based on a single tax. However, they felt it premature to decide the precise nature of the new system. The German delegate thought that the Commission's proposed directive marked an important step in the completion of the common market. He pointed out that, given that the ultimate objective was the adoption of similar rates, this would have major repercussions on the budgetary receipts and financial structures of member states, particularly in view of the differences in weight of direct and indirect taxes in their economies. Rather than allow member states some flexibility in the transition from the cascade taxes to VAT, the Germans wanted VAT to be introduced directly, with the Commission setting a date in its directive. The French delegate claimed to be in agreement with this. He thought, however, that article 4 of the Commission's directive concerning the abolition of fiscal borders was unnecessary, since the central issue was the removal of impediments to competition. The Italian delegate argued that, since there was a close interdependence between fiscal structures and economic structures, both of which had evolved over time, it would be very difficult to change the fiscal system without examining all the economic consequences. And he felt that, given the structure of the Italian economy with a predominance of small and medium-sized firms, and given that the rate for VAT would have to be as high as 15–18 per cent, there would be strong resistance to paying it.

The problem which the Dutch delegate identified was that the harmonization of indirect taxes could not be studied without also examining direct taxes.[30] Indeed, this became a point of principle for the Dutch who argued that, before fiscal borders could be abolished, the six member states of the EEC would have to agree on the relative weight of direct and indirect taxes in the national budget and accept a loss of autonomy over budgetary, social and monetary policies.

When the Council of Ministers passed the Commission directive on to the European Assembly and the Economic and Social Committee in December 1962, the Assembly expressed the wish that the common system of VAT should be introduced by 31 December 1967 at the latest, and that at that point the Commission could propose how to abolish fiscal barriers.[31] There was a fundamental difference of opinion between the Germans and the French over whether or not the Treaty of Rome called for the abolition of fiscal barriers. The Germans, who were most in favour of doing so, had to accept that it was not in fact a legal requirement of the Treaty of Rome.

It was clear that one of the many implications of abolishing fiscal barriers and taxing goods in the country of origin was that countries such as France, which imported more from third countries than they did from the Community, would lose revenue were fiscal barriers to be removed on intra-EEC trade. It was recognized that such countries would have to restructure either their trade or their taxes by raising more from direct tax. The verdict of the Economic and Social Committee was that fiscal barriers could not be abolished until other decisions had been taken in the direction of the social, political and economic integration of the EEC.

The Commission had proposed that member states should be asked to introduce VAT in two stages and have it in place by the end of the transitional period in December 1969. In the first stage, member states would replace their turnover tax with a non-cumulative tax which did not necessarily have to be a tax on value added. However, both the Economic and Social Committee and the Assembly preferred that VAT would be introduced in one go, with the Assembly calling for the deadline to be December 1967, and the Economic and Social Committee preferring the later deadline of December 1969. Within Coreper, both the Dutch and the Italians called for a flexible timetable for the introduction of VAT.[32]

While the Commission's proposed directive was being debated within the various institutions of the EEC, the German parliament voted to increase the compensatory tax on imports of a number of products, including steel. The storm of protest which this unleashed, particularly from French steel firms, was to increase the pressure on governments to reach a decision on tax reform.[33] In order to keep up some momentum, the Commission asked the tax authorities of each member state to estimate in September 1963 the rate of VAT which they would need to set in order to retain their existing level of revenue from indirect taxes. This was based on a German proposal that, notwithstanding whatever was finally agreed, the rates for VAT should cover all transactions including those in the service sector and agriculture, up to and including the retail stage. According to the Germans, there should be no more than two rates for VAT, a standard one and a reduced one, with a minimum number of exceptions. The EEC would then adopt as the rates for VAT the weighted average of all those rates. On the basis of the exercise it was estimated that this would lead to an increase in revenue for all countries except France. For France it could mean a reduction in the existing rates of VAT and, in order to maintain revenue, an increase in direct taxes.[34] One effect of the exercise was to shift opinion within the Council of Finance Ministers away from agreeing to impose VAT up to the wholesale stage to agreeing to impose it up to the retail stage, while allowing individual states the option of applying it only up to the wholesale stage if they preferred.[35]

For France, which was the only country already to have VAT in place, the prospect of the other five member countries adopting VAT was seen as economically disadvantageous, since it would reduce the handicap which the cascade tax had inflicted on the exports of the five. But the general director of taxes in France was firm that for France the risk of the five adopting VAT was less than the risk to France of the others manipulating export rebates under the cascade tax. Moreover, in taking this lesser risk, France could reap the political capital of affirming its commitment to Europe.[36]

It was not until spring 1965 that the Council of Ministers finally agreed to the principle of introducing VAT, and not until April 1967 that it approved the text of the Commission's directive committing member states to introducing VAT by 1 January 1970 on all stages of production up to and including the retail stage. Although the two-year delay has been attributed to intra-bureaucratic struggles in the Netherlands,[37] it is clear that the change in taxation was problematical for all member states. Ultimately the prospect of revenue gains resulting from the abolition of hidden export subsidies, which were inherent in the system of cascade taxes, proved to be the decisive argument in overcoming interministerial disputes.

France was able to comply with the 1967 directive immediately. However, when West Germany announced its intention of introducing VAT two years ahead of the specified date, this provoked a volley of criticism from Washington. Although the United States had shown little interest when France had adopted VAT in 1954, and had indeed attempted, unsuccessfully, to institute VAT in post-war Japan under the mission led by professor Carl Shoup,[38] it was a different matter when West Germany announced that it was going to introduce VAT on 1 January 1968. Largely owing to the size of the American trade deficit with West Germany, the US administration tried to block the introduction of VAT in West Germany, fearing that it would lead to a reduction in the price of German exports. On the grounds that direct taxes also affected prices, the American delegation to the OECD argued that the direct taxes paid by a producer should be reimbursed when a product was exported, as well as the indirect taxes. In addition, the United States stated its intention of imposing an import tax of 2.5 or 3.0 per cent on goods from Europe, whereas the average rate of indirect taxes in the United States was 1.95 per cent.[39]

The hostility of the American reaction had little impact on Europe. West Germany went ahead and introduced VAT in 1968, the Netherlands followed in 1969, Luxembourg in 1970. Belgium was one year late, while it was not until 1973 that the Italian government finally implemented the directive.[40] The French commercial attaché in Italy interpreted the Italian decision to postpone the introduction of VAT as being partly due to a predicted loss of revenue in the first year of the operation of VAT, but mainly due to the advantages which a number of exporting firms (FIAT, in particular) derived from manipulating the system of export tax rebates, under Italy's cumulative tax system.[41] The French Ministry of the Armies identified other factors as well in Italy's postponement of VAT. It rejected the official arguments of Confindustria (the Italian manufacturers' association), which warned of the social consequences of the increase in the cost of living following the introduction of VAT, seeing it rather as a fear that VAT would reduce the competitiveness of Italian industry. It also rejected the arguments of the Italian Central Bank, which claimed to fear the impact of VAT on the exchange rate of the lira. In the French view, it was the loss of foreign exchange reserves resulting from a fall in Italian exports which concerned the Italian Central Bank. It was the Italian Ministry of Finance and the Foreign Ministry which pressed for the introduction of VAT by the agreed date. The Ministry of Finance argued that the existing cascade tax allowed many firms to defraud the tax authorities and was largely responsible for Italy's budget deficits.[42] The 1967 directive meant that VAT was binding not only on the six member states but, as part of the *acquis communautaire*, it would be binding on all new member states. However in spite of repeated attempts by the European Commission since the 1967 directive to harmonize rates of VAT, there are still marked differences in the rates levied by member countries. The standard rate of VAT ranges from 25 per cent in Denmark and Sweden, to 12.5 per cent in Ireland. Over the last two decades the standard rate of VAT has risen everywhere (apart from Ireland, where it rose very sharply and then fell), but on the two occasions when the European Commission tried to introduce legislation in order to maintain a minimal degree of harmonization, the proposals were rejected by the European Council.[43] As a result the Commission has been unsuccessful in abolishing border controls in order to impose VAT in the country of origin.

Convergence through competition?

While the European Commission has clearly been unable to overcome the resistance of some member states to attempts to harmonize rates of VAT or indeed other taxes, the question to which we shall now turn is whether the market has succeeded where the Commission has failed. In view of the progressive removal of non-tariff barriers to trade within the framework of the Single European Act, national tax rates and tax systems have themselves come under increased competitive pressure. It is the effect of such competition on the whole range of member states' taxes which we shall analyse in the second part of this chapter.

With regard to tax structures, historically there have been great differences both between countries and over time in the amount of tax revenue which governments have been willing and able to extract from their citizens. In the twentieth century, the northern European social democratic states have tended to levy the greatest tax burden (tax revenue expressed as a percentage of GDP) while over the long run, the tax burden has tended to rise in times of war and preparations for war and to decline thereafter.[44] However, the combined demands of the welfare state and the cold war served to ensure that, in the years after the Second World War, not only did the tax burden fail to decline, but it continued to grow and it did so until the consensus underpinning it broke down in the 1980s. With the market-driven reforms of the 1980s and 1990s, many governments adopted a tax-cutting agenda. However, whether the tax burden has fallen in line with government rhetoric in Europe over the last two decades, and whether the experience has been similar across Europe, is open to question. Although this rhetoric usually referred to income taxes which, as the most visible of taxes, were considered to be the most sensitive politically,[45] all taxes need to be considered in answering the question.

Drawing on OECD data,[46] we can see in Figure 7.1 that, contrary to popular belief, the tax burden has risen everywhere in the EU since 1980. One country

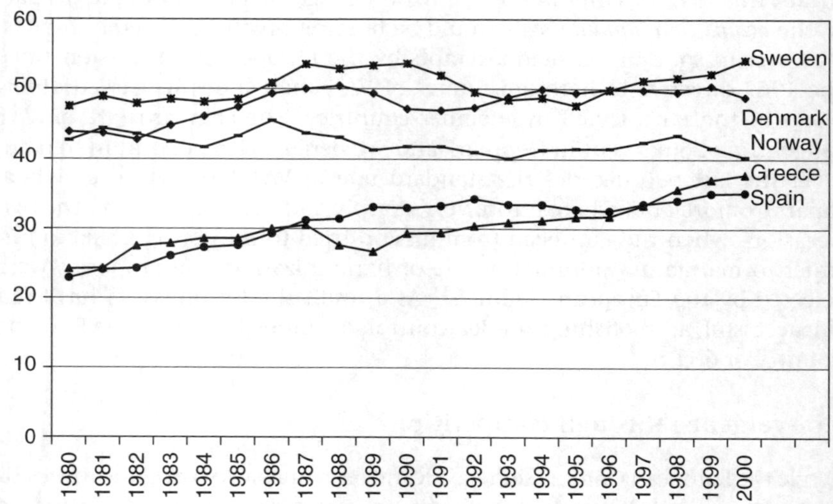

Figure 7.1 Total tax revenue as a percentage of GDP

where it has fallen is Norway, not a member of the EU. There has, however, over the same period, been a narrowing of the gap between the most heavily and the most lightly taxed countries. While the Swedish and Danish governments continue to impose the greatest tax burden (over 50 per cent of GDP), the southern European states of Greece, Portugal and Spain have all increased their tax revenue as their economies have grown. It is clear that tax competition within the EU has not led to a reduction in the overall tax burden within member states, but it is possible that membership of the EU, by stimulating economic growth and development, may have led to a greater convergence of the tax burden.

However, if there has been some convergence in the total tax burden as poorer member states increased their revenue from taxation, what we need to find out is whether there has been any convergence in the relative weight of the different taxes levied. The richer northern European states have tended to raise relatively more of their income from direct taxes and the poorer southern European states more from indirect taxes. In 1980, income tax in Denmark accounted for 52 per cent of total taxation, as compared with 14.9 per cent in Greece. By 2000, the respective proportions were 52.6 per cent in Denmark and 13.5 per cent in Greece. Indeed, across the EU there have been few changes in the relative weight of direct and indirect taxes in terms of total taxation although, apart from Denmark, France and Italy, there has been a slight reduction in income taxes as a percentage of total taxation. In France, where income taxes accounted for the lowest proportion of total taxation, this has moved from 11.6 per cent in 1980 to 18 per cent in 2000 – still well below the EU average of 25.6 per cent. The slight reduction in the relative weight of income taxes corresponds with the tax-cutting rhetoric of governments in the 1980s and 1990s. However, when we measure income taxes in terms of GDP, it was only in Belgium, Germany, Ireland, Luxembourg, the Netherlands and Sweden that income taxes were lower in 2000 than in 1980, as we can see in Figure 7.2.

It is a commonly held assumption that governments have stealthily increased social security contributions and indirect taxes while announcing that they were cutting income taxes in the last two decades. If we consider social security contributions first, the one country for which this would clearly seem to be the case is Finland.

In 1992, social security contributions as a percentage of GDP were 10.9 as compared with 2.8 in 1991. The increase, which brought Finland more into line with the European average, may have been part of Finland's preparations to join the EU (although in view of the fact that the OECD revised the Finnish data several times during the 1990s the earlier data may be unreliable). In all the other members of the EU the increase was slight apart from France, Ireland, Luxembourg and the Netherlands, where social security contributions as a percentage of GDP actually fell. If we take income tax and social security contributions together, then it is only in Ireland, Luxembourg

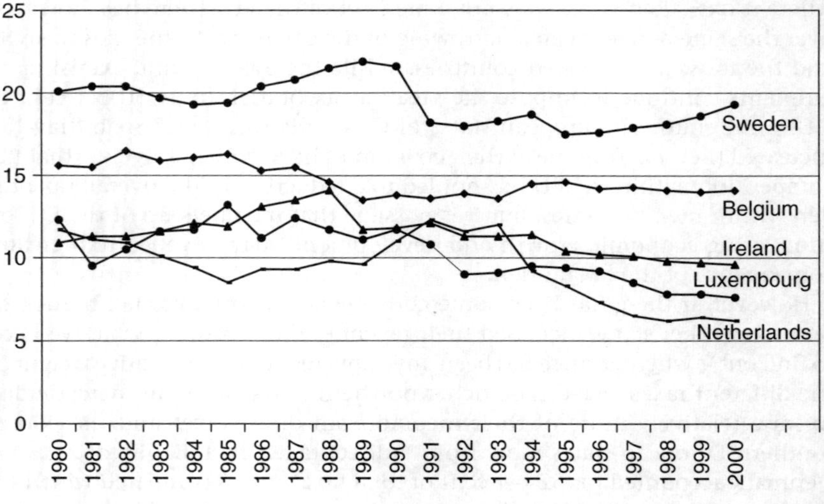

Figure 7.2 Taxes on personal income as a percentage of GDP

and the Netherlands where they fell as a percentage of GDP. Compared with personal income taxes and social security contributions, other direct taxes have been fairly insignificant, whether expressed as a percentage of total taxation or of GDP. Given the increasing mobility of capital and European governments' efforts to attract inward investment, it is not surprising that corporate taxes have accounted for a low percentage of GDP. With the exception of Luxembourg (an exceptional economy in terms of structure and size) taxes on corporate income have ranged from between 1 and 5 per cent of GDP within the EU, with only minor fluctuations over the period. On the other hand Norway, while not a member of the EU, has felt constrained to bring its corporate taxes into line with the European average from the mid-1980s.

However, while the share of GDP attributed to corporate tax revenue has remained fairly stable the proportion of total tax revenue coming from corporate income taxes has risen. In this respect, the EU has behaved quite differently from the United States where the share of total tax revenue arising from corporate income tax has fallen over time. It was largely this American experience, which fitted with the economic theory of tax competition, which provoked concern among policy-makers about the declining revenue from corporate income tax in the longer run. Action taken by the European Commission in the early 1990s to suggest minimum rates of corporate taxation may well explain differences in the European experience.

While it could be expected that corporate income taxes would account for a low proportion of GDP, due to the mobility of capital, it might be assumed that, conversely, taxes on property would have risen over the last two decades.

However, in most countries property taxes as a percentage of GDP have remained at a low and stable level. Britain is the exception due to the distinctive characteristics of the British property market. But even in Britain the contribution from property taxes, while it has fallen from the mid-1980s rate of 5 per cent to 4.4 per cent of GDP in 2000, still remains higher than the European average of 2 per cent.

Another commonly held assumption is that as governments have sought to reduce income taxes they have increased indirect taxes over the last two decades. The picture in the EU is in fact very varied. Nine countries have increased the weight of consumption taxes, namely Finland, Germany, Greece, Italy, Luxembourg, the Netherlands, Portugal, Spain and the United Kingdom, but the other six countries have reduced it.

It could be argued that global percentages are not an adequate measure of the extent to which tax competition rather than long-run historical forces have affected government tax policy, and that what is needed is an analysis of the effective rates of taxation actually paid by households and firms. Recent research into corporate income tax, while confirming that statutory rates have fallen over the 1980s and 1990s and that tax bases have been broadened, nonetheless presents a more nuanced picture in terms of effective tax rates. Michael P. Devereux, Rachel Griffith and Alexander Klemm have shown that the effective marginal tax rates have remained stable but the effective average tax rates for projects earning positive economic profits have fallen, and have fallen more at higher levels of profitability.[47]

Tax competition theory makes an implicit connection between the behaviour of taxes on corporate income and taxes on personal income, predicting that as the former fall the latter will rise. Drawing lessons from the American experience, Vito Tanzi and Howell H. Zee maintain that 'despite the absence of explicit coordination of individual income tax rates in the European Union, economic integration and factor mobility have been constraints on individual EU member's flexibility in setting tax rates substantially different from one another'.[48] However, any detailed analysis of whether or not national governments have been sensitive to changes in the effective rates in income taxes in other member countries to the extent that, in the words of Vito Tanzi and Howell H. Zee, 'a sort of decentralised harmonization, driven by market forces' has been at work, requires a much finer investigation of the tax incidence on different tax units. Drawing on data compiled by the OECD we can analyse the effective tax rates paid by two household types across the 15 EU countries since 1979: that of a single person without children, and of a one-earner household with two children, earning in both cases the average industrial wage.

These data (Figure 7.3) show that for a fairly mobile single person without children on an average industrial wage over the last two decades there have been large differences in effective tax rates across the EU and fairly stable effective tax rates in the eurozone countries, apart from Belgium where they have almost doubled in 20 years. There have, however, been reductions in the

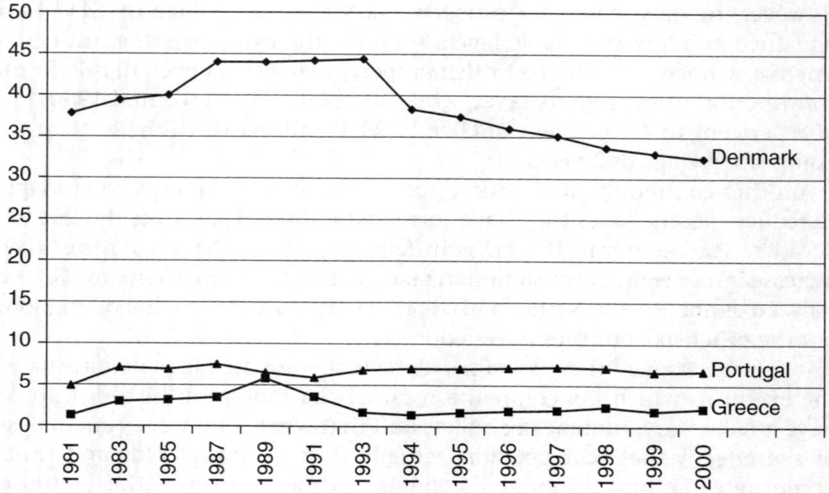

Figure 7.3 Effective tax rates of single person, without children, on average industrial wage

effective tax rates in the three countries which are not members of EMU: Britain, Denmark and Sweden. While a single person without children now pays the highest taxes in Denmark and the lowest taxes in Greece and Portugal, this was as true 20 years ago as it is today but the gap between the highest and lowest is closing slightly.

Even if we include employee social security contributions along with income tax, the pattern remains broadly the same. There is little evidence, apart from in Denmark and Sweden, of tax competition leading to a convergence of effective income tax rates and no evidence of those rates, with or without social security contributions, being forced up to counter a downward pressure on the rates of more mobile factors of production. On the assumption that a single-income household with two children is less mobile than a childless single person we might expect that the effective rates of income tax would have risen over the period for this category of household. This was indeed the case in some countries – Finland, Belgium, Italy, Austria, Greece and France – but not the case in the rest of the EU. Once again, if we include social security contributions there is no common pattern.

We have mapped out the main characteristics of the fiscal systems of EU member states in terms of their level, structure and rates. This has revealed that, in spite of the twin pressures arising from tax competition and European harmonization measures, European systems have, on the whole, displayed a remarkable resistance to change. Tax competition has not resulted in 'a race to the bottom' and a lowering of the tax burden, nor in a shift from direct to indirect taxes, nor from taxes on capital to taxes on labour, as tax competition theory predicted. Indeed, the changes which have occurred in both the tax level and the tax mix in European countries almost invariably occurred in the period 1965–1980.[49]

What emerges from this analysis of the early history of the adoption of VAT as the common turnover tax for members of the EEC, as well as from an analysis of the subsequent evolution of taxation in the EC/EU since 1980, is the resilience of national fiscal systems. While the first steps in the creation of the common market led to a detailed examination and exchange of ideas about taxation and of the impact of taxes on trade and competitiveness, the parameters of that examination were strictly limited. The French government's insistence that, in the Treaty of Rome, member states should not cede any sovereignty over taxation, has proved to be of long-lasting significance. The agreement on a common form of indirect taxation, VAT, has not spilled over into a convergence of fiscal systems in the EEC/EC/EU. Nor has the increasing openness of European economies, particularly under the Single European Act, introduced much competition between European tax systems.

Tax harmonization in the EU remains a highly divisive and emotive issue, with opinions ranging from those who argue that the Economic and Monetary Union is unworkable without formal legislation to harmonize taxes, to those who argue that legislation is necessary only to prevent the more harmful aspects of tax competition. This chapter has demonstrated the remarkable stability of national fiscal systems and fiscal outcomes in the context of increasing competition within the European and international economy. Governments, in their anxiety to prevent tax competition from eroding their revenue, and unwilling to relinquish sovereignty over taxation to the European Commission, have managed to cooperate with each other in order to remain largely in control of taxation.

Notes

*Financial support for some of the research on this chapter from ESRC Grant No. RES-000-22-1408 is gratefully acknowledged.

1 Niall Ferguson, *The cash nexus. Money and power in the modern world, 1700–2000* (London, 2001), p. 99.

2 Cf. also Joseph Thorndike's essay in this volume.

3 Andreas Haufler, *Taxation in a global economy* (Cambridge, 2001); Eric Osterweil, 'The OECD and the EU: two approaches to harmful tax competition', *The Tax Journal*, 3 (1999), pp. 89–100; Alex Easson, 'Harmful tax competition: the EU and OECD responses compared', *The EC Tax Journal*, 3 (1998), pp. 1–16; OECD, *Report on harmful tax competition: an emerging global issue* (Paris, 1998); European Commission, *Towards tax coordination in the European Union. A package to tackle harmful tax competition*, Doc. COM (97) 495 final.

4 John Douglas Wilson, 'Theories of tax competition', *National Tax Journal*, LII (1999), pp. 269–304.
5 Michael P. Devereux, Rachel Griffith and Alexander Klemm, 'Corporate income tax reforms and international tax competition', *Economic Policy*, 35 (2002), pp. 451–95.
6 Peter Birch Sørensen (ed.), *Public finance in a changing world* (Basingstoke, 1998); and idem, *Tax policy in the Nordic countries* (Basingstoke, 1998).
7 House of Lords Select Committee on the European Communities, '15th Report, Session 1998–99', *HL Paper 92*, p. 109.
8 Dirk Spierenburg and Raymond Poidevin, *The history of the High Authority of the European Coal and Steel Community. Supranationality in operation* (London, 1994), p. 83.
9 Council of Ministers of the EEC (hereafter referred to as CM) CEAB 1, no. 1856 'Exposé du point de vue de l'industrie sidérurgique allemande sur les problèmes fiscaux dans le marché commun', 19 Dec. 1961.
10 John Gillingham, *Coal, steel and the rebirth of Europe, 1945–1955* (Cambridge, 1991), p. 345.
11 Patricia Clavin and Jens-Wilhelm Wessels, 'Transnationalism and the League of Nations. Understanding the work of the Economic and Financial Organisation', *Contemporary European History*, 4 (2005), pp. 465–92.
12 CM, CEAB 1, no. 1878. Letter from Hans-Günther Sohl, president of the Economic Association of the German Iron and Steel Industry to Piero Malvestiti, president of the High Authority of the European Coal and Steel Community, 15 June 1961.
13 CM, CEAB 2, no. 2190. Haute Autorité, Division Economique, 'Etat d'avancement des travaux du comité des taxes'. 15 July 1955.
14 Frances M. B. Lynch, 'A tax for Europe. The introduction of value-added tax in France', *Journal of European Integration History*, 4 (1998), pp. 67–87.
15 French Ministry of Finance (hereafter referred to as F. Min. Fin.) Z808, letter from Meersmann, 17 Dec. 1955.
16 F. Min. Fin. Z808, 'Proposition de la délégation allemande concernant les remboursements de la taxe sur le chiffre d'affaires et les taxes de péréquation sur le chiffre d'affaires', 6 Feb. 1957.
17 F. Min. Fin. Z808, letter from P. Ramadier to C. Pineau, 26 Jan. 1957.
18 Treaty setting up the European Economic Community, Rome, 25 Mar. 1957, (London, 1967).
19 Donald Puchala, 'Worm cans and worth taxes: fiscal harmonization and the European policy process' in Helen Wallace, William Wallace and Carole Webb (eds), *Policy-making in the European Community* (London, 1983), pp. 237–65.
20 French Ministry of Foreign Affairs (hereafter referred to as F. MAE), DE-CE 678. 'Marché commun: Fiscalité, taxes compensatoires. Compte-rendu de la réunion des experts fiscaux des pays du marché commun'. Milan, 8–9 May 1959.
21 Ibid.
22 CM, CEAB 2432. Rapport Deringer.
23 Archives of the European Commission (hereafter referred to as EC) BAC 1019/1966, Document de travail, 28 Sept. 1959.
24 EC BAC 19/1996, no. 2. Minutes of meeting of 29–30 Oct. 1959.
25 EC BAC 19/1966. Meeting in Brussels, 18 Nov. 1957.
26 EC BAC 19/1966, nos. 1–12. Meetings of working groups.
27 International Bureau of Fiscal Documentation, *The EEC reports on tax harmonization: the report of the fiscal and financial committee and the reports of the sub-groups A, B, and C* (Amsterdam, 1963).

28 Ibid.
29 F. Min. Fin. B 51721. European Commission Directorate General for Competition, division Fiscal Problems. Nov. 1963.
30 F. Min. Fin. B 25335. Note from the Council of Ministers of the EEC. 13 Dec. 1962.
31 CM CEAB 2, no. 3412. Note d'information 'Harmonisation des taxes sur le chiffre d'affaires'. Brussels, June 1964.
32 Ibid.
33 CM CEAB 2 No. 2432. J. Ferry, vice-president of the Chambre syndicale de la sidérurgie française to P. Malvestiti, president of the High Authority of the ECSC. 14 Mar. 1963.
34 F. Min. Fin. B 51721. Rapport du groupe de travail spécial concernant les estimations des taux de la TVA à adopter et des conséquences générales qui pourront découler d'un taux commun.
35 F. Min. Fin. B 51721. Conclusions of meeting of Council of Finance Ministers 2–3 Apr. 1964.
36 F. Min. Fin. B 42394. Directeur général des impôts. Projet de note sur les orientations souhaitables de la politique d'harmonisation des fiscalités dans le cadre du marché commun, 15 Sept. 1966.
37 Donald Puchala, 'Worm cans and worth taxes', p. 241; and D. L. McLachlan and D. Swann, *Competition policy in the European community: the rules in theory and practice* (London, 1967), p. 34.
38 Cf. W. Elliott Brownlee's chapter in this volume.
39 F. Min. Fin. B 51716 Note for the Director of Taxes. 'Réactions américaines à l'adoption de la TVA en Europe', 6 Feb. 1968.
40 Donald Puchala, 'Worm cans and worth taxes', p. 242.
41 F. Min. Fin. B 51715. Robert Richard, commercial attaché at the French embassy in Rome, to the French minister of economics and finance. 20 Mar. 1969.
42 F. Min. Fin. B 51715. Memo from the French Ministry of the Armies. 25 Mar. 1969.
43 Kenneth Walker, 'The future of value-added tax in the European Union', *The EC Tax Journal*, 6 (2002), pp. 1–20.
44 Ferguson, *The cash nexus*, pp. 25–53.
45 Paul Johnson, Frances Lynch and John Geoffrey Walker, 'Income tax and elections in Britain, 1950–2001' *Electoral Studies*, 8 (24) (2005), pp. 393–408.
46 OECD *Revenue statistics of OECD member countries* (Paris, various years).
47 Michael P. Devereux, Rachel Griffith and Alexander Klemm, *Corporate income tax reforms and international tax competition*, pp. 451–95.
48 Vito Tanzi and Howell H. Zee, 'Consequences of the economic and monetary union for the coordination of tax systems in the European Union: lessons from the U.S. experience', International Monetary Fund working paper, 1998.
49 Ken Messere, 'Tax policy in Europe: a comparative survey', *European Taxation*, 40 (2000), pp. 526–35.

Part III
Empires and International Organizations

8

Tax Transfers: Britain and its Empire, 1848–1914

Martin Daunton

In a footnote to their influential two-volume account *British Imperialism*, Peter Cain and Tony Hopkins comment that 'taxation in Africa remains a neglected subject', despite the fact that colonial officials had to wrestle with the problem of extracting revenue in the absence of an existing tax base.[1] In India, there was a pre-existing tax base, but it was not necessarily one that British rulers saw as appropriate or sustainable. They pondered how it should be reformed in order to ensure that the Raj secured as much revenue as possible, while also contributing to political stability and encouraging economic growth. Similarly, decisions on the shape of taxation in the new white settler colonies had major implications for the nature of society, the distribution of income and wealth, the allocation of land, and the provision of welfare. In each case, taxation was linked with normative assumptions about the most desirable social and economic structure – the nature of landownership, the distribution of income and wealth, and the limits of the market – and with calculations of political stability and order.

Most writing on imperial taxation deals with the issue of the burden of imperial finance on Britain, and the vexed question of whether the result was to increase domestic taxes above the level in other European countries.[2] Surprisingly little has been written about the taxation of the British Empire from the point of view of the colonies, and the decisions about the mode of extraction of revenue. Both issues are connected, for the greater the success of securing revenues within the colonies, the greater the ability to reduce transfers of funds from the metropole, or even to reduce domestic taxation at the expense of contributions from the Empire.

The British government had a well-developed sense of how to extract revenues within the metropole, and a clear idea of how its commitment to fairness and equity, to transparency in accounts, and to involvement of taxpayers in collection, all contributed to a sense of legitimacy. How far were these approaches to taxation adopted within the Empire to secure compliance and to minimize conflict, or did other considerations apply? Rather than adopting domestic assumptions about taxation as a means of securing revenue with the minimum of disturbance to the status quo, did the imperial authorities seek to use taxation as an instrument to force colonial society into a new shape and, if so, what determined the choice? Was it to copy the social structure of the metropole or to depart from it in some respects? In other words, was the crucial consideration the transfer of ideas about taxation, or rather the transfer of assumptions about the social and economic structure, with taxes as one method of shaping the changes? Was the aim to stimulate convergence between Britain and the colonies, to allow pragmatic divergence to meet circumstances and to serve metropolitan needs, or to accept principled divergence to avoid some of the less desirable features of metropolitan society? This chapter shows that there was no simple transfer of ideas between Empire and colonies. Rather, the transfer of ideas was mediated by the specific economic conditions, by assumptions about land and property and, not least, by the power relationships between the colonial officials and the colonized peoples. The following remarks are tentative conclusions, based mostly on the analysis of available secondary material. The important question of exchanges of ideas among the colonies merits attention, but has not been considered on this occasion.

Taxation and the nexus of political legitimacy in Britain and its Empire around 1848

In *Trusting Leviathan*, I argued that the British state experienced a loss of legitimacy in fiscal extraction after the Napoleonic Wars when government spending reached 23 per cent of GNP. The reconstruction of legitimacy was a difficult and lengthy process, and was linked with a fall in government spending to a trough of around 8 per cent by the end of the century. The fiscal military state was contained at home by stressing equity in Britain and by using accounting techniques to show that taxes were used efficiently and for the intended purpose, thus ensuring a high level of voluntary compliance.[3] But the fiscal military state was also exported, as C. A. Bayly has argued. In 1831, Archibald Alison commented that the Whigs were upsetting society and politics by reducing taxation on the great cities and industrialists in Britain and by passing the fiscal burdens to the colonies. This might sound like spurious special pleading, but Bayly remarks that 'the Indian peasant bore a heavy part of the costs of Britain's world role which the British people were not prepared to bear', thereby allowing the British state at home to 'disarm and civilianize itself'.[4]

The extraction of more revenue from the Empire ran counter to the model adopted in the metropole. Domestic compliance and legitimacy were crucial; in the Empire, more draconian policies were possible. The Empire allowed Britain to escape the problems which continental Europe experienced in 1848, as distant colonies were used to ease burdens at home, both by paying taxes and bearing the costs of adjustment to free trade which contributed to domestic prosperity. The risks were high, and Britain exported the problems faced by Paris and other continental European cities in 1848 to the colonies. There was no fiscal revolt in Britain in 1848 but there was serious discontent in the Empire. Riots, civil disobedience or fiscal crisis were experienced in Montreal, New South Wales, Tasmania, Ceylon, Punjab, the Orange River and the Cape.[5]

Several factors lay behind the contrasting experiences of metropole and colonies in 1848. At home, the Whigs wished to hold down taxes on the middle classes while spending more money on defence against France. One solution was to cut defence expenditure on the colonies by replacing garrisons by local forces; another was to displace the tax burden, for example by cutting sugar duties, so that the domestic working class had a cheap commodity, at the expense of colonial planters. Such policies secured the desired effect at home and triggered discontent in the colonies, where free trade eroded incomes and made payment of taxes more difficult. The worst impact was felt in Ceylon, where the costs of the army were to be met by a land tax and new indirect taxes. The planters succeeded in blocking the land tax so that more of the tax burden fell on indirect taxes, resulting in an uprising by the peasantry. The attempt to shift the burden of taxation from the metropole to the colonies was problematic.

This chapter considers the outcomes after the crisis of 1848 by analysing processes of creating political legitimacy and transferring ideas about taxation in three areas: settler colonies such as Australia and New Zealand with elected assemblies and a degree of political autonomy; colonies with large populations and existing systems of revenue extraction such as India; and colonies with large populations without a developed tax system where methods of extraction were developed virtually *de novo*, above all in Africa. The political calculations were very different in each case, and the economies of each region and the ability to extract revenue were equally varied. In each case, the debate over taxation was connected to other issues: the nature of landownership and tenure, and the form of the labour market.

The extra-European societies were predominantly agricultural, and the most obvious way of extracting revenue was by taxing land – a commonplace in pre-industrial societies in Europe. A domain state lives on revenues of Crown estates, and goods and services from dependants. In a tax state, revenue comes from taxes – and this means a conflict with other claims on the surplus (rent, profits of the farmers). But rather than finding evidence for a clear-cut shift from a domain state to a tax state, which the economist Joseph Schumpeter found in a European context, the story in the British Empire was more complicated. Indeed, stages make less sense than a continuing process of change and adaptation. Would the result be an alliance of the Crown with the landlords to their mutual benefit against the peasant; or of the Crown with the peasant against the landlords, and how did this shift in different circumstances? Whether the tax state complemented the rise of great estates or opposed it, depended on a strategic choice about the most effective way of extracting revenue and securing political stability. It also reflected normative assumptions about the most effective way of stimulating economic growth. Would growth be encouraged by large estates able to invest in agricultural improvement, cooperating with tenant farmers who were freed of the need to purchase land and so able to use their own assets for more animals, fertilizers and tools? Or would growth be stimulated by small owner-occupying farmers who were freed of the necessity to support large landowners? The choices were contested and never finally closed.[6]

These issues were debated in nineteenth-century Britain, and had a complex political history. Small farms and free trade in land were associated with radical critics of 'parasitical' and exploitative aristocrats who had 'stolen' the land from small yeomen farmers and peasants through a misappropriation of state power. In the radicals' view, the large estates should be dissolved in turn through state power, most particularly taxation. They applauded small peasant proprietorship as socially just, dissolving the problems of poverty of the landless poor and deference to aristocratic power. But would such a system of landownership be economically efficient? The dominant view in the nineteenth century was that the divide between landowners, tenants and labourers was economically rational and efficient. At the end of the nineteenth century, more doubts were appearing as British agriculture failed to adapt to change – and some Conservatives realized that small yeomen farmers had another attraction, as a bulwark of property owners against socialism.[7] These British – and particularly Irish – debates influenced policy in the colonies, and the debates in the colonies in turn fed into British debates which drew on Australasian reforms of land registration and land taxation.[8]

The structure of landownership was also connected with ideas about the labour market. A concentrated pattern of landownership with large tenant farmers entailed a class of landless labourers with implications for welfare provision to cover seasonal unemployment. By contrast, small owner-occupied farms drew on family labour, sometimes reallocating surplus members between each other as part of the life cycle. Families might opt to use the farm to support their members rather than to maximize output for the market; even if they did adopt a highly commercial attitude, the welfare implications were different for the farm provided an asset in old age. There were advantages and disadvantages of each system. Landless labourers might become a threat to social stability, or they might provide a flexible source of labour for capitalist farming. Small family farms might offer stability, but their owners might lack the necessary capital and knowledge to develop colonial agriculture, and especially export crops. The issue was particularly significant in Africa: how could a non-commercialized system of hunting, pastoralism and subsistence cultivation be turned into commercial agriculture, and how could men be induced to work for wages on plantations or capitalistic farms, and in mines? The outcome depended on the definition of land rights and the imposition of taxation. Should capitalistic farming be encouraged by exempting this sector from taxes; and could the creation of a workforce be stimulated by taxation of Africans so that they needed to work for wages in order to meet the fiscal demand?

How would the taxes be collected, through bureaucracies (with the danger of a loss of consent in return for higher yields) or by devolving to the taxpayers or indigenous peoples (with the possibility of securing consent at the expense of yield)? The success or difficulty of securing tax revenues affected the ability to raise loans for investment in the infrastructure, and to make a transition to a fiscal state which combined tax revenues and large-scale borrowing at low interest rates and without the threat of default. The tax authorities needed to have an eye to resistance from the taxpayers, and also to the bond market in London which carefully assessed the risk of lending – and the payment of interest to bondholders outside the society had the potential for political resentment on the part of taxpayers.

The colonial officials and metropolitan politicians implementing tax policies in India and Africa, as well as the legislative assemblies of settlers in Australasia, were aware of the fiscal assumptions and approaches of Britain, and were often experienced in both metropole and colonies. For example, James Wilson, a free trader, founder of *The Economist*, and Liberal MP, served as secretary of the India Board of Control where he was responsible for finance and revenue, before becoming financial secretary of the (British) Treasury, and then in 1859 financial member of the Council in India – in effect, chancellor of the exchequer for India. He had the difficult task of resolving the financial crisis created by the Indian mutiny, seeking to use the insights of Cobdenite political economy in the subcontinent. The link with the 'Manchester School' was direct and controversial. Similarly, Gladstonian finance and India were linked by Stafford Northcote and his son Henry. Stafford was private secretary to Gladstone, secretary of state for India, and Chancellor of the Exchequer from 1874 to 1880. Henry served as his father's secretary at the Treasury and in 1900 became governor of Bombay where he launched a programme of reform of the land revenue, before he moved to Australia as governor general in 1903. Alfred Milner was secretary to George Goschen, the chancellor, moving to be director-general of accounts and under-secretary of finance in Egypt, returning to Britain as chairman of the Inland Revenue before returning to the colonies as governor of the Cape and high commissioner of South Africa, and eventually colonial secretary. Matthew Nathan provided another link, moving from his initial career in the Royal Engineers to colonial administration in Sierra Leone in the aftermath of a tax revolt; in 1911, he became chairman of the Board of Inland Revenue, returning to colonial service as governor general of Queensland in 1920–25.[9] Personal careers, quite apart from the writings of political economists, linked domestic and imperial taxation. But were ideas transferred from one locale to another, or did circumstances dictate different approaches and techniques of fiscal extraction?

The transfer of ideas, the taxation of land and the white settler colonies

What was the connection between land and taxes in the white settler colonies? The existence of large amounts of public land meant that the white settler colonies had some features of a domain state able to raise revenue from its lease or sale, which posed the question of what system of tenure should be adopted. If ownership or occupation of land was widespread, some of the costs of welfare could be reduced by passing the burden to the family farm. Small farms might be viewed as a source of stability, creating a society of property owners and escaping the extremes of landed aristocrats and landless labourers. But reliance on small family farms also had certain disadvantages in sacrificing economies of scale and, in the case of owner-occupation, forgoing the ability to share risk and investment between tenant and landholder. They might be seen as a route to inefficiency, leading to a misuse of resources by settlers who lacked capital or knowledge to use the land to good effect. These issues were debated and contested both in Britain and in the settler colonies of Australia and New Zealand – leaving aside a further major topic of the rights of indigenous peoples.[10]

The development of white settler colonies required large-scale investment in public works such as roads, railways and ports which exceeded their tax income in any year. As with the fiscal military state, 'lumpy' investment required loans, supported by the certainty of a flow of income to pay interest, and confidence that the government would not default. The result was a similar debate over the costs and benefits of loans in the white settler colonies as in the fiscal military state. After the defeat of the French in 1815, the high costs of funding the wartime debt led to a radical attack on the fiscal system, for the removal of the income tax in 1816 and the failure to revise the land tax since the 1690s meant that much of the tax burden fell on workers and producers through customs and excise duties, with the benefits taken by aristocrats and *rentiers*. The removal of this perception of inequity and misuse of political power was a major task of politicians in the 1830s and 1840s.[11] Similarly, in a settler society, public works might lead to higher land prices with the benefits taken by large 'squatters' or the colonial gentry, with the wider population paying taxes to service the debt which was largely held outside the colony.

The recipients might see British investment in the white settler colonies as the provision of a scarce resource on reasonable terms, or as an exploitative and imperialistic drain on their economies. The political situation varied according to the institutional systems and social structures of the debtors, and changed over time. In Australia before the First World War, for example, government loans were in the hands of representative bodies and most non-governmental loans went to Australian owned and operated concerns. Consequently, capital imports were for the most part not problematical, compared to the situation in Argentina, a settler economy outside the Empire. There, most of the loans were to companies registered in Britain with British directors, and there was direct competition between British and Argentinean concerns or at least a sense that outside capitalists were extracting income.[12] The backlash against global capital flows became more intense after the First World War, when the price of primary products fell sharply, placing strains on the balance of payments and on domestic prosperity: even in Australia there was growing resentment at the costs of loans, and in Argentina there was a nationalistic backlash against British interests.

Taxation was, therefore, intimately connected to issues of landownership, both in terms of welfare provision and investment in the infrastructure. One outcome was an interest in land taxation, not just to secure revenue, but also to shape the social structure. A tax on land is administratively convenient, for it is visible, an obvious taxable entity in societies where it was difficult to measure incomes. It was usually a major element in taxation in agrarian societies, without any ulterior motive beyond securing revenue for the state. But a land tax could also have a wider ambition that went beyond revenue considerations to a desire to shape the structure of settler society. Land taxation appealed to opponents of large holdings as a device to break them up for small farmers. For example, the proposed land tax in New South Wales in 1860 was linked to the ambition of stopping the emergence of large estates when public lands were thrown open for sale. Land taxation was opposed by advocates of large landholdings, and was not welcome to many others who feared a wider radical attack on property and wealth. A further issue which was debated at the time was whether it was fair to impose a tax on land rather than on other forms of property and income from trade and industry. These debates could have a variety of outcomes and the form taken by taxation was central to debates over the nature of settler societies, and to their ability to extract revenue.

New Zealand provides one case study of the debates over taxation and land in white settler societies, and the transfer of ideas about landholdings between the metropole and the colonies.[13] Initial attempts to introduce an income tax modelled on British precedent did not succeed, and attention turned to a land tax based on the unimproved value of land and not (as in the British income tax) its annual value. Underlying the tax was the assumption that while landowners were not paying their fair share of taxes, they were taking the benefits of public works in increased land values. Whether the law would pass was doubtful, given the influence of the landed gentry in the Upper House, and progress was delayed. The state of Victoria set a precedent in 1877, introducing the first land tax in Australia with the intention of breaking up large estates above 640 acres. New Zealand followed in 1878–79, when John Ballance, the colonial treasurer, introduced a land tax. However, Ballance diverged from Victoria, for New Zealand had incurred larger loans, especially during the premiership of Julius Vogel, and the land tax applied to all land and not just extensive holdings. Income from personal exertion (that is, salaries, professional fees or the profits of trade and industry) was untaxed, going further than the advocates of differentiation in Britain in the 1850s and 1860s. The British advocates of differentiation argued that 'unearned' income from land or bonds continued regardless of the health or age of the owner, and left an asset to support dependants. 'Earned' or 'industrious' income from salaries and profits depended on the health and age of the individual, and ceased without leaving an income for dependants. As a result, part of the earned income needed to be saved and should therefore be encouraged by a lower rate of tax. Gladstone refused to accept this case for differentiation, on the grounds that it would turn the income tax into a source of conflict between different forms of income and property, rather than integrating classes in a common endeavour as he wished. At most, he allowed a tax break on the actual sums paid into life insurance policies to provide support for retirement and dependants.[14] By contrast, the New Zealand tax of 1879 did not tax income from employment at all, whereas landed property was taxed even if it produced no income.

Ballance advocated denser land settlement by smaller farms and land nationalization, and in 1885 he introduced a Land Act in order to encourage settlement by offering leases of small holdings of Crown land and by making government loans available. He believed that large pastoral farms blocked economic progress and prevented access to land by new settlers; unlike many contemporaries, he did not argue that the Maoris should surrender their land in order to encourage settlement. In the election of 1890, he campaigned for radical land reform, arguing for a tax on the 'unearned increment', and advocating the programme of Henry George as a means of 'bursting up the great estates'. The election brought Ballance to power as both premier and colonial treasurer, and he worked with John MacKenzie, the minister of lands from 1891 to 1900, to implement his proposals. In 1891, the Liberal government replaced the existing property tax with a progressive land tax and a progressive income tax. In 1892, further legislation led to government purchase of land from large estates for settlement, with the threat of compulsion against those who did not sell voluntarily. Between 1892 and 1912, the government purchased 223 estates and settled 7000 farmers on the land.[15]

The tax system was both an instrument for creating a particular social structure by breaking up large estates, and a means of funding other social policies – not least non-contributory pensions in 1898. The Liberals wished to spread landownership more widely, and to create a more open society with higher levels of social mobility.[16] The New Zealand tax system became a model for the colonies in response to the depression of the 1890s. Four factors shaped the transfer of ideas to the debates in New Zealand and the Australian colonies. First, the cost of public works meant that there was a need to raise revenue for loans for roads and railways, and also to fund the costs of land settlement. Second, the desire to break up large estates and to differentiate against those who did not live by their own exertions, was a major concern of Liberal politics. Third, the depression of the 1890s created difficulties in the settler societies. Finally, there was the issue of welfare. Financial pressure meant that public authorities tried to pass more of the cost of support from the Poor Law to family members by widening the definition of family responsibilities which led to concern that family farms were overloaded with social costs. An alternative form of tax-funded welfare emerged.[17] The policies adopted by Liberals in New Zealand exceeded the limits of acceptable taxation in the metropole, where the income tax was still flat rate and undifferentiated. These colonial ideas on taxation and other topics returned to Britain. Old age pensions were the most obvious area of interest in Britain, and there was also considerable debate over the use of arbitration in labour disputes. The British Liberal government moved to differentiation and progression in the income tax, and to the use of a land tax to attack large estates, as a free trade response to Conservative support for tariff reform.

Taxation and political legitimacy in India

In India, the British faced an existing system of land tenure and fiscal extraction, with a large indigenous population without formal political rights in shaping policy. This gave the transfer of ideas a different shape from the one to and from the white settler colonies. The key problem was how to move from a complex hierarchy of rights where proprietorship and revenue extraction were overlapping and multiple. The solution reflected assumptions about the most desirable pattern of landownership and understandings of the course of growth, both of which were influenced by English precedents, mediated by administrative and political expediency in India.

The permanent settlement in Bengal in 1793 offered one solution. The *zamindars* possessed a clear right of ownership that was linked with collection of revenue for the government. Payments were fixed and failure to pay meant loss of proprietorship. An alliance was created between the East India Co. and *zamindars* against peasants, so creating intermediaries to contain revolt against taxation. The *zamindars* might be seen as equivalent to large aristocratic landowners in England, who would encourage agricultural development and provide a force for stability in rural society.[18]

The English land tax was itself a form of 'permanent settlement', as it had been fixed in the 1690s and formed a decreasing proportion of income from the land as rents rose in the later eighteenth century. By analogy, the *zamindars* might react in the same way as large English landlords, investing their profits in order to encourage growth and prosperity. However, the permanent settlement also had a serious disadvantage: the East India Co. and later the Crown did not share in the profits of agriculture as the value of land rose, and taxes had to be imposed on other groups in society which might be viewed as inequitable and a source of political controversy. In other words, land tenure and the tax system were linked with visions of growth based on a particular view of the English agricultural revolution and the benefits of great estates – or of their drawbacks. English landowners were also criticized by radicals as parasites, expropriating common land, increasing rent levels, and ignoring their social obligations. Similarly, the *zamindars* were open to criticism for extracting more rent without reinvesting and without fulfilling their obligations to maintain water supplies and other communal services. The outcome in the North West Provinces in 1833 was a temporary settlement which allowed renegotiation of the government's claim to revenue, so ensuring that revenue rose in line with rising rents and land values, or according to the needs of the government. However, the temporary settlement also created practical problems, for renegotiation led to tensions and involved closer Company or Crown involvement in fiscal extraction. Hence the British government in India shifted back to the use of permanent settlement on the grounds that it led to growth and minimized resistance.

Not everyone agreed that the use of settlement was desirable, not least James Mill who was responsible for the revenue letters from the Board of Control in London to the government of India. He followed other political economists – above all David Ricardo and Thomas Malthus – in arguing that rent was an unearned income from land, offering the best source of revenue without distorting the allocation of labour and capital. Mill argued that in districts not covered by the permanent settlement, taxation should be based on the share of rent in the total produce of land. By levying a tax directly on the cultivator, exploitative middlemen could be removed, and by varying the tax by the quality of land, the unearned surplus (the so-called Ricardian rent) produced by superior land could be captured. The task was entrusted to R. K. Pringle, a student of Malthus, who set to work recording the extent of each holding, its quality, and estimating the net produce left after all costs had been met, including a reasonable return to family labour and capital; the government should then claim 55 per cent as its share. It was implemented in 1828, without success, for the collection of data was flawed, and the revenue demand was too high. The solution was to adjust Pringle's approach, without abandoning the search for Ricardian rent. Of course, the ideas of economists and theoreticians in London collided with practicalities on the ground where administrators were obliged to follow local custom and to be concerned with social order. However, it would be wrong to deny that the ideas had some impact, despite the constraints on action.[19]

The adjustment formed the basis of the *ryotwari* system which asserted the rights of cultivators or peasants (*ryots*) who paid taxes direct to the government. From 1835, the Bombay Survey and Settlement evolved as a means of preventing exploitation of cultivators by tax farmers, and encouraging increases in productivity and efficiency through incentives to the cultivators to accumulate capital and increase their revenues. The land was surveyed to establish occupation and soil quality; and rather than make unrealistic calculations of the amount of net produce, payments were assessed according to the condition of the occupier and the amount paid from the area in the past. The *ryot* would then be assured the payment of the same amount for a defined period before a new settlement was implemented – a highly complex and time-consuming exercise. In theory, all land belonged to the state, but so long as the *ryot* paid tax to the government, he had security of tenure and could sell and bequeath the land. The amount of tax varied with the quality of land, so that inefficient *ryots* would be encouraged either to improve their techniques to pay the tax, or transfer their holdings to someone who could. The Bombay Revenue and Settlement thus rested on a particular vision of the connection between tenure and economic growth.[20]

Whether the system had the desired effect is another matter, for contrary to the intentions of the reformers, the tax might act as a disincentive by imposing a high charge on the cultivator; and the intrusion of tax collectors might generate tension. Perhaps the tax system was securing revenue at the expense of growth. In 1901, the Famine Commission complained that the proponents of the *ryotwari* system 'expected the accumulation of agricultural capital: but their plans did not promote thrift, nor did they conduce to the independence of the *ryot*. They looked for the capitalist cultivator; and we find the *sowkar's* serf.'[21]

Many Indian nationalists complained that the burden of the land revenue rose as a proportion of output over time with serious economic consequences. The reality was different, particularly when the amount of land tax collected per acre is compared with the amount of output sold to pay the tax.[22] In the Bombay Presidency, the nominal tax per acre was reduced in the initial settlement and continued to fall during its term; although the amount was increased at resettlement, it remained lower than before the initial settlement. Changes in prices meant that the tax demand varied in real terms as a proportion of income: prices rose over this period, so the real value of the tax declined to a greater extent.[23] Certainly, the land tax remained the major source of central government revenue, but it did decline as a proportion of net revenue from 52.8 per cent in 1865 to 48.1 per cent in 1895 and 40.1 per cent in 1910.[24] The decline accelerated after the war, as a result of political protest such as the Bardoli campaign in the Bombay Presidency against reassessment of the land settlement that led to refusal to pay. The collection of land revenues collided with constitutional reform, for the tax was the responsibility of the executive rather than the representative legislative councils.[25]

The declining contribution of the land tax meant that the government of India had to turn to other sources of revenue. At the time of the transfer of power from the Company to the Crown in 1858, the major sources of revenue were the monopolies on opium and salt. Not surprisingly, James Wilson felt that his Cobdenite principles had been offended, and he aimed to bring Indian finances in line with the principles adumbrated by Peel in 1842 and Gladstone in 1853. Peel and Gladstone had been anxious that taxes should not divide classes and interests, but serve to create a sense of common interest by reducing indirect taxes and allowing the poor to share in the consumption of goods. Hence, in his first budget in 1860, Wilson urged that '[a]ll taxation must be based on the postulate of perfect equality and justice between the different classes of the community'. Furthermore, 'taxation must be in accordance with sound commercial and financial principles' – that is, the level should not distort or reduce trade and production.[26] He aimed to introduce free trade and an income tax to India. How successful was he in achieving this ambition of importing the principles of metropolitan equity in taxation to the Raj?

The income tax was only a small part of net revenue: in 1865 it amounted to 2.1 per cent, in 1895 to 3.9 per cent, and 1910 3.7 per cent. The tax was initially introduced in 1860 as a temporary measure to pay for the costs of the mutiny, and most members of the council felt it should expire in 1865. Although the viceroy, John Lawrence, had his doubts, the finance member, Charles Trevelyan, allowed it to end in the face of strong opposition from both *zamindars* (who claimed exemption as a result of the permanent settlement), and the British community. Trevelyan's choice had more in common with 1816, when the income tax was allowed to expire after the Napoleonic Wars, than with 1842 when it was reintroduced and linked with free trade. Instead, Trevelyan proposed export duties: since he could not have both an income tax and free trade, he was forced to sacrifice the former at the expense of the latter. However, the government in London did not permit the export duties. Instead, licence and certificate taxes were introduced in 1867 and 1868, amounting in effect to a form of income tax. Wilson's proposals for equity and balance were sacrificed. Although the income tax was reintroduced in 1870, it was again abandoned in 1873 as a result of strong opposition from both Indians and British civilians, despite the concern of administrators that rich Indians were exploiting the mass of the population.[27]

The costs of government were rising in the later nineteenth century as a result of the depreciation of the rupee, military spending, and investment in economic development. Indirect taxes became more important and changed in character. The revenue from opium fell as a proportion of net revenue, as a result of changing judgements about the morality of the trade and Chinese hostility to imports. The importance of the salt monopoly initially rose but then fell as a result of political protests. In 1865, opium was 19.7 per cent and salt 14.6 per cent of net revenue; by 1895 the figures were 10.8 and 18.1 per cent; and in 1910 14.6 and 6.5 per cent. Meanwhile, customs revenue rose from 5.7 per cent of net revenue in 1865 to 10.5 per cent in 1895 and 14.9 per cent in 1910, and excise duties from 5.1 to 12.0 and 15.4 per cent.[28] In 1865, the aim was to introduce export duties that would ensure that India remained open to British goods; obviously, the Indian business community preferred import duties, a policy not acceptable in London or Lancashire.[29] As the financial situation became more pressing with the rising fiscal pressure of the later nineteenth century, import duties became more appealing to the British authorities in India and were introduced in 1894. However, they were strongly opposed in Lancashire which saw a serious threat to its markets from tariffs and the deterioration in the exchange rate of the rupee. The solution was to impose an excise duty on Indian cloth as a counterpart to the import duty to ensure that the market was not distorted.[30]

When India was granted fiscal autonomy after the First World War, the share of customs duties rose still further, reaching 39.9 per cent of net revenue in

1930 as the land tax declined to 22.7 per cent. By then opium and salt had declined to 1.6 and 4.9 per cent, and excise to 12.7 per cent. There was a fundamental shift to customs duties, continuing the pre-war trend.[31] This is not surprising, given the political calculations of rising nationalist pressure. An increase in taxation led to a demand for wider political participation – and in the words of Peter Robb 'resistance to British rule was fuelled by attempts to extend the amount and scope of taxation'.[32]

The transfer of British conceptions of taxation to India was, therefore, highly constrained. In the case of land taxation, different assumptions about the connection between land tenure and economic growth were in conflict, as a result of ideological differences within Britain and the dictates of administrative expediency on the ground. Similarly, metropolitan principles of free trade and equity collided with political realities in India, forcing a shift towards indirect taxes and particularly customs duties which were anathema at home.

The transfer of ideas and the African colonies

Africa posed problems which were different from India, as there was no pre-existing revenue system (or at least, not one recognized by the British authorities) and no commercialized agriculture or land tenure on the lines understood by the British. This had important consequences for the transfer of ideas about taxation. There were two broad outcomes, with various intermediary forms of tenure and agriculture. At one extreme, there was reliance on small farms and African cultivators, with land held directly by the farmers or on trust by the Crown. This pattern could be found in Uganda and West Africa, where there was little large-scale European production except in mining, and the imperial authorities encouraged peasant production, even by means of coercing cotton planting. At the other extreme, white settlers operated large farms and metropolitan companies ran plantations, with a large amount of land alienated from the Africans on the assumption that it was not properly utilized. This pattern applied most obviously to South Africa. Other parts of Africa fell somewhere between the two extremes: in Kenya, for example, white settlers relied on indigenous labour but there were no large-scale capitalist land concerns; in central and southern Africa large farms and plantations coexisted with African cultivators. The outcome varied according to three factors: chronology, with land more likely to be alienated in the early stages of colonization; geography, with more alienation where the climate was more attractive for European settlement; and self-government, for alienation was easier where white settlers had more control over the political process.[33]

In all cases, the colonial rulers had to establish some way of raising revenue in order to pay for administration and long-term economic development, of encouraging Africans to grow crops for the market, or of securing a workforce for European farms, mines and plantations. The colonial authorities or the local assemblies used a number of techniques to encourage commercialization and the emergence of a waged labour force. One was to demand specified periods of work from Africans, which was unusual except in Kenya and Uganda, and even there it did not last long. A second and more common approach was to place pressure on chiefs to provide 'volunteers' to European enterprises or to grow particular crops. However, this technique declined in the face of hostility from the metropolitan authorities. Much more common were three other approaches: land policy to create a waged workforce on the reserves, as in southern and central Africa; contracts, sometimes with penal sanctions, in South and East Africa; and taxation to encourage the growth of commercial crops and waged labour.[34] Above all, the imperial power relied on the hut tax.

Initially, there was some concern about the implications of the hut tax. In 1855, George Grey, the governor of the Cape, explained his policy on taxation to the second session of the colonial parliament. More revenue was needed to cover authorized expenditure, and Grey argued that the solution was indirect taxes, given the difficulties of collecting a direct tax in a country with a highly dispersed population, and 'barbarous or semi-barbarous tribes' who could not easily be induced to pay. Indirect tax would be paid without knowing it, and would in effect be voluntary; and the yield would increase as the natives were raised in the social scale and used more goods.[35] Indeed, the authorities might even decline payment of the hut tax, for it was closely linked to rights to land. In 1855, the special commissioner on the eastern Cape was concerned about the influx of population, and refused to accept payment of the hut tax on the grounds that there was no room for the incomers who took the receipt of the tax as a claim to land – a position endorsed by the prime minister, Lord John Russell.[36] However, Grey's confidence in indirect taxes was misplaced. Could revenue rise sufficiently unless Africans were forced into a commercialized and monetized economy that produced taxable goods and income to meet tax liabilities? And could crops be grown for the market, or mines developed, unless a waged labour force was created? Such considerations led to an increasing reliance on the hut tax as a means of forcing economic and social change. Of course, there were many other reasons for migration – a traditional response to dry seasons, ecological disasters caused by disease and famine, or a collapse of the pre-colonial social system – but taxation was certainly one force for change.[37]

The use of the hut tax to create a labour force was most explicit in South Africa, where the policy of Cecil Rhodes was encapsulated in the Glen Grey Act of 1894. Land was divided into smallholdings in order to replace communal property with individual plots. Of course, there was a danger that Africans would remain on their smallholdings, so competing with white farmers in product markets and refusing to provide a waged workforce. But Rhodes was confident that the process of subdivision of holdings would soon force men into the labour market. As he pointed out, 'every black man cannot have three acres and a cow [. . .]. It must be brought home to them that in future nine-tenths of them will have to spend their lives in daily labour, in physical labour, in manual work.' The process of economic and social transformation would be encouraged by a hut tax of 10s. on men who had not worked for wages for three months.[38]

South Africa was extreme in the transformation of land rights. In Nyasaland, the approach was somewhat more cautious. The administrator, Harry Johnston, was initially in the pay of Rhodes who wished to create landless labourers to work on large plantations. Instead, Johnston opted to grant land to the Africans and to rely on the hut tax to create waged labour and, above all, commercialized cultivation. In 1901, the full rate of hut tax was 6s., but this was reduced to 3s. on condition that the taxpayer worked for a European for a month; in 1911, the rate was raised to 8s., with a lower rate of 4s. for men who worked for a European or sold rice, tobacco or cotton to a European. The local colonial officer approved the list of Europeans for whom the Africans could work and with whom they could trade. Although this system was open to exploitation, small African cultivators did have some independence for they could raise money to pay the tax through their own economic activities and could avoid sinking into waged labour and dependence as further south.[39]

The appeal of the tax was obvious. Huts are visible and could be easily counted, and were known to the chiefs who could be co-opted into assessing and collecting the taxes. In Nyasaland, for example, the chiefs received a commission of 10 per cent, and they might well be more effective than direct collection by officials, at least in the initial stages. Subsequently, collection in Nyasaland was transferred to officials.[40] Not surprisingly, officials with an eye to the legitimacy of the tax in the eyes of missionaries, bodies such as the Aborigines Protection Society, and wary civil servants in London who feared disorder, stressed the ease of collection and high level of compliance. 'The settled population may fairly be said to discharge its tax liabilities almost to the last shilling with little or no pressure', it was reported from Nyasaland in 1910.[41] In fact, reality was somewhat different from the comforting picture of contented Africans willingly paying for protection by a beneficent British administration.

Collection of the hut tax could be carried out with a degree of brutality and force. In Nyasaland and Kenya, for example, collection was enforced by destroying or forfeiting huts, seizing wives or imprisoning defaulters.[42] The system was open to abuse by farmers and traders who failed to record work or sales, so that Africans were forced to supply more labour or goods than legally necessary. The wage rate or price of goods set by the tax system might diverge from the market rate in order to encourage more waged labour and production.[43] Further, the assessment of the tax might collide with local customs. In Swaziland, for example, a tax of £2 was imposed on males, and an additional £2 on each wife after the first – an imposition that was deeply resented.[44] The tax system was in any case highly regressive. The hut tax fell on Africans whereas European settlers and companies paid little or nothing. European incomes were usually not taxed, and in some cases export duties were levied on African and not European production. As a result, African farmers paid a much higher proportion of their income in taxes, an effective transfer from poor to rich so that Africans paid for the infrastructure and labour needed by colonial enterprises. The Labour Commission in Kenya in 1927 estimated that direct taxes were about 30 per cent of the earnings of an African family on a reserve, before taking account of indirect taxes.[45] In John Lonsdale's words, 'taxation which was levied on all made it possible for public expenditure to subsidize the few, to make them more attractive to outside investors'.[46]

Not surprisingly, the hut tax and its wider implications for social and economic structures led to periodic resistance, and 'officials feared rebellion as much as they desired taxation'.[47] One of the first and most serious rebellions was the 'hut tax war' in Sierra Leone in 1898.[48] The experience meant that the British administration was cautious about imposing direct taxation or challenging the chiefs' control of land in Nigeria and the Gold Coast, where capitalist agriculture on plantations or larger African farms failed to materialize. In Nigeria, the emirs in the Islamic north of the colony collected taxes and retained power as native administration, with part of the tax revenue handed over to 'native treasuries' and the remainder passed to the Crown. By giving them security and relying on 'indirect rule', the governor, Frederick Lugard, hoped that they would be bound to the British state and turn to cultivation in place of slavery and warfare. As John Lonsdale remarks, the British authorities 'conceded defeat and called it principle. It enshrined the nebulous concept of communal land tenure under tribal authority, in order to hide the nakedness of British weakness and ignorance.'[49] In South Africa, the authorities were more robust. The Zulu rebelled against the hut tax in 1896, and the imposition of a further £1 poll tax on adult males triggered armed revolt in 1907 that led to the death of between 1000 and 4000 Africans, and the imprisonment of 7000.[50] At the Colonial Office, Churchill criticized the 'disgusting butchery of natives' that made the colony 'the hooligan of the British empire'.[51] An approach to disturbances that would not have caused too much concern a decade earlier was now unacceptable. But the British government did little to remove the underlying grievances in South Africa where land was alienated, men forced into the labour market on unfavourable terms, and the fiscal system highly regressive.

The relationship between land and taxes in Africa was therefore variable, from the survival of African proprietorship and administration in Nigeria to the loss of land and proletarianization in South Africa. Taxes were linked to a desire to create a more commercialized and capitalistic society by different means, varying from inducing African cultivators to produce for the market to forcing them into waged labour on large plantations or mines. Taxation was used not only to produce revenue for development and administration, but as a lever to shift the structure of society. Unlike in Britain, the administrators showed little concern for balance and equity in the tax system: it was biased between groups, as a deliberate act of policy. British precedents offered little or nothing to the fiscal administration of Africa, and neither did precedents elsewhere in the Empire. The aim was to create a commercialized society producing for export markets, and in the process stratagems were used to raise revenue that led to resistance and a lack of legitimacy. African nationalists were placed in a difficult position, for opposition to taxation was central to their campaigns; the problem was that opposition to the tax system imposed by the British as lacking in legitimacy and consent also weakened the African state.

Conclusions

The transfer of ideas about taxation within the British Empire was varied and complicated. In most cases, the transfer did not entail a direct application of the British fiscal system to the colonies, unlike in the French Empire where the metropolitan cadastral survey was adopted. Even in the white settler colonies, the application of the income tax diverged from the metropole, reflecting local concerns over the stimulation of earned income and the desire to contain large landed estates. The income tax took on a more radical edge than in Britain, pre-empting the policies adopted by the Liberal government after 1906. Similarly, fiscal policies in India rested on a different connection between direct and indirect taxes than in Britain, with a shift towards customs duties in order to resolve the problems of raising revenue caused by the difficulties of imposing an income tax and the lack of buoyancy in the land revenue. In the white settler colonies, India and Africa, debates over taxation were more concerned with the nature of land tenure and assumptions about the generation of economic growth than with the application of British definitions of equity and balance in the fiscal system. Further, the debates over land tenure did not rest on the imposition of a single norm based on the dominant tripartite structure of large landowners, tenant farmers and landless labourers found in Britain. This did apply to the *zamindars* of India, and the belief that they would stimulate economic growth much as the great aristocratic landowners of Britain during the agricultural revolution. But the assumption was contested on ideological grounds (as in India by James Mill and in New Zealand by John Ballance) as well as on purely practical grounds as in Nigeria. The outcome also shaped the capacity of the colonial state, its ability to fund long-term development, secure loans on favourable terms, and pay for welfare and the social infrastructure. Should taxes be used to pay for welfare within the colonies, and in particular should the English Poor Law be adopted in the white settler societies? Might money be better spent on education, as in Scotland? How should the disasters of famine and devastation of cattle by disease be dealt with in India and Africa? How much should be spent on defence, and how much transferred to Britain to pay for the Empire, or transferred from Britain to stimulate development? These issues remained open as long as the Empire survived.

Notes

1 P. J. Cain and A. G. Hopkins, *British imperialism: crisis and deconstruction, 1914–1990* (London 1993), p. 205. But see T. Garba, 'Taxation in some Hausa emirates, 1880–1939', PhD thesis, University of Birmingham, 1986; the issue does appear in many more general books but there is no systematic study.

2 For this debate, see L. E. Davis and R. Huttenback, *Mammon and the pursuit of empire: the economics of British imperialism* (abridged edition, Cambridge, 1988); P. K. O'Brien, 'The costs and benefits of British imperialism, 1846–1914', *Past and Present*, 120 (1988), pp. 163–200; Paul Kennedy, 'The costs and benefits of British imperialism, 1846–1914', *Past and Present,* 125 (1989), pp. 186–92.

3 Martin Daunton, *Trusting Leviathan: the politics of taxation in Britain, 1799–1914* (Cambridge, 2001), pp. 63–76.

4 A. Alison, 'On the financial measures of the reformed parliament, No. 1. The Whig budget', *Blackwood's Edinburgh Magazine,* 29 (June 1831), 975, quoted in A. Gambles, 'Rethinking the politics of protection: conservatism and the corn laws, 1830–52', *English Historical Review,* 113 (1998), p. 946; C. A. Bayly, 'Returning the British to south Asian history: the limits of colonial hegemony', *South Asia,* 17 (1994), pp. 16, 18–19 and 'The British military fiscal-state and indigenous resistance: India, 1750–1820', in Lawrence Stone (ed.), *An imperial state at war: Britain from 1689–1815* (London, 1994), pp. 322–54.

5 Cf. on this and on the following Miles Taylor, 'The 1848 revolutions and the British empire', *Past and Present,* 166 (2000), pp. 146–80.

6 Joseph Schumpeter, 'The crisis of the tax state', in A. T. Peacock et al. (eds), *International Economic Papers,* no. 4 (London and New York, 1954); for a more recent development of his ideas, R. Bonney and W. M. Ormrod, 'Introduction: crises, revolutions and self-sustained growth: towards a conceptual model of change in fiscal history', in idem (eds), *Crises, revolutions and self-sustained growth: essays in European fiscal history, 1130–1830* (Stamford, 1999). For a controversial account of the interplay between rents and taxes and agrarian social structure, see R. Brenner, 'Agrarian class structure and economic development in pre-industrial Europe', *Past and Present,* 70 (1976), pp. 30–75.

7 F. M. L. Thompson, 'Changing perceptions of land tenures in Britain, 1750–1914', in Donald Winch and P. K. O'Brien (eds), *The political economy of British historical experience, 1688–1914* (Oxford, 2002); cf. also Avner Offer, *The First World War: an agrarian interpretation* (Oxford, 1989), ch. 8.

8 A good example is the system of land registration designed to create a free market in land which was implemented in South Australia in 1858, often (and inaccurately) named after one of its advocates, Robert Torrens, who attempted to introduce the reform in England. The issue is discussed in a forthcoming PhD thesis by Edmund Rogers, University of Cambridge. See also Avner Offer, *Property and politics, 1870–1914: landownership, law, ideology and urban development in England* (Cambridge, 1981), p. 33.

9 Cf. Thomas J. Spinner jun., 'Goschen, George Joachim, first Viscount Goschen (1831–1907)', *Oxford dictionary of national biography* (Oxford, 2004), online edn, May 2006 [http://www.oxforddnb.com/view/article/33478, accessed 29 Aug. 2006]; Colin Newbury, 'Nathan, Sir Matthew (1862–1939)', ibid. [http://www.oxforddnb.com/view/article/35189, accessed 29 Aug. 2006]; idem, Colin Newbury, 'Milner, Alfred, Viscount Milner (1854–1925)'; ibid., online edn, May 2006 [http://www.oxforddnb.com/view/article/35037, accessed 29 Aug. 2006];

W. D. Rubinstein, 'Northcote, Stafford Henry, first earl of Iddesleigh (1818–1887)', ibid. [http://www.oxforddnb.com/view/article/20328, accessed 29 Aug. 2006]; P. Lucas, 'Northcote, Henry Stafford, Baron Northcote (1846–1911)', rev. H. C. G. Matthew, ibid. [http://www.oxforddnb.com/view/article/35256, accessed 29 Aug. 2006].

10 Cf., for example, the contentious work of H. Reynolds, *The law of the land* (Ringwood, Victoria, 1987) and, for a more sophisticated analysis, P. G. McHugh, *Aboriginal societies and the common law: a history of sovereignty, status and self-determination* (Oxford, 2004). The older study by S. H. Roberts, *The squatting age: Australia, 1835–47* (Melbourne, 1935) retains its interest.

11 See P. K. O'Brien, 'The political economy of British taxation, 1660–1815', *Economic History Review*, 41 (1988), pp. 1–32; Philip R. Harling and Peter Mandler, 'From 'fiscal-military' state to laissez-faire state, 1760–1850', *Journal of British Studies*, 32 (1993), pp. 44–70.

12 L. E. Davis and R. E. Gallman, *Evolving financial markets and international capital flow: Britain, the Americas and Australia, 1865–1914* (Cambridge, 2001), pp. 817–19, 822–5; see also Donald Denoon, *Settler capitalism: the dynamics of dependent development in the Southern Hemisphere* (Oxford, 1983).

13 These comments largely rely on Peter A. Harris, *Metamorphosis of the Australasian income tax, 1866–1922* (Canberra, 2002).

14 On this debate see H. C. G. Matthew, 'Disraeli, Gladstone and the politics of mid-Victorian budgets', *Historical Journal*, 22 (1979), pp. 615–44 and M. Zimmeck, 'Gladstone holds his own: the origins of income tax relief for life insurance purposes', *Bulletin of the Institute of Historical Research*, 58 (1985).

15 See his collection of essays *A national land policy based on the principle of state ownership* (1887); Tim McIvor, 'Ballance, John (1839–1893)', *Oxford Dictionary of National Biography* (Oxford, 2004) [http://www.oxforddnb.com/view/article/1225, accessed 29 Aug. 2006]; idem, *The rainmaker: a biography of John Ballance* (1989); D. Hamer, *The New Zealand Liberals: the years of power* (1988).

16 For the policies of Richard Seddon, see David Hamer, *The New Zealand Liberals: the years of power* (Auckland, 1988) and idem, 'Seddon, Richard John (1845–1906)', *Oxford dictionary of national biography* (Oxford, 2004); online edn, May 2006 [http://www.oxforddnb.com/view/article/36002, accessed 29 Aug. 2006].

17 D. Thomson, *A world without welfare: New Zealand's colonial experiment* (Auckland, 1998).

18 Cf. T. N. Travers, ' "The real value of the lands": the *Nawabs*, the British and the land tax in eighteenth-century Bengal', *Modern Asian Studies*, 38 (2004), pp. 517–38.

19 E. Stokes, *The English Utilitarians and India* (Oxford, 1959), pp. 93–102; M. B. McAlpin, *Subject to famine: food crises and economic change in Western India, 1860–1920* (Princeton, 1983), pp. 108–9. For a denial of the importance of Ricardian rent in practice, see M. Mann, 'A permanent settlement for the Ceded and Conquered provinces: revenue administration in north India, 1801–33', *India Economic and Social History Review*, 32 (1995).

20 McAlpin, *Subject to famine*, pp. 110–13.

21 Quoted in A. K. Bagchi, 'Land tax, property rights and peasant insecurity in colonial India', *Journal of Peasant Studies*, 20 (1990), p. 40.

22 Cf. Travers, ' "The real value" '.

23 McAlpin, *Subject to famine*, pp. 198–202.

24 P. J. Thomas, *The growth of federal finance in India* (Madras, 1939), p. 500.

25 N. Charlesworth, 'The problem of government finance in British India: taxation, borrowing and the allocation of resources in the inter-war period', *Modern Asian Studies,* 19 (1984), pp. 522–3.
26 Thomas, *Growth of federal finance,* 121.
27 M. Naidis, 'A note on Sir John Lawrence and the income tax', *Bengal Past and Present,* 80 (1960); S. Chandra, 'The income tax (1860–1873): a study in basic contradictions', *Indian Economic and Social History Review,* 3 (1966); I. Klein, 'Wilson v Trevelyan: finance and modernization in India after 1857', *Indian Economic and Social History,* 7 (1970).
28 The figures are from Thomas, *Growth of federal finance,* p. 500.
29 Naidis, 'Note on Sir John Lawrence', p. 78.
30 A. W. Silver, *Manchester men and Indian cotton, 1847–72* (Manchester, 1966); P. Harnetty, 'Lancashire and the Indian cotton duties, 1859–62', *Economic History Review,* 18 (1965) and 'The Indian cotton duties controversy, 1894–6', *English Historical Review,* 77 (1962); I. Klein, 'English free traders and Indian tariffs, 1874–1896', *Modern Asian Studies,* 5 (1971) and 'Politics and public opinion in Lytton's tariff policy', *Journal of Indian History,* 45 (1967); C. Dewey, 'The end of the imperialism of free trade: the eclipse of the Lancashire lobby and the concession of fiscal autonomy to India', in C. Dewey and A. G. Hopkins (eds), *The imperial impact: studies in the economic history of Africa and India* (1978).
31 Thomas, *Federal finance in India,* p. 501.
32 P. G. Robb, *Ancient rights and future comfort: Bihar, the Bengal Tenancy Act of 1885, and British rule in India* (Richmond, 1997).
33 D. K. Fieldhouse, 'The economic exploitation of Africa: some British and French comparisons', in P. Gifford and W. R. Louis (eds), *France and Britain in Africa: imperial rivalry and colonial rule* (New Haven and London, 1971), pp. 616–22.
34 Fieldhouse, 'Economic exploitation of Africa', pp. 620–2.
35 *Cape of Good Hope: further papers relative to the state of the Kaffir tribes,* 'Governor's address to the Legislative Council and the House of Assembly, at the opening of the second session of the Colonial Parliament', p. 524.
36 *Cape of Good Hope: further papers relative to the state of the Kaffir tribes,* 'Report of special commissioner, appointed to inquire into the present state of the Fingoe locations on the Eastern Frontier, especially in the division of Victoria, Fort Beaufort, and Queen's Town, and the location of the Zitzikama', W. Calderwood, 22 Jan. 1855, p. 505; 'Copy of a despatch from the Right Hon. Lord John Russell to Governor Sir George Grey', 26 May 1855, p. 533.
37 M. Wright, 'East Africa, 1870–1905', in R. Oliver and G. N. Sanderson (eds), *The Cambridge history of Africa,* vol. VI: *From 1870 to 1905* (Cambridge, 1985), p. 590.
38 Shula Marks, 'Southern and central Africa, 1886–1910', in Oliver and Sanderson (eds), *Cambridge history of Africa,* VI, pp. 462–3.
39 L. White, *Magomero: portrait of an African village* (Cambridge, 1987), pp. 85–90; C. Baker, 'Tax collection in Malawi: an administrative history, 1891–1972', *International Journal of African Historical Studies,* 8 (1975), pp. 49–50, 52, 53; Marks, 'Southern and central Africa', p. 456; A. J. Hanna, *The beginnings of Nyasaland and North-Eastern Rhodesia, 1859–95* (Oxford, 1956), pp. 241–4; R. I. Rotberg, *The rise of nationalism in Central Africa: the making of Malawi and Zambia, 1873–1964* (Cambridge, Mass., 1966), pp. 40, 41–3, 46–7.
40 Baker, 'Tax collection', pp. 40–5, 55–7.
41 Baker, 'Tax collection', pp. 46–7.

42 Baker, 'Tax collection', pp. 47–9; Marks, 'Southern and central Africa', p. 456; R. D. Wolff, *The economics of colonialism: Britain and Kenya, 1870–1930* (New Haven and London, 1974), p. 117.
43 Rotberg, *The rise of nationalism in Central Africa*, pp. 33–4.
44 D. H. Gillis, *The Kingdom of Swaziland: studies in political history* (Westport, Conn. and London, 1999), p. 136.
45 Cf. the case study of one colony by V. Jamal, 'Taxation and inequality in Uganda, 1900–1964', *Journal of Economic History*, 38 (1978), pp. 418–28; also Wolff, *Economics of colonialism*, pp. 118–19; Fieldhouse, 'Economic exploitation of Africa', pp. 614–15.
46 John Lonsdale, 'The conquest state of Kenya', in J. A. de Moor and H. L. Wessling (eds), *Imperialism and war: essays on colonial wars in Asia and Africa* (Leiden, 1989), p. 88.
47 John Lonsdale, 'The European scramble and conquest in African history', in Oliver and Londsale (eds), *Cambridge history of Africa*, VI, p. 752.
48 L. Denzer and M. Crowder, 'Bai Bureh and the Sierra Leone hut tax war of 1898', in R. I. Rotberg and A. A. Mazrui (eds), *Protest and power in black Africa* (New York, 1970); A. Abraham, 'Nyagua, the British and the hut tax war', *International Journal of African Historical Studies*, 5 (1972); A. Abraham, 'Bai Bureh, the British and the hut tax war', *International Journal of African Historical Studies*, 7 (1974).
49 J. Lonsdale, 'The European scramble and conquest in African history', in Oliver and Sanderson (eds), *Cambridge history of Africa*, VI, pp. 744, 761, 764–5.
50 Marks, 'Southern and central Africa', p. 457; eadem, 'The Zulu disturbances in Natal', in Rotberg and Mazui (eds), *Protest and power.*
51 Marks, 'Southern and central Africa', p. 455.

9

The Transfer of Tax Ideas during the 'Reverse Course' of the US Occupation of Japan*

W. Elliot Brownlee

Imperial nations have often attempted to transplant ideas about taxation in the soil of less powerful societies. Historians are well aware of how the expansion of empires, both formal and informal, has spread institutions of *private* finance.[1] But less well understood is how imperial expansion spread, or at least attempted to spread, ideas of *public* finance, including taxation. This essay seeks to help launch an exploration of this phenomenon in the context of the history of the economic and political expansion of the United States, especially during the period following the Second World War. The transfer of tax ideas may have been an important aspect of reconstruction of international economic institutions and programmes that the United States undertook in the wake of the Great Depression and the Second World War.[2] This essay explores the transfer of tax ideas associated with one important aspect of this reconstruction – the American occupation of Japan (1945–52). The essay undertakes this exploration through an in-depth study of government decision making, including the ideas of key policy-makers, both American and Japanese, during the occupation.

The early occupation, 1945–47

At the outset of the American occupation in 1945, Japan's system of public finance rested on income tax and heavy corporate taxation, as well as a highly centralized fiscal structure. In Japan, as in the United States, the wartime crisis had prompted a major restructuring of taxation that emphasized both income taxes and dominance of fiscal policy by the central government. Wartime tax reforms undertaken by the Japanese government in 1940 included a personal income tax built on what economist Jinno Naohiko has described as 'two planks, consolidated income tax levied with graduated rates, and classified income tax levied with proportional rates'.[3] Under the classified tax, sometimes called a schedular tax, the flat rates varied by type of income. The tax exempted capital gains and imposed a lower rate on interest from national bonds than any other form of taxed income. The 1940 reforms included, in addition, special corporation taxes, including, among other provisions, a net income tax of

35 per cent on domestic corporations, an excess profits tax graduated from 10 to 40 per cent, and a substantial tax on capital stocks. To this system, Japan added a collection-at-the-source system (several years in advance of the United States and Great Britain) for normal tax liability on salary and wage income. These reforms sought to increase the tax burden, both absolute and relative, of the modernized sector of the economy. Also in 1940, the central government undertook a complicated set of reforms in local taxation and intergovernmental transfers designed to reinforce, in Jinno's words, 'the capability of local communities to maintain order'. In practice, however, these reforms increased the ability of the central government to control the way in which local governments provided public services. Through this tax reform, as Jinno has written, 'a centralized-deconcentrated system operated by means of fiscal-resource control was formed in embryo'.[4]

During the initial years of the occupation, from 1945 to late 1947, General Douglas MacArthur – the Supreme Commander for the Allied Powers (SCAP) – did not undertake any radical reforms of either the structure or the administration of the Japanese tax system. But SCAP did force the Japanese government to adopt some modest reforms. In 1946, for example, SCAP arranged the enactment of a stiff progressive tax on capital. SCAP designed the tax to reinforce the early occupation's effort to dissolve the *zaibatsu* groups. In 1947, to tax dividends, interest and high earned incomes more heavily, SCAP replaced the schedular personal income tax with one that consolidated earned incomes, dividends and interest in its base and imposed a more steeply graduated rate structure. While creating a somewhat more progressive tax system, the primary effect of these reforms in 1947 was to reinforce both the importance of the income tax and the dominance of the central government within the Japanese fiscal order.[5] The American occupation also kept in place the powerful Japanese Ministry of Finance (MOF) – a decision that augmented the centralizing force of tax reform. With this bureaucracy in place, the American occupation faced an inherent barrier to the transfer of tax ideas, particularly those that threatened the power of the central government.[6]

Taxation and the 'reverse course', 1947–49

Fostering economic and social stability had been more important than promoting democracy in the tax policy of the early American occupation. But soon after the tax reforms of 1947, a shift in the general objectives of the occupation pushed American tax policy in Japan in even more conservative directions. SCAP embraced what became known as the 'reverse course', in which the goal of economic recovery became even more important. To implement this goal, the administration of President Harry S. Truman allowed the departments of the Army, Treasury and State, supported by powerful elements of the American business community, to take over occupation policy. The lead agency in this de facto reorganization of the occupation was the National

Advisory Council on International and Financial Affairs (NAC), chaired by John W. Snyder, Truman's secretary of the Treasury from 1946 until 1953. In the 'reverse course', SCAP became largely a 'transmission belt' for the NAC and the cabinet departments.[7]

As early as 1947, the Treasury department began to shift the direction of SCAP's tax policy.[8] The long-run goal was to build a strong Japanese economy that would be the foundation of an anti-Communist stronghold in East Asia. A vibrant Japanese economy, in the eyes of the Treasury, required both higher rates of Japanese savings (and investment) and the revival of Japanese export industries.[9] The most important challenge was to control inflation, which was accelerating in 1947. Inflation damaged the Japanese economy by eroding savings and raising the cost of Japanese exports. Mounting Japanese budget deficits in fiscal 1947–48 seemed to make both problems more severe. And inflation threatened to destabilize the Japanese government. A secondary challenge was to reduce the cost of the occupation to American taxpayers. The cost was rising, threatening to fuel an isolationist backlash to prosecuting the cold war in Asia. Increasing taxes in Japan would, the Treasury was confident, help both to control inflation and to stabilize the political environment for both the Japanese and American governments.

The intense effort in 1947–48 to balance the budget through increasing tax revenues led to efforts to strengthen the ability of the Japanese government to collect taxes. In January 1948, the powerful Economic and Scientific Section (ESS) of SCAP, using Eighth Army personnel, implemented what it called 'field surveillance' over the eight regional bureaux and 450 district tax offices that comprised the national tax service. Over 100 officers and enlisted men fanned out to monitor tax collections through the remainder of fiscal year 1947–48. The ESS also worked with the MOF to impose a significant tax increase at the national level. In early 1948, the MOF and the American occupation agreed on what became known as the 'transactions tax' – a 1 per cent levy on most monetary transactions.[10]

In 1947, the department of the Treasury, the ESS and SCAP also concluded that balancing the budget in the short run and establishing a strong revenue foundation in the long run would require further strengthening of Japanese tax administration, and possibly reforms of the Japanese tax structure. To lead this programme, the Treasury loaned to SCAP one of its international experts in the Bureau of Internal Revenue, L. Harold Moss, along with a team of 'experienced tax technicians and economists'. SCAP created a new division, the Internal Revenue Division (IRD), within the ESS, and made Moss its chief.[11]

During 1948, Moss and his staff outlined a programme for reform. At the national level, Moss wanted reforms that would enable personal income and corporate taxes to generate more revenue. Part of Moss's approach was to crack down administratively on individuals who filed returns as self-assessors and under-reported incomes. He believed that many members of both the traditional sector (farmers and small merchants) and the most modern (wealthy businessmen and corporations) were guilty of doing so. To reinforce this programme, Moss sought to lighten the most progressive aspects of the Japanese tax system and thereby encourage voluntary compliance. Most important, he hoped to reduce the highest marginal rates of taxation. He believed that it was necessary to make 'drastic revisions in the rate structure' of the personal income tax, in particular, because had it 'gone beyond the point of diminishing returns'.[12]

At the local level, Moss wanted to enhance the taxing capability of local governments. This policy also had a potentially significant democratization element in that it would also promote the independence of local governments. Other divisions of SCAP had already forced local reforms on behalf of democratization, such as the popular election of prefectural governors and the dismantling of the Home Ministry. However, this decentralizing thrust had limited effects because it had prompted other ministries of the central government to react, countering by setting up outposts throughout Japan to concentrate the delivery of public services. Thus, despite SCAP's programme of local reform, fiscal control from the centre had tightened further, and the civilian bureaucracy had gained even greater power. Moss hoped to succeed in challenging this bureaucracy where other entities of SCAP had failed. But, for Moss, democratization at the local level was to be more a means to an end – enhancement of the fiscal capacity of government – than an end unto itself.[13]

Moss believed that the existing bureaucracy within SCAP was not capable of undertaking the reforms he had in mind to enhance fiscal capacity. He worried, in particular, that he might face opposition from other divisions within SCAP to his efforts to reduce high marginal tax rates. And he anticipated significant opposition from the Japanese government, particularly over democratization at the local level. In the spring of 1948, Moss began to organize a mission of tax experts to help with both problems.

Moss had effective control over the appointment of expert personnel for the mission, and used his power in ways that would produce the kind of tax policy recommendations that he favoured. The appointment of a leader for the mission was key. As an experienced hand within the wartime Treasury and the Bureau of Internal Revenue, Moss appreciated in particular the work of one influential economist – Carl S. Shoup – and was able to appoint him as 'Director of the Tax Mission'.

During the early 1930s, Shoup had participated in a number of important cooperative studies of tax policy and had become, in the words of historian Joseph Thorndike, 'a charter member of the expert policy community taking shape around New Deal taxation'.[14] Shoup had begun his Treasury career as an expert on business taxation and had sympathy with the anti-monopoly orientation of much of New Deal tax policy. But he had stopped short of supporting the New Deal's most punitive anti-business measure, the undistributed profits tax. Later, during the Second World War, he had counselled against adopting the kind of extreme excess profits taxation that had characterized

American taxation of corporate incomes during the First World War. In Japan, Shoup was quite likely to advocate reform of corporate taxes to make them more economically efficient. Shoup was also well known in the Treasury for supporting both broadening the base of the income tax – thereby advancing a Haig–Simons model of income taxation – and reducing the highest marginal rates of the income tax.[15]

The other members of the mission, whom Shoup was largely responsible for recruiting, reinforced Shoup's views. William Vickrey, a colleague and former student of Shoup's at Columbia, had a particularly well-developed interest in advancing reform along Haig–Simons lines and worried about how high marginal tax rates at the top of the progressive scale 'merely drive more taxpayers to the use of . . . loopholes'.[16] Stanley Surrey and William Warren, law professors at the University of California, Berkeley and Columbia University, respectively, reinforced this interest with a powerful commitment to closing loopholes in the personal income tax. In 1989, in response to an interviewer's question regarding his selection of Surrey for the mission, Shoup recalled how hostility to tax preferences shaped his choice of colleagues: 'My own prejudices determined the selection of the members of the Tax Mission, and if Surrey had been an advocate of tax preferences, I might not have asked him to join the mission.'[17]

In promising to advance a Haig–Simons model of income taxation and reduce high marginal rates, Shoup, Vickrey and the two law professors represented a line of reform – one that emphasized economic efficiency and horizontal equity – that had not won popular support in the United States or had a significant impact on tax policy there. However, experts within the Department of the Treasury had championed the line as early as the 1920s.[18] Thus, in staffing the Shoup mission, Moss was embracing for Japan a reform programme that was based more on American ideas than on American practice. In effect, Moss invited Shoup, Vickrey and Surrey to reform Japanese taxation according to models that they had been unable to implement in the United States. Moss offered them an opportunity to design a progressive income tax that they believed would be the most economically efficient and horizontally equitable of any in the world. Reinforcing the American orientation of the mission was the failure to appoint to it any experts on Japanese public finance.[19]

Over the months in which Moss slowly organized the Shoup mission, discussions within Washington and SCAP over fiscal policy took a frantic turn. In the autumn of 1948, MacArthur resisted belt-tightening by either SCAP or the Japanese government. In the context of increasing inflation in Japan and the desire of Truman and the NAC to revitalize the Japanese export economy, MacArthur's stubbornness prompted the Treasury and the Federal Reserve to unite in an effort to increase even further their influence over the occupation. In particular, in December 1949 they forced the Joint Chiefs of Staff to promulgate a directive that established a 'Nine-Point Programme' for economic recovery in Japan. In February 1949, the Truman administration sent a mission into Japan ahead of the Shoup mission and charged it with the responsibility for implementing the nine points. In command, at the personal invitation of President Truman, was a Detroit banker, Joseph Dodge. The nine points became known as 'the Dodge line'.[20]

Dodge was a blunt, hard-nosed banker with strong, well-formed views on the fiscal situation in Japan. In September 1948, he had sketched out the principles that produced the Dodge line. For one thing, he was sceptical about the commitment of the Japanese government to balancing its budget. He believed that 'the combined forces of Japanese political, bureaucratic, business, and other elements is constantly being applied to an effort to lower tax rates and revenues'. For another, he believed that Japanese tax policy ought to be tied to the objectives of the United States and, in particular, 'to the final elimination of the need for United States aid, and the prevention of a revival of inflation'. He suggested a criterion for evaluating Japanese tax policy: 'One of the yardsticks probably we should apply in granting foreign aid is the measurement of the tax practice of the aided country against our own. If the American taxpayer is to be highly taxed to provide the aid, foreign nations should not be allowed to pay a disproportionately lesser tax.'[21]

A new Japanese government, organized in October 1948 by the conservative leader of the Democratic Liberal Party, Yoshida Shigeru, shared the general goals and approach of Dodge's programme. Prime minister Yoshida and his finance minister, Ikeda Hayato, were in essential agreement with the Treasury Department and the Federal Reserve that Japanese inflation had become dangerously high, and that counter-cyclical fiscal policy was appropriate. Consequently, Ikeda had cooperated with Moss's effort to increase tax collections through tighter enforcement of the income tax.[22]

The vigorous enforcement effort and the new transactions tax – and the inflationary process of 'bracket creep' – produced dynamic tax revenues throughout 1948. But the accelerating pace of collections prompted widespread public hostility to occupation taxes. Particularly resented was the practice of the MOF, supported by the Eighth Army's 'field surveillance', to set income tax revenue goals for each of the local tax offices. Many heads of these offices assessed taxpayers arbitrarily and collected taxes from whom they could. There was nothing new in this capricious practice, but the high post-war rates aroused resistance, especially among taxpayers who had been used to evading self-assessed income taxes. When Yoshida called a general election in January, opposition politicians, including Communists, made major issues out of high taxes and the costs that Japanese taxpayers had to bear for the occupation. In response, the Liberal Party promised to repeal the transactions tax and to reduce income taxes. In the elections, on 24 January, the Communist Party gained a significant number of seats in the Diet, but the anti-tax message of Yoshida and the Liberals helped them win a decisive victory.[23]

The victory, however, created a political problem for Yoshida and Ikeda. On the one hand, they believed they had to follow through on their campaign promises to reduce taxes. On the other hand, they knew that Dodge would take a hard line against tax reduction. The stage was set for serious conflict between Ikeda and Dodge, despite their agreement that the inflation called for Keynesian counter-cyclical medicine.

In February, the Dodge mission arrived in Tokyo. Dodge and Ikeda soon locked horns over tax cuts. On the one hand, Dodge believed that balancing the budget would require not only expenditure cuts but also increases in tax revenues, probably through further improvement in collections. On the other hand, Ikeda proposed abolishing the transactions tax and increasing income tax exemptions. In numerous meetings, the two got nowhere. In March, however, Dodge apparently decided that the conservative Ikeda administration was, indeed, in political trouble and that taxes had become too high. Dodge softened his line. Behind the scenes, he and Moss decided that in return for cuts in expenditures by Ikeda they were willing to support some income tax cuts, but they did not want to accept any cuts in a way that would make it seem as if they had caved into the Japanese government. Dodge proposed to Ikeda that they leave it to the Shoup mission to propose cuts, and then enact them retroactively. Ikeda accepted the compromise. The key for both Ikeda and Dodge was publicity. A highly visible announcement of the Shoup mission would give the Japanese public the impression that tax cuts would be coming, and would therefore get Ikeda and the MOF off the hook for not cutting taxes immediately. And publicity would seem to make the Shoup mission, rather than SCAP, responsible for agreeing to tax cuts.[24]

In settling on this compromise, Ikeda believed that the purpose of the mission was to recommend tax cuts and provide advice on tightening tax administration, rather than to propose fundamental tax reform. Later, Ikeda recalled: 'I had no particular intention that Shoup should give me theoretical recommendations for the Japanese tax system.' He was insulted by the implication that the Japanese government and its experts required instruction on what was best practice in public finance. 'The tax *system* as such was based on a fairly careful study of various European systems', Ikeda observed, 'and its theoretical underpinnings were well developed, so there was no particular need to seek the guidance of foreigners on the system itself.' Ikeda was correct with regard to the attention that Japanese policy-makers had paid to European experience. They had begun doing so soon after the Meiji Restoration. In crafting Japan's first income tax, adopted in 1887, finance minister Matsukata Masayoshi and other members of the government studied both the British and the Prussian income taxes. For example, in his 1884 draft of legislation Matsukata closely followed the British tax with regard to both its classification of income and provision for collection at the source, but by 1887 had abandoned collection at the source in favour of the Prussian lump-sum approach. More recently, in drafting the 1940 reforms of personal and corporate income taxes, the MOF borrowed ideas from the United States, Germany, England and France. The intention, economist Shiomi Saburo wrote, 'was to adopt all advanced systems of other countries'.[25]

The linkage between Ikeda's campaign for tax cuts and the Shoup mission shaped Ikeda's interpretation of the chronology of the mission. He recalled that the decision 'to get Shoup to come [to Japan] originated' not in the autumn of 1948 but 'from about the time when in February of that year [1949] I failed in my negotiations with Dodge for tax reductions'.[26] Ikeda made no reference to tax reform. Symmetrically and consistently, Secretary of the Treasury Snyder recalled that he had sent the Shoup mission to Japan 'to back up' Dodge in implementing his austerity programme.[27]

Three days after a press release announcing the Shoup mission had appeared, Moss broke the news to Shoup that 'your group will be walking into the hottest political issue this side of Frisco: taxes'. Moss explained the history of the Dodge mission, emphasizing that the tough adherence of the Japanese government to a programme of tax cutting had led to Dodge's decision to advertise the Shoup mission. 'You made headlines in the Japanese press throughout the country', Moss wrote, 'and millions of people are expecting Dr. Shoup and his mission to solve all Japanese tax problems'.[28] In effect, Moss was telling Shoup that his mission would not only provide technical advice to SCAP and the Japanese government but also participate in the public debate over taxation that was under way as a consequence of the large tax increases during 1947 and 1948, the elections in January 1949, and the Dodge–Ikeda decision to trumpet the promise of the Shoup mission.

Before the Shoup mission arrived, Dodge further increased pressure on it by hardening his position on potential tax cuts, having concluded that Ikeda had not been sufficiently vigorous in pursuing expenditure cuts. Dodge became worried that Japanese politicians might persuade the mission members, unless 'forewarned and careful', to recommend excessive short-term tax cuts. Consequently, he worked hard to stiffen the backbone of the mission in anticipation of pressure from the MOF and public opinion. The mission, he wrote, 'will require thorough indoctrination' regarding 'work already done here'.[29]

Overnight, the Shoup mission had moved into a political spotlight. Both the Japanese government and American occupation officials entertained high hopes for the mission, yet each side had different priorities. The former emphasized the goal of significant tax cuts. The latter, represented by Joseph Dodge, stressed cuts in expenditures and inflation fighting. Further increasing the pressure on the Shoup mission, Harold Moss and the IRD looked forward to reform of income taxation and a fundamental restructuring of intergovernmental finance.

The Shoup recommendations

While Moss had correctly anticipated the general nature of the recommendations of the Shoup mission, neither he nor anyone else had fully reckoned on the energy and ambition of the Shoup mission. In August, after three months of intense work, Shoup and his colleagues completed an exceptionally elaborate and intricate proposal for not only tax cuts but also a thoroughgoing reconstruction of the Japanese tax system.

At the heart of the Shoup reforms was an effort to place a greater emphasis within the Japanese tax system on horizontal equity – 'equal treatment of those equally circumstanced', as Shoup defined it two decades later.[30] Such taxation, Shoup believed, would help implement the key American goals of augmenting revenue flows. Shoup and his colleagues recognized that an income tax along Haig–Simons lines would conflict with the Japanese preference for using the income tax to create investment incentives. Thus, throughout the Shoup report, its authors emphasized that a Haig–Simons income tax would promote economic efficiency. In 1989, Shoup emphasized that the mission had avoided proposing specific incentives to economic growth. 'How did we know', Shoup asked, 'what kind of economic growth was desirable?' He explained that since 'we did not know which economic activities were to be preferred', the mission had sought instead a tax system that was 'economically neutral'. The mission had faith in the 'marketplace' and the productive capacity of Japan, and 'wanted to be careful that the tax system did not impede spontaneous economic rehabilitation'.[31]

With regard to the personal income tax, Shoup and his colleagues focused on (1) promoting horizontal equity through base broadening and (2) reduction of the marginal rates of personal income taxation, including a cut of the top rate from 85 to 55 per cent. To encourage compliance with the personal income tax by small businesses, Shoup recommended limiting the deduction of depreciation only to those unincorporated non-farm business filers who maintained good records. Such filers would submit special returns (the 'blue-return' system) and would be reassessed only after examination of their books. The mission also recommended two new national taxes: (1) a net worth tax to offset partially the regressive effects of the rate cuts; and (2) an accessions tax, which would replace all estate and gift taxes with a tax on the total of gifts or bequests received over a beneficiary's lifetime. In the realm of corporate taxation, the mission proposed a variety of changes. Perhaps the most important was a revaluation of assets to take account of wartime and post-war inflation. The intent was to allow corporations to build up depreciation reserves and to avoid paying huge capital gains taxes. In addition, the mission recommended (1) reducing the normal rate of corporate income taxation to 35 per cent; (2) taking some modest steps towards integrating personal and corporate income taxation (including reduction of the taxation of dividends under the personal income tax); and (3) adopting a modest undistributed profits tax to encourage payment of dividends. Also, the mission proposed repeal of excess profits taxation and the unpopular transactions tax.[32]

The Shoup mission had recommended a significant number of tax cuts, but their scale and timing were much less aggressive than the Yoshida government had proposed in the general elections and the budget for 1949–50. Shoup had caved in to overt pressure from Dodge and provided unqualified support to Dodge's desire for budget 'overbalancing' (debt reduction as well as balancing), even though Shoup, and perhaps other members of the mission, personally regarded the Dodge line as too severe.[33] In the report, Shoup went so far as to reinforce the claim of Joseph Dodge that Ikeda had found the least compelling and most irritating during their arguments. This was the claim that Japan's tax burden was relatively light. Shoup and his colleagues understood the limitations of comparative measures of tax burden among nations, but they nonetheless emphasized that the ratio between all taxes to net national product in Japan in 1949–50 'may be no more than 20 percent or so', compared with 24 per cent in the United States and 38 per cent in Great Britain in 1948. 'There is no evidence in these data', the Shoup report concluded, 'that the Japanese tax total is unusually large.'[34]

The most ambitious of the Shoup proposals for fiscal reform were those that called for the reorganization of public finance at the local level. Shoup recommended creating a Local Finance Commission that would have considerable powers to (1) determine central government grants, (2) extend emergency taxing authority to localities, and (3) adjust property tax rates across localities. And Shoup recommended the transformation of local taxation. Under the Shoup programme, all localities would move away from dependence on funding from the central government and develop their own revenue sources. Prefectures would rely primarily on an existing local tax on business income. This tax, called the 'enterprise tax', would be transformed into a value added tax.[35]

Shoup, in outlining this programme for MacArthur, claimed that he was not trying to turn Japan into a social laboratory to test out new fiscal instruments. 'In our recommendations', Shoup told MacArthur, 'we have attempted to adhere to the principle expressed during the interview in your office the day after my arrival – a minimum of experimentation, no "guinea pig" approach'. However, Shoup admitted: 'the value-added tax is not being used elsewhere in just this form, so far as we are aware'.[36] In 1989 Shoup said that in proposing the VAT the mission had not violated their pledge to MacArthur, but 'we thought that maybe one new thing would be all right'.[37]

In his comments to MacArthur, and in Shoup's 1989 recollections, he slipped by the fact that *other* new taxes that he and his colleagues had recommended verged on the experimental. Only Puerto Rico had adopted an accessions tax. The United States had abandoned its experiment with an undistributed profits tax, and had never adopted a net worth tax. Perhaps most significant, no modern nation, including the United States, had explicitly and comprehensively embraced the Haig–Simons concept of income taxation.[38]

Shoup and his colleagues believed their understanding of public finance had enough intellectual power to lift their proposals for innovative taxes above the level of risky experimentation. Consequently, they thought of their work as cautious reform rather than daring experimentation. 'We have tried', Shoup wrote to the Department of the Army when he completed his report, 'to keep a judicious balance between no undue experimentation and no slavish adherence to the past.' He explained: 'We are recommending for Japan a tax system that is dependable, but that is also modern.' But Shoup and his colleagues believed that if the Japanese government adopted the entire reform programme, the result would be more than 'modern'. It would be unique and, in their view, uniquely superb. Shoup declared: 'We believe that the Japanese people should have the opportunity to be able to say, within five or ten years, that they have the best tax system in the world' – even better, in other words than the American tax system. 'We have formulated our recommendations with this aim in mind', Shoup continued. 'The rest will be up to them' (the Japanese people). The expert missionaries from America believed they had presented Japan with the means for fiscal salvation.[39]

Shoup had chosen his words carefully. He and his colleagues had prepared their reform proposals with the Japanese people, rather than the Japanese government, in mind. Shoup must have had a very good idea of what the reaction of the Yoshida government would be. He had to understand that the new taxes – the net worth tax, the accessions tax, the undistributed profits tax and the value-added tax – were certain to prove objectionable to Yoshida and Ikeda. He had to understand as well that the creation of the Local Finance Commission would pose a direct threat to one of the key elements of the MOF's power. Indeed, when Shoup had met with finance minister Ikeda to discuss his preliminary report, Ikeda presented a string of difficult problems with regard to the Local Finance Commission. Shoup had to admit to General William Marquat, the chief of the ESS, that 'these were real problems, which our mission had not solved in detail'. However, he made his distaste for Ikeda's position clear: 'I fear the repetition of the same old story – national-government influence penetrating every organization that is set up primarily to safeguard the localities' interest.'[40]

Two days after Shoup presented a preview of his findings to the Department of the Army, he went public with them. He delivered an extended speech at a press conference, and released a 3000-word summary of his findings, inviting public comment. He hoped, he said, 'that through the publication of this report an intelligent discussion of the Japanese tax system will develop, in the press, in national and local tax offices throughout the country, in business circles, in women's organizations, and in the universities and secondary schools'.[41] This amounted to a calculated challenge to the Yoshida government, which had not yet formally received Shoup's report. Moss and Shoup had come to the conclusion that only broad, democratic pressure would bring about adoption of the report, and had decided to launch a direct appeal for popular support.[42] Perhaps from the outset, when Dodge made the work of the mission highly visible, Moss and Shoup had decided that the Yoshida government was unlikely to make a good faith effort to consider the proposed reforms. It is entirely possible as well that Moss and Shoup may have calculated that the occupation would continue for a long period of time – the 'five or ten' years Shoup referred to in his challenge to the Japanese people. Shoup and Moss may have believed that 'five or ten' years would provide enough time for the coming to power of a government that would be more sympathetic than Yoshida's to at least the mission's proposals. A socialist government, for example, would have been much more likely to support the Shoup proposals for local reform.[43]

Implementing the Shoup report

Problems implementing the Shoup report began even before SCAP formally transmitted it to the Japanese government. The mission had declared: 'All of the major recommendations, and many of the minor ones, are interconnected.' Shoup and his colleagues warned that 'If any of the major recommendations are eliminated, some of the others will thereby become of less value, or even harmful.' They declared that they would 'disclaim responsibility for the results that may follow the adoption of only part of our recommendations'.[44] Nonetheless, significant opposition emerged even within the IRD and other divisions of the ESS to some of the most innovative Shoup proposals: the value added tax, the net worth tax, the accessions tax and some of the base-broadening measures. Critics within the occupation found these untried measures too uncertain in their revenue potential and beyond the administrative capacity of the Japanese government.[45]

In light of the disagreements within SCAP, MacArthur formally asked the Japanese government only to follow 'the broad principles and objectives set forth in Dr. Shoup's recommendations'.[46] However, SCAP informally pressed the Yoshida government to take action on much of the programme, and to act swiftly on local finance and tax enforcement. 'Unless substantial pressure is brought to bear' on the Japanese government, Moss told Marquat in September, it would not 'vigorously' implement the recommendations for reform of local public finance and of tax enforcement.[47]

Moss increased even further the pressure on the Yoshida government. Just as Shoup had done at the end of August, Moss went around the government and appealed directly to the Japanese people. In August, Moss had secretly organized the translation of the report into Japanese. At the same time that SCAP delivered the report to Yoshida, Moss widely distributed the copies in Japanese. He also sent 50,000 copies of a 160-page summary in Japanese to all regional tax administration agencies and offices. This launched a publicity campaign that went on for a year. By the time it was over, SCAP and the MOF had produced two motion pictures, three trailer films, 344 radio broadcasts and 433 newspaper advertisements.[48] Moss modelled this publicity campaign explicitly on the pay-your-taxes campaigns that the Bureau of Internal Revenue and other federal agencies had conducted within the United States during the Second World War.[49]

On 16 September, prime minister Yoshida wrote that he had received the report and believed that it 'is bound to mark a new era in Japan's fiscal policy'. He explained: 'I fully realize the fact that the recommendations are not to be accepted eclectically, but they should be taken as a whole if they are to serve as the basis for a rational and equitable tax system such as envisaged by Dr. Shoup.'

He went on to promise: 'It is with this fact in mind that my government will study the Report and formulate a taxation program to be submitted to the coming Diet.'[50]

This response did not reassure Moss. He believed that Ikeda and Yoshida had taken a positive tone simply to strengthen their bargaining position with Dodge over tax cuts. He worried that Ikeda and Yoshida would succeed in separating the issue of tax cuts from that of tax reform, which included significant tax increases. They would enact the tax cuts but evade tax reform. They planned, Moss believed, 'to put a lot of the recommended language on the books, even while disagreeing with the basic philosophy, and let it stagnate there'.[51]

Yoshida's public statement did, indeed, contain significant elements of ambiguity. He had not, in fact, clearly endorsed the report. His government remained focused on the need for substantial tax cuts, and what they believed was a need for deeper cuts than Shoup had recommended. But Ikeda was vigorously opposed to most of the other elements of the Shoup proposals, especially those that sought local reform.

In considering the Shoup recommendations within the Diet, Ikeda avoided taking them 'as a whole', just as Moss feared he would. By breaking up the Shoup plan into separate legislative proposals and stringing out debate over them, Ikeda effectively mobilized opposition to specific tax increases and blamed SCAP for unpopular measures. There was little that Moss could do about this in light of the reservations within SCAP's bureaucracy over the Shoup recommendations; SCAP was not willing to insist on comprehensive legislation. In fact, American reservations grew about the tax increases Shoup had proposed because, beginning in June, both deflation and rising unemployment took hold, to a large extent as a consequence of the Dodge line. The widespread unpopularity of the Dodge line increasingly turned into public hostility to the Shoup report. His strategy of appealing to the Japanese public had backfired.[52]

Joseph Dodge himself encouraged a piecemeal approach. In November 1949, he returned to Tokyo to negotiate a supplementary budget for the current fiscal year and the new budget for the next year. He was far more cooperative with Ikeda than he had been earlier in the year. Dodge was happier with deflation than inflation, and he could see that Ikeda was working to curtail spending. Moreover, tax collections were strong, despite the deflation. Dodge decided not to insist on concessions on tax reform. He and Ikeda readily reached agreement on cuts in the personal income tax and repeal of the transactions tax, and announced that their programme of cuts 'would follow the Shoup recommendations'. This outcome was favourable to Ikeda. The cuts were larger and on a faster timetable than Shoup had recommended, and Ikeda had not had to pay the price of agreeing to substantial reform.[53]

The outcome of the second major round of negotiations between Dodge and Ikeda had again shown that the goal of economic stabilization dominated the American occupation under the 'reverse course'. When the largely unreformed tax system had proven sufficiently productive of revenue, American interest in promoting horizontal equity and the fiscal viability of local government waned. Although Harold Moss, the IRD and SCAP had continued pressing for tax reform, Joseph Dodge and the Truman administration eased off.

Once Dodge had returned home, Moss, the IRD and SCAP lobbied the Japanese government to adopt many of the reforms that Shoup had recommended. Ultimately, the Diet agreed to put on the books most of the Shoup recommendations for national-level reform. But negotiations with Ikeda proved especially difficult on the reform of local finance, particularly since the prior enactment of the Shoup tax cuts had weakened SCAP's bargaining power. Yoshida and Ikeda saw the Shoup proposals for local reform as directly threatening to the power of the central government, and especially to the MOF. They mired Moss and the IRD in discussion of the complex tangle of tax rates, tax limits, tax sharing, equalization grants, and redistribution of taxing powers. Matters became so confused that Moss pressed the Shoup mission to return for another consultation. In December 1949, Moss complained to Shoup about the 'difficulties we are encountering in the local tax field'. He explained: 'The Japanese proposed local tax bills are vague and indefinite, and in many respects appear to be down-right inconsistent with your report and the understanding we reached with them several weeks ago as the principles to be followed in drafting the legislation.'[54]

By March, Moss despaired of any progress and arranged for MacArthur to pressure the Yoshida government to take action on local reform. 'I am convinced', MacArthur wrote to Yoshida, 'that democratic government for Japan must evolve from the thousands of local communities administering to the needs of the public under a sound program of local administration to include an acceptable fiscal system.'[55]

The negotiations over local finance dragged on, nonetheless. Ikeda proved adept at exploiting differences of opinion within the occupation government. In May, he even travelled to Washington, DC to lobby the Treasury directly over local finance.[56] Finally, in July, the Diet seemed to cave in and adopt the Shoup proposals for reform of local finance, including the creation of the Local Finance Commission. However, the Diet did so only 'partially and eclectically', as John Dower has written. Once the legislation was in place, Yoshida, as John Dower put the matter, 'effectively killed the Local Finance Commission by the most elemental of oppositional tactics: he did not appoint sufficient personnel to render it workable'.[57] And, although the Diet put the value added tax on the books, it kept extending its effective date until 1954, when it formally repealed the tax.[58] The second Shoup mission visited Japan for two months during the summer of 1950, and issued a follow-up report.[59] But it had almost no impact on the design of the Local Finance Commission, or any other significant matter in the realm of local reform. The Korean War had begun in June. From that point on, American support for the Yoshida government was unwavering, and an early end to the occupation and SCAP seemed clearly on the cards.

After the end of the occupation, Japan steadily rolled back the national-level Shoup reforms. In 1953, it repealed the net worth tax and gutted the accessions tax; in 1954 it did the same thing to the undistributed profits tax. Most important, the Japanese government revived the practice, which it had vigorously employed during the Second World War, of using the income tax to create economic incentives. The government returned to taxing personal income on a schedular basis and carving out of loopholes in the income tax. For example, in 1953, the Diet returned to the pre-Shoup policy of excluding 50 per cent of capital gains from taxation, and in 1955 the Diet made bank interest free of tax. Other examples of incentives included accelerated depreciation for certain industrial equipment, a deduction for income from exports, and allowance of tax-free reserves for losses from export transactions. In the view of the Japanese government, special incentives for investment were desirable because, in general, the broad-based, progressive income tax unwisely advantaged consumption over saving, and because, in certain instances, the market would fail to recognize strategic growth opportunities.

Within a year after the end of the occupation, the Japanese government had eradicated most of the recommendations of the Shoup report for fundamental fiscal reform. This counter-reform movement occasioned little comment on the part of the United States, which increasingly valued its anti-Communist partnership with Japan and the Yoshida government.[60]

The Shoup legacy and the transfer of tax ideas

During the second phase, or 'reverse course', of the occupation of Japan, an effort to transfer tax ideas, largely through the Shoup mission, figured prominently in an American programme to strengthen Japan as a cold war ally. This effort, however, had limited success in shaping Japanese tax policy. In fact, the net effect of the American occupation was to reinforce the tax regime that the Japanese government had established during the Second World War.[61] And the reinforcement may have been very long term in its effects; the 'centralized-deconcentrated' fiscal system created in 1940 still remains largely in place today.[62]

The history of the Shoup mission testifies to the inherent difficulty of imposing tax ideas on powerful, resilient societies like Japan, especially through top-down reconstructions. Such societies normally have effective, flexible mechanisms of public finance for helping to maintain social stability, and are reluctant to subject them to major reform, especially if their revenue systems, like the Japanese tax system created in 1940, have proven to be sufficiently flexible to meet national emergencies.

To be sure, the Japanese government kept in place some Shoup reforms even after the end of the occupation. But these more or less permanent reforms were only those that reinforced the existing inclinations of government. In fact, the Japanese government probably would have adopted them in some manner had there been no Shoup mission. They included enhancements of central administration of income taxation, the revaluation of assets to take account of inflation, the 'blue-return' system, increasing the deductibility of dividends, and an array of tax cuts, including repeal of the transactions tax, reduction of the high marginal tax rates on personal and corporate income, and repeal of the excess profits tax.

Would better tactics on the part of SCAP have led to a more effective transfer of tax ideas, in the sense of having a greater impact on Japanese taxation? On the one hand, SCAP could have promoted the Shoup reforms in a more diplomatic fashion, trying to avoid the patronizing approaches that offended the Yoshida government. SCAP could have, for example, elevated Japanese economists to the status of full members of the mission. Nonetheless, less patronizing tactics probably would not have made the Yoshida government any more receptive to fundamental reform involving the adoption of a Haig–Simons income tax and creating fiscal autonomy at the local level. Moss, Shoup and SCAP, of course, also might have moderated their public efforts to promote the reform agenda of the mission. SCAP's approach bred resentment and stiffened the resistance of Yoshida and Ikeda, as well as the Japanese public, and one might argue that if Dodge and SCAP had kept the tone of Shoup low-key, just as Moss had originally planned in 1948, it might have had greater influence on the course of democratic tax reform. But the major objections of Yoshida and Ikeda to fundamental reform along Shoup's lines would have almost certainly remained.

On the other hand, SCAP could have adopted tougher tactics. The occupation might have been more unified in support of Shoup, and aggressively insisted on comprehensive legislation. The result would no doubt have been the enactment of even more of the Shoup programme between 1949 and 1952. But it is highly unlikely that the additional reforms would have survived the end of the occupation. In fact, the Japanese backlash to the occupation reforms might well have been even more severe.

Only if a less conservative government had come to power in Japan would SCAP have had the potential of greater success in advancing the Shoup agenda. Under a socialist government, for example, the idea of promoting fiscal autonomy for local government would have received a warmer welcome. But enacting a highly experimental VAT probably would still have been a non-starter; some other fiscal instrument for local autonomy would have been necessary. And other proposals of Shoup's might not have fared any better than they did with Yoshida in power. Income taxation along Haig–Simons lines might not have had any greater appeal. And, some of the successful Shoup proposals, such as the cuts in the highest marginal rates of taxation and the repeal of the excess profits tax, might have failed to win approval. Moreover, even under a socialist government, the Japanese civilian bureaucracy would have continued to limit the possibilities for tax reform. In any event, while Shoup and Moss might have welcomed a socialist government, the architects in Washington of the 'reverse course' would not have, and their vigorous support of the Yoshida government worked against whatever hopes Shoup and Moss might have had for a more favourable political environment for reform.

By the beginning of the Korean War, Shoup himself had begun to recognize the limited effect his specific recommendations were likely to have. He began to emphasize, instead, the long-run importance of the mission's direct appeals to the Japanese people. In June 1950, he wrote to MacArthur: 'I am inclined to think that the most lasting, and ultimately the most beneficial, effect of our work may turn out to be the widespread interest in the aims and techniques of taxation that has been aroused in Japan, chiefly because you authorized the printing and distribution of the full text of the report.'[63] In 1989, Shoup made an even more expansive claim for the mission as a democratizing force. He declared: 'When we came, ... Japanese tax policy was a closed little secret between the Finance Ministry and some members of the Diet.' He went on: 'we broke that open – broke that shell, that secrecy'.[64]

Examination of the impact of the Shoup report on Japanese tax politics lies outside the scope of this essay. But, with regard to the short run, it is worth noting that if Japanese tax politics became more democratic during the occupation, this happened before Shoup's arrival. Popular resistance to tax increases, linked to increasingly widespread resentment of the American occupation and the its deflationary policies, played a significant political role during 1948 and shaped the elections of January 1949. And, there is little evidence that Japanese tax politics became more democratic during the consideration of the Shoup reforms, despite his direct appeals to the Japanese public. With regard to the longer run, it is possible that the Shoup mission did help widen the circle of participation in tax politics.[65] In subsequent years, the Shoup report, because of its broad scope and the clear and non-technical nature of Shoup's writing, often served as a useful textbook and may well have facilitated discussion of tax options by the Japanese tax policy community. (However, with the exception of value added taxation, the Shoup report did not introduce any ideas that were new to Japanese tax experts.) Also, in the years following the occupation, the Japanese government seemed to follow Shoup's recommendation to encourage the production of tax accountants, lawyers and economists, the systematic study of public finance, and the formation of professional organizations such as the Japan Tax Association. However, this policy of encouraging tax professionalism did not necessarily represent anything undamentally new in Japan. And, the new programmes for promoting tax professionalism were not necessarily a consequence of the Shoup mission.

A clearer long-run effect of the Shoup mission was the enhancement of the reputation of tax missions within the tax policy community in the United States. The credentials of the members of the Shoup mission and the myth that it had great success in Japan, made the Shoup mission a model for subsequent missions launched by the United States and entities, such as the International Monetary Fund (IMF), charged with restructuring tax systems of 'developing' or 'emerging' nations.[66] The Shoup mission may still influence American policy-makers. For example, some tax experts suggested that it might serve as a model for go-it-alone efforts by the US Treasury to reconstruct the tax system of Iraq. But before the United States ever adopts the Shoup mission as a model of an instrument of top-down reconstruction on behalf of democracy and economic growth, the Treasury would do well to review carefully the history of tax reform during the American occupation of Japan.[67]

Notes

*This essay is based on two substantially longer essays, 'The Shoup mission and the "reverse course" of the occupation of Japan' and 'The American occupation of Japan and the transfer of tax ideas, 1945–1952', that I wrote for a book-length study of the history and long-term significance of the Shoup mission. Professor Jinno Naohiko of the University of Tokyo, Professor Andrew DeWit of Rikkyo University and I are collaborating on this book. I delivered the first essay at the Conference on Historical Perspectives on Tax Law and Policy, UCLA School of Law, 18 July 2005 and the second at the Conference on Transfers of Ideas about Taxation, Centre for Research in the Arts, Social Sciences and Humanities, University of Cambridge, 17 Sept. 2005.

1 The scholarly literature on this topic is vast, covering the histories of many nations. For analysis of the role of informal empire in the nineteenth-century economic development of the United States, for example, see Mira Wilkins, *The history of foreign investment in the United States to 1914* (Cambridge, Mass., 1989), and Lance E. Davis and Robert J. Cull, 'International capital movements, domestic capital markets, and American economic growth, 1820–1914', in Stanley L. Engerman and Robert E. Gallman (eds), *The Cambridge economic history of the United States*, vol. II (Cambridge, 2000), pp. 733–812 and 950–9 (bibliography).

2 There is much important scholarship on the origins and significance of many of these institutions, such as the International Monetary Fund (IMF), the General Agreement on Tariffs and Trade, the World Bank and the Marshall Plan. But no scholars have asked whether or not in the immediate post-war period, the United States carried its efforts at institutional globalization (or economic Americanization) into the realm of taxation and public finance.

3 See Jinno, 'The "Japanese-model" fiscal system', in Tetsuji Okazaki and Masahiro Okuno-Fujiwara, *The Japanese economic system and its historical origins* (Oxford, 1999), pp. 228–9. Jinno's essay (ibid., pp. 208–38) is the best survey available in English of the history of Japanese taxation and public finance. Among its strengths is its close analysis of the broad institutional setting of public finance. Another fine study of the history of Japanese taxation with the same strength is Andrew P. J. DeWit, 'Trench warfare on the tax fields: fiscal sociology and Japan's centralized tax state' (Ph.D. dissertation, the University of British Columbia, 1997). See also Andrew DeWit, 'Caught over a pork-barrel: decentralizing Japan's 1940 fiscal regime', *Studies in Political Economy*, 57 (1998), pp. 103–27. The most important early studies of the history of Japanese taxation during the American occupation were Saburo Shiomi, *Japan's finance and taxation, 1940–1956* (New York, 1957), which provides excellent detail on the 1940 reforms (pp. 33–52, 127–9), and Martin Bronfenbrenner and Kiichiro Kogiku, 'The aftermath of the Shoup tax reforms' (Parts I and II), *National Tax Journal*, 10 (1957), pp. 236–54, 345–60. Shiomi was a Japanese adviser to the Shoup mission, and Bronfenbrenner served as a tax economist for SCAP during 1949 and 1950.

4 See Jinno, 'The "Japanese-model" fiscal system', p. 233. For reference to other important scholarship by Jinno, see n. 62 below.

5 For the history of SCAP reforms from 1946 into 1948, see Henry Shavell, 'Taxation reform in occupied Japan', *National Tax Journal*, 1 (1948), pp. 127–43, and 'Postwar taxation in Japan', *Journal of Political Economy* (1948). In 1948, Shavell was taxation adviser in the Finance Division, Economic and Scientific Section (ESS), SCAP, and may well have contributed to two other useful histories of Japanese taxation during this period. These are unpublished documents in the SCAP files located in Record Group (RG) 331 of the holdings of the National Archives and Record Administration (NARA). Unless otherwise indicated, all of the archival citations in this chapter are to documents in RG 331 NARA. The two unpublished histories are: General Headquarters (GHQ), ESS, Internal Revenue Division (IRD), 'General survey of Japanese taxation', 6 May 1949, Box 2144, file folder: 'Taxes, Shoup mission 1949'; and Moss, 'Historical summary of the Japanese tax system', 30 June 1951, Box 8377, file folder: 'Historical summary of the Japanese tax system'. See also Shiomi, *Japan's finance and taxation, 1940–1956*, pp. 62–73, 130–2.

6 As John Dower has pointed out, while SCAP eradicated the military and abolished the Home Ministry, the traditional bastion of control over police and local government, SCAP left in place and reinforced the rest of the 'civilian bureaucracy'. SCAP recognized that it 'lacked the linguistic and technocratic capacity to effectively govern the country directly'. See John Dower, *Embracing defeat: Japan in the wake of World War II* (New York, 1999), pp. 212–13.

7 For the 'transmission belt' metaphor, see Theodore Cohen, *Remaking Japan: the American occupation as New Deal* (New York, 1987), p. 426.

8 John Dower writes that there was 'no concrete, systematic attempt to stabilize the Japanese economy and to gear industry for export production' until Jan. 1949, with the arrival of the Dodge mission in Japan. Dower's choice of the adjective 'systematic' is well founded, but the 1947 shift in tax policy by the Department of the Treasury certainly constitutes a 'concrete' effort to stabilize the Japanese economy. And the Treasury's shift in 1947 was important; it was, in fact, the first step in developing a 'systematic' programme. Dower, *Japan in war and peace: selected essays* (New York, 1993), p. 175.

9 At this point, the Treasury's central goals did not include promotion of American capital investment in Japan or the stimulation of American exports to Japan. In this regard, the policy of the United States for stimulating the recovery of Japan seems to have departed significantly from its approach to encouraging the recovery of Germany and, more generally, Western Europe.

10 The ESS had about 500 employees and had the powerful responsibility of supervising the economic ministries, including the MOF and the Bank of Japan. SCAP defined this responsibility to include clearing legislation, including amendments, which had fiscal implications, before the Diet acted upon it. See Justin Williams, 'Completing Japan's political reorientation, 1947–1952: crucial phase of the Allied occupation', *American Historical Review*, 73 (1968), p. 1457; Major General J. A. Lester, Headquarters Eighth Army, 'Surveillance of Japanese tax administration', 21 Jan. 1948, Box 7629, file folder: 'Organization of tax bureau'; Shavell, 'Tax reform in occupied Japan', p. 142.

11 President Truman's secretary of the Treasury, John W. Snyder, described Moss as 'my representative from the Treasury'. See 'Oral history interviews with John W. Snyder', Truman Presidential Library, http://www.trumanlibrary.org/oralhist/snyder36.htm, p. 1415; General Headquarters, Economic and Scientific Section, Internal Revenue

Division, 'General survey of Japanese taxation', 6 May 1949, Box 2144, file folder: 'Taxes, Shoup mission 1949'.

12 Moss to Carl Shoup, 5 April 1949, Box 7637, '9 TR-60 Shoup tax mission'.

13 On both the reforms of local government by SCAP during the early occupation and the offsetting measures undertaken by the Japanese ministries, see Jinno, 'The "Japanese-model" fiscal system', pp. 233–4, and DeWit, 'Trench warfare on the tax fields', pp. 91–6.

14 On Shoup in the New Deal, see Joseph J. Thorndike, III, 'The price of civilization: taxation for depression and war, 1932–1945' (Ph.D. dissertation, Department of History, University of Virginia, 2005), pp. 377–83, 500. In addition to advising the Treasury on national tax policy, Shoup had conducted extensive research on sales taxation and had participated in a Treasury study of public finance in Cuba. See Carl Shoup, *The sales tax in the American states: a study made under the direction of Robert Murray Haig* (New York, 1934); Carl S. Shoup, *The sales tax in France* (New York, 1930); and Roswell Foster Magill, *The Cuban fiscal system: a study made at the request of the secretary of the Treasury* (New York, 1939).

15 Robert M. Haig had defined income as 'the money value of the net accretion of one's economic power between two points of time'. Henry Simons made this definition more explicit, describing income as the 'sum of (1) the market value of rights exercised in consumption and (2) the change in the value of the store of property rights between the beginning and the end of the period in question'. See Robert M. Haig (ed.), 'The general concept of income', in *The federal income tax* (New York, 1921), p. 7, and Henry Simons, *Personal income taxation* (Chicago, 1938), p. 50.

16 William Vickrey, *Agenda for progressive taxation* (New York, 1947), p. 14. This book, based on Vickrey's dissertation, had just appeared, and Shoup recommended it to Moss. Shoup to Moss, 30 Sept. 1949, Box 7637, file folder: '9 TR-60 Shoup tax mission'.

17 Mark Ramseyer and Carl Shoup, 'Japanese taxation: the Shoup mission in retrospect, an interview', *The Japan Foundation Newsletter*, 16 (1989), pp. 5–6.

18 On the post-First World War support for both the Haig–Simons model and cutting the highest marginal rates in the Treasury, see W. Elliot Brownlee, 'Tax regimes, national crisis, and state-building in America', in W. Elliot Brownlee (ed.), *Funding the modern American state, 1941–1995: the rise and fall of the era of easy finance* (Washington, DC and Cambridge, UK, 1996), pp. 99–101; and M. Susan Murname, 'Selling scientific taxation: the Treasury department's campaign for tax reform in the 1920s', *Law & Social Inquiry: Journal of the American Bar Foundation*, 29 (Fall 2004), pp. 819–56. On the cooperation between Shoup and Surrey in the Treasury during the 1930s, see Ramseyer and Shoup, 'Japanese taxation: the Shoup mission in retrospect', p. 5.

19 Moss and Shoup, however, had sought to appoint Japanese economists to the team. Economists Tsuru Shigeto of Tokyo University, Shiomi Saburo of Kyoto University and Ito Han'ya of Hitotsubashi University apparently agreed to serve, but SCAP was willing to appoint them only as 'advisers' to the mission, rather than full-fledged members. Moss to Shoup, 15 January 1949; Moss to Shoup, 10 February 1949; Moss to Shoup, 5 April 1949; Shoup to Moss, 14 April 1949; Moss to Shoup, 23 April 1949; and 5 May 1949, Box 7637, file folder: '9 TR-60 Shoup tax mission'.

20 Secretary of the Treasury Snyder recalled that he intervened to send Joseph Dodge to Japan after General MacArthur 'had had a great number of his staff officers try to undertake ... monetary and educational operations and had not had great success'. Snyder explained: 'We even went so far as to have it specifically understood that

Mr. Dodge could report directly to Washington on his programs.' See 'Oral history interviews with John W. Snyder', Truman Presidential Library, pp. 1405–6.

21 'Tentative preliminary comments on SCAP C-51322 by Ambassador Joseph W. Dodge', Box 8355, file folder: 'Joseph M. Dodge'.

22 Typescript, 'Taxation investigating committee appointed to study improvements in system', Box 7637, '9 TR-60 Shoup tax mission'.

23 Bronfenbrenner and Kogiku, 'The aftermath of the Shoup tax reforms, Part I', pp. 237–8.

24 On the compromise with Ikeda, see Joseph M. Dodge, 'Summary of meeting with Finance Minister Ikeda from 1415 to 1530, 28 March', March 28, 1949, Box 5976, File folder: 'Dodge mission – Jan.–May 1949 meetings with Fin Min Ikeda'.

25 Ikeda quotation, reported by Yoshida Shigeru in *Kaiso Junen* ['Ten Years of Memoirs'] (Tokyo, 1957–58), pp. 231–2, and translated by Jason C. James, 'Japanese tax policy in the wake of the Shoup mission' (Dissertation for Part Two of the tripos in Oriental Studies: Japanese Studies at Cambridge University, 1987), p. 19, in Oriental Studies Faculty Library, University of Cambridge. Shoup later took note of Ikeda's statements in Shoup, 'The tax mission to Japan, 1949–50', in Malcolm Gillis (ed.), *Tax reform in developing countries* (Durham and London, 1989), p. 220, and Shoup, 'Melding architecture and engineering: a personal retrospective on designing tax systems', in Lorraine Eden (ed.), *Retrospectives on public finance* (Durham and London, 1991), p. 23. On the influence of the experience of other nations in establishing the income tax in Japan, see Kotaro Ikeda, 'The establishment of the income tax in Japan (a historical and sociological study)', *Public Finance*, 12 (1957), pp. 161–5, and Shiomi, *Japan's finance and taxation, 1940–1956*, pp. 114–30. The Shiomi quotation is from p. 27.

26 Ikeda quoted by Yoshida Shigaru in Jason C. James, 'Japanese tax policy in the wake of the Shoup mission', p. 19.

27 'Oral history interviews with John W. Snyder', Truman Presidential Library. pp. 1405 and 1927.

28 Moss to Shoup, 5 April 1949, Box 7637, file folder: '9 TR-60 Shoup tax mission'.

29 Radiogram 'For West from Dodge', 19 April 1949, Box 5976, file folder: 'Dodge mission – Jan.–May 1949 reference folder'.

30 Shoup, *Public finance* (New York, 1969), p. 23.

31 Ramseyer and Shoup, 'Japanese taxation: the Shoup mission in retrospect: an interview', pp. 2–3.

32 *Report on Japanese taxation by the Shoup mission* (Tokyo: Supreme Commander for the Allied Powers, 1949), vol. I, pp. 51–5, 83, 105–12; vol. II, pp. 123–31, 165–7, 224.

33 In July, as the mission was drafting its final recommendations, Dodge came down hard on a tentative proposal by Shoup to provide about 100 billion yen of additional tax relief. Dodge reminded Shoup of what he regarded as the basic purpose of revisions in Japanese tax policy. They 'should directly contribute to the development of the means for meeting United States objectives, including the final elimination of the need for United States aid, and the prevention of a revival of inflation'. See 'Tentative preliminary comments on SCAP C-51322 by Ambassador Joseph W. Dodge', Box 8355, file folder: 'Joseph M. Dodge, Teleconference transcript, "Taxation in Japan – Ref. Cable 51322" ', July 1949, Box 8355, file folder: 'Shoup tax mission'.

34 See *Report on Japanese taxation by the Shoup mission*, vol. I, pp. 4–8.

35 Shoup to SCAP, 12 Aug. 1949, enclosed in Radiogram, SCAP to Vorhees, 'Taxation progress report', Aug. 12, 1949, Box 6369, file folder: unmarked.

36 Radiogram, SCAP to Vorhees, 'Taxation progress report', 12 Aug. 1949, Box 6369, unmarked file folder. For the Gillis quotation, see Malcolm Gillis, 'Legacies from

the Shoup tax missions: Asia, Africa, and Latin America', in Eden, *Retrospectives on public finance*, p. 32.

37 Ramseyer and Shoup, 'Japanese taxation: the Shoup mission in retrospect', p. 4.

38 In 1989, Shoup described the net worth tax and undistributed profits tax as 'minor innovations'. Ibid., p. 4.

39 'To West from Shoup', 24 Aug. 1949, Box 6836, file folder: 'Taxation'.

40 Shoup to General Marquat, 27 Aug. 1949, Box 5980, file folder: 'Shoup tax report-1949'.

41 'CIE press conference on summary of recommendations of tax mission, 1000 hours, 26 August, 1949', Box 5386, file folder: 'Shoup tax mission'.

42 The same day Shoup held his news conference, Moss told General Marquat that he recommended bringing the Shoup report 'into the open for free discussion and debate'. Howard Moss, 'Analysis of Shoup tax mission final report', 26 Aug. 1949, Box 5980, file folder: 'Shoup tax report-1949'.

43 Martin Bronfenbrenner claimed that in May 1955 Shoup had told him that he 'anticipated a new Government which might combine Premier Yoshida's willingness to listen to American advice with greater sympathy for fiscal equity than the Yoshida Cabinet's'. See Bronfenbrenner and Kogiku, 'The aftermath of the Shoup tax reforms, Part II', p. 346. At least one of the Japanese advisers to the Shoup mission, Tsuru Shigeto, may have reinforced Shoup's political judgement. Tsuru had been an adviser in the socialist government of Katayama Tetsu in 1947–48 and apparently supported the Shoup proposals for the reform of local government. See Shigeto Tsuru, *Japan's capitalism: creative defeat and beyond* (Cambridge, 1993), pp. 16–18, 53–4. Also, there were signs in 1949, particularly at the prefectural level, that the Socialist Party was making a comeback from its defeat in January. See Robert A. Fearey, *The occupation of Japan, second phase: 1948–50* (New York, 1950), p. 111.

44 *Report on Japanese taxation by the Shoup mission*, vol. I, p. ii.

45 Among the critics was Henry Shavell, the deputy chief of the IRD, who opposed both the value added tax and the accessions tax. His critique of the latter suggested that there had been friction between himself and William Vickrey; Shavell reported that the accessions tax was Vickrey's brainchild and that as an adviser to Puerto Rico Vickrey had forced it on that nation. See Shavell to File, 'Exceptions to the Shoup report – accessions tax, Oct. '9, 1949', Box 7637, file folder: '9 TR-60 Shoup tax mission'; Henry Shavell, 'Value added tax', 3 Dec. 1949, Box 7637, file folder: '10 PE-80 Shoup report and recommendations'.

46 MacArthur to the Prime Minister, 15 Sept. 1949, Box 7637, file folder: '9 TR-60 Shoup tax mission'. In 1989, Shoup recalled incorrectly that MacArthur 'accepted the report in toto and recommended to the prime minister that it be accepted and implemented without change, as a package'. See Shoup, 'The tax mission to Japan, 1949–50', p. 179.

47 Moss to General Marquat, 'Formal release of the Shoup tax report', 10 Sept. 1949, Box 5980, file folder: 'Shoup mission [1949–1950]'.

48 On the crucial leadership role by Moss in this publicity effort, see Stanley S. Surrey to Moss, 17 Oct. 1949, Box 7637, file folder: '9 TR-60 Shoup tax mission'; and Tax Administration Agency, the Japanese Government, 'Table of information activities concerning Shoup recommendation', Box 7631, file folder: 'Shoup recommendations'.

49 On the Second World War models, see Carolyn C. Jones, 'Mass-based income taxation: creating a taxpaying culture, 1940–1952', in Brownlee (ed.), *Funding the modern American state, 1941–1945*, pp. 107–47.

50 Yoshida Shigeru to MacArthur, 16 Sept. 1949, Box 7637, file folder: '9 TR-60 Shoup tax mission'.

51 This was Bronfenbrenner's description of Moss's position. See Bronfenbrenner to Shoup, 22 Oct. 1949, Box 7631, file folder: '9 TR-60 Shoup tax mission'.

52 On the deflationary effects of the Dodge line, see Tsuru, *Japan's capitalism*, pp. 54–5.

53 Moss to Dodge, 'The progress report', 31 Oct. 1949, Box 7637, file folder: '11 RF-11 Dodge reports'; Bronfenbrenner to Shoup, 22 Oct. 1949; Moss to Jerome B. Cohen, 18 Nov. 1949, Box 7631, '9 TR-60 Shoup tax mission'. For the much more harmonious conferences between Dodge and Ikeda, see the various meeting notes kept by Dodge, Box 5977, file folder: 'Dodge mission Nov.–Dec. 1949 meetings'. See also 'State of the national economy speech by finance minister on the occasion of the introduction of the 1949–59 supplemental budget, Nov. 15, 1949', Box 5977, file folder: 'Dodge Mission – November–December 1949 memoranda'.

54 Moss to Shoup, 15 Dec. 1949, Box 7637, file folder: '9 TR-60 Shoup tax mission'.

55 MacArthur to the Prime Minister, 21 March 1950, Box 2144, file folder: 'Equalization grant'. Bronfenbrenner to Carl Shoup, 27 March 1950, Box 8377, file folder: 'Memorandum for Shoup'.

56 On his return to Japan, Ikeda avoided the ESS and the IRD and submitted revised tax proposals directly to Yoshida and MacArthur. Shavell to Shoup, 29 May 1950, Box 7507, file folder: 'Memorandum for Shoup'.

57 See Dower, *Empire and aftermath*, p. 361. Dower comments on this aspect of the Shoup programme as part of an excellent discussion of the issue of local autonomy during the occupation. See, in particular, pp. 356–61. The most thorough discussion of the Shoup programme and public finance is DeWit, 'Trench warfare on the tax fields', especially pp. 96–109.

58 By the time of the quasi-adoption of the VAT, the Americans had given up on it, despite the fact, which Shoup pointed out to MacArthur, that France had adopted a VAT early in 1950. In May 1950, Shoup concluded that adoption of the value added tax should be deferred, perhaps agreeing with Henry Shavell that: 'were it not deferred, I fear that the tax would have been heartlessly sabotaged by the Japanese administrators'. However, in 1950, Shoup did not apologize for the VAT recommendation; in June he pointed out to MacArthur that France had just adopted a VAT. In 1989, however, Shoup suggested that proposing a value added tax had been 'premature'. The net worth tax was 'administratively difficult', he added. 'I'm not sure we would have recommended it had we had more time to think about it.' He concluded: the undistributed profits tax 'perhaps . . . wasn't worth the fuss. 'Shavell to Shoup, 29 May 1950, Box 7507, file folder: 'Memorandum for Shoup'; Shoup to MacArthur, 2 June 1950, Box 5980, file folder: 'Shoup tax report-1949'; Ramseyer and Shoup, 'Japanese taxation: the Shoup mission in retrospect', pp. 3–4.

59 See *Second report on Japanese taxation by the Shoup mission* (Tokyo, Supreme Commander for the Allied Powers, 1950). This follow-up report went to the Japanese government on 20 Sept. 1950. W. F. Marquat to the Japanese government, 'Shoup mission report on Japanese taxation', 20 Sept. 1950, Box 7631, file folder: 'Shoup projects'.

60 For an excellent scorecard for the legislative implementation of the Shoup recommendations, see Bronfenbrenner and Kogiku, 'The aftermath of the Shoup tax reforms', Part I, pp. 245–54. See also Tsuru, *Japan's capitalism*, pp. 104–6.

61 Recently, support for this position has grown among students of the history of Japanese taxation. In 1991, Minoru Nakazato, for example, wrote: 'By the mid-1950s the Japanese tax system bore little resemblance to the report's recommendations', and 'the tax system based on the Shoup report was short lived'. In 1993,

Jinno concluded: 'The Shoup Report ... served mainly to endorse the tax system formed during the war period.' Thus, scholars have come to agree more or less with Bronfenbrenner and Kogiku who wrote in 1957 that the Shoup mission 'proved only a limited and partial success'. See Minoru Nakazato, 'The Shoup report and Japanese development', in Eden (ed.), *Retrospectives on public finance*, pp. 57, 64; Jinno, 'The "Japanese-model" fiscal system', p. 234; and Bronfenbrenner and Kogiku, 'The aftermath of the Shoup tax reforms, Part I', p. 237.

62 For suggestions as to why this may be so, see Jinno, 'The "Japanese-model" fiscal system', especially pp. 235–6, and DeWit, 'Caught over a pork-barrel: decentralizing Japan's 1940 fiscal regime'. Jinno has also addressed this question in his *Shisutemu Kaikaku no Seijikeizaigaku* ['The political economy of structural reforms'] (Tokyo, 1998). Unfortunately, this work is not available in English, but Andrew DeWit has written an extensive review in English. See Andrew DeWit, 'Book review', *Tax Notes International*, 31 Jan. 2000, pp. 533–6.

63 Shoup to MacArthur, 2 June 1950, Box 5980, file folder: 'Shoup tax report-1949'.

64 Ramsayer and Shoup, 'Japanese taxation; the Shoup mission in retrospect', p. 7. For a more detailed account of how Shoup believed his mission improved the tax 'atmosphere' in Japan, see Shoup, 'The tax mission to Japan, 1949–1950', pp. 206–7.

65 For suggestions along these lines see Gillis, 'Legacies from the Shoup tax mission', pp. 41–2.

66 Shoup himself directed reform missions to Venezuela (joined by Stanley Surrey) and Liberia, and undertook a major study of Brazilian public finance in 1964. See Gillis, 'Legacies from the Shoup missions', pp. 42–8, and Charles E. McClure, Jr, 'Income tax reform in Venezuela: thirty years after the Shoup mission', in Eden (ed.), *Retrospectives on public finance*, pp. 67–85; and Carl S. Shoup, 'Retrospectives on tax missions to Venezuela (1959), Brazil (1964), and Liberia (1970)', in Gillis (ed.), *Tax reform in developing countries*, pp. 252–314.

67 For these suggestions, see, for example, Bruce Bartlett, 'Taxing from scratch: Iraq might want to use the Russian flat-tax model', *National Review Online*, 12 April 2003 (http://www.nationalreview.com/nrof_bartlett/barlett042103.asp) and Thomas F. Field, 'The litmus test: taxation in post-Saddam Iraq', *taxanalysts*, 14 April 2003 (http://www.taxanalysts.com). Field, however, did not endorse an independent approach to tax reconstruction. He pointed out that, in contrast with the period of the occupation of Japan, there are now international agencies, most notably the IMF and the World Bank, with 'broad experience in introducing new and restructured tax regimes in a variety of settings'.

10

Tax Policy Transfer to Developing Countries: Politics, Institutions and Experts

Miranda Stewart

> [Tax reform] does not depend merely on the individual goodwill of ministers or on the correct intellectual appreciation of the technical problems involved. It is predominantly a matter of political power.
>
> Nicholas Kaldor[1]

> We are increasingly governed by experts.
>
> David Kennedy[2]

Introduction

Tax ideas have always been transferred across borders. However, since the early 1980s, the transfer of tax ideas has had an increased global significance. Many have identified the 1980s as a global 'decade of tax reform'.[3] To some, this signalled the generation of global tax norms,[4] or a 'remarkable consensus' of experts reflecting a 'virtual revolution in applied tax policies in developed, developing and transition economies'.[5] Others have suggested that 'the tax systems of the major developed countries, if not all countries, will increasingly tend to resemble each other'.[6] These global developments in tax reform were spurred by two significant shifts in the broader economic context. First, the 1980s was 'a decade of economic crisis for many developing countries and slow growth for industrialized countries'.[7] Second, and partly in response to this crisis, the 1980s saw the ascendance of a neo-liberal paradigm which advocated export-led growth and a free market economy, understood as a reduction of the engagement of the state in economic development. Many developing countries undertook structural adjustment reforms under this new paradigm, as a condition of loans and aid from the International Monetary Fund (IMF), World Bank and major country donors such as the United Kingdom.

This chapter discusses the transfer of tax ideas to developing countries since the 1980s through a process of mass production of tax reform in the context of structural adjustment. It examines the specific example of Ghana, which has a history as 'one of the more interesting and successful cases of adjustment in Africa', in an era which also encompassed a peaceful political shift from an authoritarian to a democratic government.[8] This chapter examines Ghana's tax reforms from the start of structural adjustment in 1983, culminating in the effort to enact a value added tax (VAT) in the late 1990s. The chapter aims to illustrate the complex layering of politics and expertise in tax reform at international and national levels, in the context of these particular tax reforms.

Politics and paradigms in tax reform

Tax reform in developing countries since the 1980s has generally been driven by an elite of policy-makers, seeking to apply expert knowledge about new technologies or ideas to enhance revenue-raising, as well as to achieve other policy goals. However, revenue-raising is a coercive political process, requiring negotiation by interests and elites with the state as a locus of power, social organization and redistribution.[9] Taxing and spending 'shifts resources from one segment of society to another, directly or indirectly'.[10] For a government to carry out successful tax reform that will significantly increase tax revenues, it must have political legitimacy and the tax reform itself must be perceived as justified in the broader context of the government's activities. Thus, leaders or elites must negotiate a stable 'fiscal bargain' that achieves quasi-voluntary compliance in the tax system.[11] Ideally, this is achieved through establishing a tax system that is widely perceived as fair, through public processes, 'accompanied by a high degree of negotiation from a wide range of potential taxpayers'.[12]

Since the 1980s, fiscal bargaining by governments has taken place in the context not only of domestic political negotiation but also of international structural adjustment and with the goal of attracting international capital. Conditions and rules established by the international financial institutions (IFIs), the IMF and the World Bank, and the World Trade Organization (WTO) and regional economic organizations, were established that had a significant influence on developing country tax policies. It has been suggested that for many developing countries, external accountability to the IFIs may have become more important than domestic accountability in taxation.[13] Within the IFIs, the paradigm of neo-liberalism established the framework for tax experts engaged in developing country tax reform.[14] The neo-liberal paradigm is most frequently associated with a reduction of the role of government in the economy, including deregulation of markets for capital, goods and services; the liberalization of international trade and investment and removal of protectionist measures; restrictive macroeconomic policy requiring elimination of deficit financing; and a reduction of barriers to national and cross-border investment. Sandford defines tax policy in the 1980s in the following terms:[15]

> Tax reform was part of a programme of pushing back the boundaries of the state, de-regulating, freeing exchange rates, privatizing, promoting

> competition and, in the remaining private sector, increasing managerial efficiency. ... Tax reform in the 'eighties was primarily aimed at minimizing tax distortions, at removing or reducing tax hindrances to the free working of markets ... The phrase which became current in the economic world was that of the 'level playing field'.

For developing countries undergoing structural adjustment, neo-liberalism was associated with a wholesale change in development policy. During the 1950s and 1960s, after independence, many developing countries, including Ghana, adopted protectionist policies and aimed for economic self-sufficiency. Development economists at that time advocated state-managed economic development, giving high priority to industrialization and self-sufficiency.[16] The international context was relevant in that framework only to the extent that since colonial times, many developing countries, including Ghana, had relied heavily on international trade taxes. Tariff protection for domestic industry, input subsidies and favourable domestic tax regimes for particular activities and investments were combined with high taxation of agricultural and mineral export sectors as tools for intervening in the economy.[17]

The call for export-led growth in an open market economy led to a reversal of these policies. Economic globalization, or the influence of global capital, was clearly important in this recasting of tax policy for development, although the extent of this influence is hard to gauge.[18] Bates and Lien suggest that global capital, rather than national capital, farming or labour, may exercise disproportionate influence on developing country economic policies even though it is 'not seizing power nor being conferred political representation'.[19] Whether or not the influence is as significant as that model suggests, the institutionalization of the neo-liberal paradigm and the leverage of international aid and loan flows have directed tax reforms in a manner that is generally amenable to global capital. The influence of global capital may have worked *against* some attempts by tax reformers in IFIs to strengthen tax systems; the continued widespread use of tax incentives for foreign investment may be an example of this.

Two further features of neo-liberalism in the early 1980s had implications for tax reform. First, neo-liberalism was associated with a reduced emphasis on equality and distributive justice. It took more than a decade for development discourse to shift towards a notion of development 'with a human face'.[20] In line with this broader trend, tax policy shifted decisively away from progressive policies. Experts explained that this was a consequence of the failure of tax systems to achieve significant redistribution.[21] This discursive shift has made it more difficult for tax reform discourse to engage with issues of fairness, although acceptance of a tax reform as *fair* may be crucial for the political legitimacy of the reform. Second, a paradox of neo-liberalism in the context of developing countries was its aim of using the mechanisms of the state in order to *reduce* the role of the state in economic development activity.[22] Successful implementation of significant tax reform in developing countries has usually required a major enhancement of state capacity and bureaucratic 'ownership' of tax reform. At the same time, developing country governments were under significant pressure to keep civil service wage bills down and to trim the size of the bureaucracy. This could lead to tensions within bureaucracies for governments seeking to implement reform.

Although the neo-liberal paradigm was fundamental to the shape of tax reform in developing countries in the 1980s, tax reforms did of course take different forms in different times and places. To explain how tax ideas are 'selected, articulated, and then stabilized' in particular developing country tax reforms, this chapter argues, as stated by Kjaer and Pedersen, that 'ideas are always embedded in discourses'.[23] Tax reform discourse at a particular time and place involves the generation of an expert consensus on tax policy within a historically contingent and specific political process. Expert engagement in tax reform has political meaning and analysing the politics of expertise helps to explain differences in application of neo-liberal tax policy, or resistance to the transfer of tax ideas.[24] Steinmo suggests that expert scepticism about the ability of governments to intervene in the economy through the tax system, based on expert professional experience and economic training in the 1970s, was important in the formulation of neo-liberal tax policy during the 1980s.[25] At the same time, tax ideas may themselves help to 'establish the basis for a new and altered politics of taxation', so that tax reform becomes politically feasible following the absorption of new ideas into the discourse.[26]

Institutions, ideas and experts in tax reform

In a developing country context, neo-liberal tax ideas were mediated primarily though experts in the IFIs who combined scepticism about government involvement in the economy with a strong drive to increase tax revenues. Developing countries engaged in structural adjustment faced serious constraints of state capacity and domestic political instability but had to account to the IFIs in carrying out tax reform.

In the 1980s, the IMF became the lead international institution engaged in tax reform in developing countries.[27] Historically, the IMF had not dealt directly with tax and spending policy, considering that these 'were and should remain the government's responsibility': this 'kept the Fund from entering into areas that require[d] judgment of social and political priorities'.[28] The World Bank tended to focus on lending and aid for specific projects or sectors and did not usually address general tax reform.[29] However, under the leadership of capable economists with an interest in tax policy, most importantly Richard Goode during the 1970s and Vito Tanzi, who headed the IMF Fiscal Affairs Department for 20 years from 1981, structural adjustment programmes were expanded to encompass 'the structural and social aspects of fiscal policy' including tax policy, law and administration.[30] Structural adjustment tax reforms were monitored with targets, such as the enactment of a tax law or increasing tax revenues as a proportion of GDP.[31] Failure to perform conditions could lead to interruption or termination of a loan programme. The IMF and World Bank also provided technical assistance in tax reform to many developing countries.[32]

Tax reform under the leadership of the IFIs was primarily the domain of economists. This was in part a consequence of the predominant position of economists in those institutions. In particular, the IMF had always been 'primarily the preserve of economists', while during the 1980s, economists in the World Bank began to be 'heavily involved in all major decisions'.[33] IMF and World Bank economists were also at the heart of the shift towards neo-liberal economic ideas and so tax policies which fit this paradigm became dominant. The 'internationalization of economic training', in part through doctoral study at leading US and European universities and growing employment within the international institutions, created a cadre of economists in developing countries who sought to apply these ideas.[34]

In this context, tax reform quickly grew in importance as part of structural adjustment, as economists deemed that the most significant actions to be taken by developing country governments were *fiscal* – tax increases and expenditure reductions.[35] By the end of the 1980s, Bird could observe that tax reform in developing countries had become a 'speciality' of public finance.[36] In the mid-1990s, Thuronyi listed as necessary for tax reform the involvement of macroeconomists and specialists in public finance, who can determine revenue targets and cash-flow requirements; economists to estimate tax revenues; and economists to help predict the effects on the economy of alternative tax structures, including the effects of taxation on savings, investment, work effort, consumption choices and production methods.[37]

The process of development of tax policy for developing countries – of 'puzzlement' in policy formation, in Hall's analysis, increasingly came to be located within the IFIs, more than in developing country governments, and in that site it was linked to the power associated with external finance.[38] During the 1980s, as in earlier times, IMF economists were well aware of the political sensitivity of taxation.[39] Nonetheless, the practice and writings of IMF experts established a general package of tax reforms for developing countries that emphasized a reduction of taxes on income, capital and exports and an increase in taxes on consumption. The IMF package included a broad-based VAT, at a rate higher than 15 per cent; a low rate, broad-based corporate income tax; a personal income tax with high thresholds and low marginal rates; the goal of 'neutrality' in all taxes achieved by eliminating tax incentives; excises, particularly on petroleum; and the reduction and eventual elimination of import and export tariffs.[40]

While economists dominated tax policy formulation, the implementation of tax reform requires a cooperative interdisciplinary effort.[41] It requires tax administration specialists; technical tax specialists (usually lawyers, accountants or in some cases economists), who are familiar with the detailed operation of particular types of provisions and can design detailed rules; and legislative drafters with experience in drafting tax legislation.[42] Tax lawyers played a significant role in transplanting models of tax law, as did lawyers who worked on other adjustment reforms, such as the establishment of corporate regulatory regimes and bankruptcy laws. Many such reforms were carried out through a 'massive transfer of legal code'.[43] Tax law expertise came from the IMF Legal Department and consultants to the IMF and the World Bank, as well as developed country treasuries, or consultants such as the UK Crown Agents, a non-profit company that is linked to the UK Department for International Development. Sometimes, tax laws were transplanted from other countries or model laws were developed and applied by tax experts.[44] More broadly, neo-liberalism incorporated a certain faith in law reform to establish the rules for the global market; in particular, lawyers were crucial in establishing the WTO system for international trade. The WTO does not directly regulate taxation (in general) but WTO rules and principles generate the powerful global norm of the 'level playing field' for trade taxation and tariff reduction. The move to enact the VAT to replace export taxes in developing countries world-wide is largely because of its conformity with WTO norms. Yet this trade-focused tax reform has sometimes led to a 'fiscal squeeze' for developing countries, putting increased pressure on raising tax revenues.[45]

Many commentators have observed that the VAT is the success story of global tax policy transfer since the 1970s.[46] The IMF has been pre-eminent in the spread of the VAT into developing countries, and this process is argued by the IMF to have been largely successful.[47] From the mid-1980s to the mid-1990s, 16 middle-income countries engaged in structural adjustment introduced some form of VAT.[48] Since the mid-1990s, more than 20 low-income countries, including Ghana, have introduced a VAT. If properly implemented and administered, experience in developed and developing countries indicates that the VAT is a very successful revenue-raiser. In its ideal form, the VAT taxes imports uniformly and exports are free of tax. Nonetheless, the VAT is a fairly complex tax.[49] In the more common 'invoice-credit' method, it is levied at a flat rate on each tier of business in the supply chain from producer to consumer, in respect of all goods and services consumed domestically. In practice, the VAT commonly has a number of exemptions or reduced rates because it is perceived as being regressive, or unfair, in imposing a heavy tax burden on poor consumers.

As mentioned, the VAT is attractive because it complies with WTO norms and it should generate a steady revenue stream for governments. On the other hand, it is frequently unpopular with taxpayers and businesses, who must collect and remit the tax. It requires significant compliance activity, while the business bears the risk of slow or no refunds and of difficulty in passing on the tax in consumer prices. Country experiences with newly introduced VATs have varied significantly. Many countries implemented VATs with 'undesirable features' that departed from 'best practice' structures.[50] These VATs usually had numerous exemptions and differential tax rates and frequently continued to tax exports. The IMF has required countries to carry out ongoing reforms to their VATs, in particular the removal of exemptions; modifying taxation of imports and zero-rating exports; decreasing the number of rates and increasing the main VAT rate.

The tax reform experiences of the 1980s brought home to tax experts that good administration was essential to the successful transfer of tax ideas. By 1990, an influential reformer in the IMF said, '[i]n developing countries, tax administration *is* tax policy'.[51] However, the increased attention given to tax administration reform by experts in the IFIs did not necessarily mean that the simplest tax structures were established. The VAT in particular was a new and complex tax that required significant compliance and monitoring activity. It seems to have been favoured by the IMF as a 'catalyst' for reform of governmental tax agencies *because* it required a substantial effort in administration.[52] Tax experts sought increased intervention and (re)construction of agencies of the reforming state, for example, the establishment of a new revenue agency, taxpayer identification systems or audit and collection processes, to enable implementation of the VAT.

The transfer of tax ideas to Ghana

1. The historical context

The independent state of Ghana was established in 1957, under the leadership of Nkrumah, based on the territory of the British colony of the Gold Coast.[53] Slave trading had been the mainstay of the Gold Coast economy in earlier times, but in the twentieth century export staples of cocoa and gold were established. Cocoa remains a primary export of Ghana today. Ghana began independence in a relatively good economic position, in terms of infrastructure, foreign exchange and the quality of its civil service. However, from the 1960s, Ghana's economy began to decline. Killick chronicles this decline as a failure of development economics in action.[54] Herbst puts it more strongly: 'the Ghanaian experience stands out for the comprehensiveness with which successive governments pursued economic destruction'.[55]

Like many other newly independent countries, Ghana was heavily dependent on trade taxes: in 1951, 35 per cent of Ghana's tax revenues were import duties; 24 per cent were export duties (largely on cocoa); and 20 per cent were income taxes collected mostly from companies conducting import or export activities.[56] The state Cocoa Marketing Board also levied a large implicit tax on cocoa exports by maintaining producer prices at a rate considerably lower than the export price. The structure of Ghana's economy has meant that over-reliance on cocoa export revenues has been a particularly difficult habit to break. The late 1960s saw an apparent shift in the tax mix towards corporate and personal income taxes and certain excise and import taxes but this did not last. As the world cocoa price increased, reliance on cocoa revenues increased again, so that in the early 1970s, cocoa was again the 'milch cow of the Ghanaian state'.[57]

Nonetheless, Ghana's 'tax effort' reached 16 per cent of GDP in 1965, large by comparison with other developing countries. Killick observed that 'it cannot be said of the Nkrumah government that it lacked the will to tax the country to finance its expenditure proposals'.[58] Nkrumah's goal was self-sufficiency and Ghana sought out and received little foreign financial assistance or investment. However, the Nkrumah government could not control expenditures and was continually in deficit; further, most of its expenditures generated little return, a source of 'popular disenchantment with the regime'.[59] In 1965, Nkrumah's government sought IMF and World Bank financing but did not agree to the conditions of a substantial reduction of government spending. Nkrumah was ousted in a coup in 1966.

The new government formed by the National Liberation Council (NLC) did obtain an IMF stand-by loan in 1966–68 and over the next few years, Ghana received substantial foreign aid and concessional trade credit from several countries including the UK and the United States.[60] This engagement with international lenders entailed conditions of reducing the fiscal deficit, which could not be met by the NLC, as it failed to decrease expenditures significantly, or to increase tax revenues. Indeed, the NLC aimed to reduce the tax burden 'on the majority of our people' by cutting taxes on income and on imports.[61] Personal income taxes seem to have been keenly felt, although collecting relatively little revenue, while import taxes were unpopular because they kept the price of many goods high. The NLC also attempted to introduce a more open trade and capital policy at this time, by decontrolling imports and devaluing the currency. This led only to an explosion of imports and a massive trade deficit and the liberalization was soon wound back.[62]

No further attempt at major economic reform occurred in the 1970s and commentators argue that under successive governments, Ghana dived 'into the abyss' of national poverty.[63] The people responded to a 'vampiric' government[64] by shifting activities from the formal market economy to subsistence; through widespread profiteering – *kalabule* – and corruption; and through mass emigration of skilled and unskilled workers. In 1979, charismatic leader Jerry Rawlings came to power by a coup. In 1983, against all expectations, Rawlings and the National Democratic Council (NDC) set Ghana on a course of sustained engagement with the IMF and international donors that has lasted to the present day. This effort at structural adjustment led Ghana to be held up as a model borrower with an 'astonishing' record of compliance with IMF conditions.[65] In 1992, Ghana adopted a system of parliamentary democracy. It continued to carry out structural adjustment reforms in a democratic environment.[66]

2. Tax reform under structural adjustment

By 1982, Ghana's tax revenue had declined to 4.6 per cent of GDP. There is no doubt that 'the fiscal needs of the state were the prime force driving reform'.[67]

The decline in revenues seems to have been caused by the withdrawal of the taxpaying community from the formal market and the shrinking of production, as well as poor tax administration.[68] The public had come to perceive the tax system as unfair and it was believed that evasion was prevalent among those who remained in the formal economy, for example, 'lawyers, medical practitioners, accountants and property owners'.[69] One of the first actions of the NDC was to constitute a Citizens Vetting Committee and a National Investigations Committee, aimed at carrying out a 'war' against tax evaders in the self-employed sector.[70]

The first goals of tax reform under structural adjustment were to increase tax revenues through improved enforcement and to shift the tax burden away from the export cocoa sector. Tax collections were affected by other economic changes required by the IMF, most importantly a large devaluation of the currency. Revenues in this early phase were increased by the windfall derived from export taxes generated by currency devaluation. Increased tax was collected on petroleum, following an increase in import prices. The shift from taxing exports to imports, particularly petroleum, caused price increases and an effective redistribution of the tax burden from rural to urban populations in Ghana and has been an ongoing source of hardship and discontent, with ramifications for later tax reforms including the VAT reform.[71]

Tax reforms later in the 1980s focused on reducing taxes on income and capital and introducing incentives for investment. Ghana provided tax incentives to domestic and foreign investors in the 1985 Investment Code. Between 1988 and 1991, the corporate tax rate was lowered from 55 to 35 per cent for a range of industries. The capital gains tax rate was reduced to 5 per cent and certain share gains were exempt. Dividend withholding tax was reduced from 30 to 15 per cent. Personal income taxes were reduced through adjustments in personal allowances and tax brackets in 1987–89 and 1991 and a cut in the top marginal rate from 55 to 25 per cent. Ghana also reformed its domestic sales tax at this time, increasing the rate to 15 per cent. While most of these reforms comprised tax *cuts*, corporate tax revenues increased 'owing in large part to a strengthening in company profitability and major improvements in tax administration', so that tax revenues reached 12 per cent of GDP in the early 1990s.[72] Administrative reforms included establishment of an autonomous revenue service which was considered 'the most "dynamic" and "highly motivated" department in a public service otherwise characterized by lethargy'.[73] Revenue officials were by far the greatest beneficiaries of World Bank grants to study abroad during this period.[74]

In spite of this success, tax revenues again fell short of budgeted levels by 1990. Unlike in earlier decades, Ghana had by this time become heavily dependent on *external* financing: external loans and aid made up more than 10 per cent of GDP in 1990. In 1993, the year after the first democratic election, Ghana had large deficits and failed to meet most conditionality targets. Finance Minister Botchwey stated in 1995 that 'the basic issue of voluntary compliance is still far from satisfactory'.[75] In an attempt to bolster the flagging economy, Ghana enacted more incentives for foreign investment. The Ghana Investment Promotion Centre Act 1994 reduced corporate tax for exports (apart from cocoa) as low as 8 per cent and for hotels to 25 per cent, and allowed 75 per cent of capital investment to be written off against tax in the first year of operation, as well as providing tax holidays in real estate, agriculture and banking, accelerated depreciation and loss carryovers.[76]

3. The VAT

Ghana's VAT reform of 1995 was 'probably the most significant economic regulation in Ghana since the inception of the country's structural reform program in 1980'.[77] The Value Added Tax Act 1994 and accompanying Regulations were passed by the Ghanaian parliament in February 1995. The VAT had a flat rate of 17.5 per cent and exempted education, health and basic foodstuffs, financial services and some kinds of machinery and equipment. The threshold for registration of businesses in the VAT system was set at 25 million cedi (about USD15,000), an amount that brought into the tax base many in the traditionally 'untouchable' small business sector.[78] Although it was initially to be collected by the customs service, an independent VAT service was established to administer the VAT. The VAT replaced the old Ghanaian sales tax, which had a rate of 15 per cent and a significantly smaller base.

In March 1995, the VAT began to be collected. Two months later, in May 1995, the VAT was repealed, following riots. Labour unions, the unemployed, youths and students joined in a coalition called *Kume Preko* ('kill me now') and mounted what has been called 'one of the most extensive and effective anti-government demonstrations in Ghana'.[79] The protestors referred to the VAT as the 'value added troubles' or 'value added toothache' and confrontations between pro-VAT and anti-VAT supporters left four dead, many injured, and considerable property damage, a shocking event in a generally peaceful country.[80]

Many specific reasons have been suggested for the dramatic failure of the VAT reform in 1995.[81] The VAT rate of 17.5 per cent was higher than the 15 per cent rate of the pre-existing sales tax, covered a broader range of goods and services and was also significantly higher than the VAT rate in neighbouring Nigeria, recently enacted at only a 5 per cent rate. Many small businesses were included within the VAT collection base because of the low business registration threshold. Implementation appears to have been rushed and there was a tight timeline of one month for registration of suppliers. The VAT requires the use of accounting and invoice systems in the taxpayer businesses and there were many fears about complexity. The interaction of the VAT with tariffs caused problems. There was internal politicking and difficulties in the administration, as a result of the establishment of the new VAT collection agency in place of the customs service.

There is also a broader issue of failure of political legitimacy of the VAT reform. Panford's interpretation that 'the demonstrations may have symbolized deeper and growing popular discontent with the onerous cost of living in Ghana' seems plausible:[82]

> The bloodshed and injuries suffered during the anti-VAT demonstrations signify the deep-seated and popular dissatisfaction with living and working conditions in Ghana ... The repeal of the VAT marked a turning point in Ghana: in a rare moment, public pressure led a government to abandon an unpopular policy.

Although enacted by an elected parliament (albeit under the continuing autocratic leadership of Rawlings), the VAT reform of 1995 was the product of significant engagement of external and domestic expertise. It was led by a bureaucratic and political elite in need of increased tax revenues, in a long-standing relationship with external tax experts in the IFIs and lender governments. Some have suggested that the VAT policy originated from the Ministry of Finance 'as part of an effort to strengthen the economic recovery program supported by the World Bank and the IMF'.[83] Ghanaian bureaucrat Seth Terkper, a member of the team that introduced the VAT, states that design of the VAT began in November 1992 within the Ministry of Finance, and included 'two years of careful planning by a technical committee, a supervisory body to this committee and consultants from Crown Agents (UK)'.[84] He also refers to 'a joint study by Crown Agents (UK) and the Harvard Institute for International Development' which, 'together with other reviews of Ghana's tax regime' was 'unambiguous in suggesting an overhaul of both the structure and administration of the sales tax regime'.[85] Technical assistance was provided by the UK Crown Agents, the World Bank and the UK Overseas Development Administration.[86]

The lack of attention paid to domestic political issues in pushing through the reform can be largely explained by this close historical engagement of Ghana's governmental elite with the IFIs. From 1983, the structural adjustment programme seems to have been agreed through secret policy negotiations between the Rawlings government and the IMF.[87] While commentators are unable to agree on whether the 1983 economic programme was 'indigenous or a World Bank/IMF diktat',[88] all have highlighted the ongoing involvement of the IMF and World Bank in Ghana's policy formulation. This influence was assured by the need for external surveillance of the structural adjustment programme, requiring 'constant interaction among the IMF, the World Bank, and Ghanaian civil servants'.[89]

The Ghanaian parliament, in existence only since 1992, appeared to be aware of public apprehension about the VAT before its initial enactment. The Finance Committee of the parliament postponed debate to allow public education and held some hearings, and submissions were made by some business and labour organizations expressing fears about regressivity and compliance issues. However, rather than seriously addressing these concerns, the chairman of the committee took the view publicly that the VAT was the only course of action – 'there was no known alternative to a VAT for widening the tax base in Ghana'.[90] In the end, the legislation was rushed through with little parliamentary debate and it was noted in the parliament that there had been no locally prepared economic, legal or political research or statistics on distribution of the tax burden, compliance issues and other sensitive factors.[91] Terkper states that early in the VAT process, there were 'seminars and consultations with academics, private sector groups, and senior government officials'.[92] However, the little consultation that took place did not focus on negotiation or compromise in policy formation with business, labour or politicians. Few formal policy consultation processes existed, although sometimes special interests, most influentially the local directors of multi-national corporations, could get a hearing.[93] Non-government experts, such as lawyers or economists in the university or the professions, were not involved in the two-year process of policy formation and design of the VAT. Ghana had experienced a significant 'brain drain' in previous decades, so that there was a lack of local expert resources, and the pattern of policy formation established by Rawlings had excluded non-government experts, perhaps because they were perceived to be anti-adjustment and critical of the government. Thus, 'the only sources of technical analysis and evaluation remained the government itself, the multilateral and allied agencies, and various consultants associated with these'.[94]

The 1995 VAT failure led to the resignation of Minister Botchwey, who had been a key player in Ghana's economic reforms since 1983.[95] The former sales tax was immediately reinstated, with some expansion of a tax on services. Nonetheless, the Rawlings government succeeded in obtaining re-election in 1996. It did not abandon the VAT and Ghana's IMF Letters of Intent indicate its serious revenue needs and the government's intention to re-enact the VAT as soon as possible. It succeeded in doing so in 1998, with further assistance from the UK Department for International Development.

The 1998 VAT reform involved a concerted effort of political consultation and compromise. A year after the riots, the government initiated a consultation with individuals, labour unions and professional groups, moderated by the World Bank, which resulted in a recommendation to reintroduce the VAT. Business leaders, in particular local directors of multinationals such as Unilever, called strongly for its reintroduction.[96] A VAT Oversight Committee was established which included professional associations and industry bodies, such as the Ghana Urban Traders' Association. The government also carried out further widespread consultations and education of members of parliament and of the public.[97] The opposing party continued to express its opposition to the VAT and there appears to have been a broad public debate about it. The government obtained feedback on key concerns of the public, which included the potential for corruption in VAT administration and, more fundamentally, whether the public would benefit from the increased tax revenues.[98] This public debate led to some important compromises. Most importantly, the VAT was introduced in 1998 with a rate of only 10 per cent, recommended by the parliamentary Finance Committee and by most industry and labour groups, and with an increased range of exemptions.[99] The registration threshold for businesses was significantly increased to 200 million cedi (approximately $80,000 at that time), several times that enacted in 1995. This carved out most of the small traders engaged in the Ghanaian economy. In effect, the problem of taxing that 'hard to tax' informal sector was left for another day.

The successful implementation of the VAT in 1998 reveals a new fiscal bargain, entailing significant concessions made by the government both to popular expectations of fairness and to specific interests. This compromise meant that the VAT would raise less revenue than had been hoped, and it has continued to constrain VAT reform. After pressure from the IMF, the government increased the VAT rate to 12.5 per cent in 2000, at the cost of another political compromise, in which the government promised to match the additional revenues in a specific education trust fund designed to ease the burden on families posed by the gradual elimination of higher education subsidies.[100] A year later, the NDC lost the 2001 elections, which saw the first transition of power to a new government since 1983. The new government (who in opposition had always opposed the VAT) stated that it would not increase the VAT rate further.[101]

The politics of tax policy transfer

In the last two decades, the transfer of tax policy ideas into developing countries has come to be mediated largely through the IFIs. Developing countries have had to generate a significant increase in tax revenues, so as to ensure payment of international debt and the funding of development policies. This revenue imperative has put pressure on state administrative capacity and on political negotiations in establishing tax reform in many countries. At the same time, developing countries have sought increased foreign investment and export-led growth, so that reforms have focused on the reduction of taxes on trade and capital and a shift of the tax burden to domestic consumption.

This chapter examined the case study of Ghana's tax reforms in the context of structural adjustment from the 1980s, following two decades of economic decline. After more than a decade of structural adjustment, the discourse of tax reform in Ghana was forged through an 'intimate articulation'[102] of international experts and the close-knit governmental elite. In this context, the VAT was perceived as a necessary economic reform that would satisfy the requirements of the IFIs, comply with WTO requirements and achieve the revenue goals of the government. The previous decade of IMF-led VAT reforms had enabled development of a substantial body of expert knowledge about the VAT, which expertise could be transferred, it seemed, to Ghana without too much difficulty.

In 1995, Ghana's VAT was introduced in a context where, in spite of improved tax administration, the state had reached the limits of its capacity in collection of taxes on capital and income. High taxes on petroleum and imports, currency devaluation and lack of government services had contributed to hardship in peoples' daily lives and to scepticism about government expenditures. In the context of a newly formed democracy, the people had become exhausted by structural adjustment. The visibility of the VAT, its high rate and broad reach, combined with the lack of consultation, rushed implementation and the public's fear of increased prices, led to a breakdown in the 'fiscal bargain' and to the VAT revolt.

It was another three years before a new 'fiscal bargain' could be instituted in Ghana. By 1998, collective knowledge about the VAT and the engagement of the public in the process of tax reform enabled the VAT to be enacted, with significant compromises in terms of revenue collection and coverage of the VAT. Since then, the VAT has proved to be a stable revenue-raiser, generating revenues of about 5 per cent of GDP in 2003, while Ghana's overall tax level increased to 20 per cent of GDP by 2003.[103] Ghana's economic position has been improved as significant changes have taken place in the international economic arena. Most importantly, Highly Indebted Poor Country debt relief, for which Ghana is eligible, was agreed by the IMF and other external creditors and Ghana is engaged in a poverty reduction strategy process in close consultation with the IMF and the World Bank.

Kaldor wrote, perhaps despairingly, in 1963 that successful tax reform is ultimately a matter of political power not technical expertise. However, during the 1980s, the global institutional response to the 'failure' of economic development was to enhance the power of experts in the IFIs, who entered into a close engagement with structural economic reform, including tax reform, particularly in poor countries. Leveraged through conditionality of loans and aid, the detailed engagement of the IFIs in tax reform continues to this day. The IMF has consolidated a body of tax expertise that has enabled it to lead a mass response to fiscal crisis. This has contributed to the generation of global tax norms including lower tax rates on capital and a reduction in trade tariffs, and to the spread of particular taxes, most importantly the VAT, across the globe.

Like other governments that maintained structural adjustment over a significant period, the Ghanaian government built long-term relationships with experts in the IFIs. The close-knit relationship of key individuals within the Rawlings government with external advisers in the IFIs facilitated this expert governance and enabled translation of neo-liberal tax policy into Ghanaian law. During the 1980s, the Ghanaian government reduced taxes on exports, increased them on petroleum and imports, reduced income taxes on capital, enacted incentives to encourage foreign investment and created a new revenue agency. It ultimately sought to shift towards mass consumption taxation through enactment of the VAT. Yet, to be successful in the context of Ghana's history of 'belt tightening' under structural adjustment, the tax reform consensus regarding the VAT had to reflect political, institutional and economic conditions within Ghana. Policy-makers in the international sphere are prone to imagining themselves as operating 'beyond culture and politics', in 'a neutral world of expertise'.[104] Sustainable tax policy transfer requires domestic political legitimacy, although the fiscal bargain is increasingly negotiated subject to global discursive constraints.

Notes

1 Nicholas Kaldor, 'Will underdeveloped countries learn to tax?' *Foreign Affairs*, 41 (1963) pp. 410–18, at p. 418.
2 David Kennedy, 'Challenging expert rule: the politics of global governance', *Sydney Law Review*, 27 (2004), pp. 5–28, at p. 6.
3 See Joseph Pechman (ed.), *World tax reform: a progress report* (Washington, DC, 1988); Michael J. Boskin and Charles E. McLure Jr (eds), *World tax reform: case studies of developed and developing countries* (San Francisco, 1990); Cedric Sandford, *Successful tax reform: lessons from an analysis of tax reform in six countries* (Bath, 1993); Malcolm Gillis (ed.), *Tax reform in developing countries* (Durham, 1989).
4 John L. Campbell and Ove K. Pedersen (eds), *The rise of neoliberalism and institutional analysis* (Princeton, 2001), 'Introduction', pp. 1–23, at p. 1.
5 Glenn P. Jenkins, 'Introduction' to Ward Hussey and Donald Lubick, *Basic world tax code and commentary* (Virginia, 1996), at p. iii.
6 Sandford, *Successful tax reform*, p. 222.
7 Miles Kahler, 'Orthodoxy and its alternatives: explaining approaches to stabilization and adjustment' in Joan Nelson (ed.), *Economic crisis and policy choice: the politics of adjustment in the third world* (New Jersey, 1990), pp. 33–61, at p. 33.
8 Stephen Younger, 'Estimating tax incidence in Ghana using household data' in David E. Sahn (ed.), *Economic reform and the poor in Africa* (Oxford, 1996), pp. 231–53; and see Sergio Pereira Leite, Anthony Pellechio, Luisa Zanforlin, Girma Begashaw, Stafania Farbizio and Joachim Harnack, *Ghana: economic development in a democratic environment*, IMF Occasional Paper 199 (Washington, DC, 2000).
9 Sven Steinmo, *Taxation and democracy: Swedish, British and American approaches to financing the modern state* (New Haven, 1993); Andrew C. Gould and Peter J. Baker, 'Democracy and taxation', *Annual Review of Political Science*, 5 (2002), pp. 87–110, at p. 91; John Campbell, 'The state and fiscal sociology', *Annual Review of Sociology*, 19 (1993), pp. 163–85.
10 United Nations, *World economic and social survey* (New York, 1997), p. 65.
11 Margaret Levi, *Of rule and revenue* (Berkeley and Los Angeles, 1988), p. 49.
12 Ibid.
13 Siri Gloppen and Lise Rakner, 'Accountability through tax reform? Reflections from Sub-Saharan Africa', in Mick Moore and Lise Rakner (eds), *The new politics of taxation and accountability, Institute of Development Studies Bulletin*, 33 (2002), pp. 30–40, at p. 38.
14 Campbell and Pederson, *The rise of neoliberalism*, pp. 170–1; Peter Hall, 'Policy paradigms, social learning and the state: the case of economic policy making in Britain', *Comparative Politics*, 25 (1993), pp. 275–96, at p. 279; Ha-Joon Chang, *Kicking away the ladder: development strategy in historical perspective* (London, 2002), p. 1.

15 Sandford, *Successful tax reform*, p. 21.
16 Dharam Ghai (ed.), *The IMF and the south: the social impact of crisis and adjustment* (London, 1991), 'Introduction', pp. 1–9, at p. 3.
17 Ibid.; and see Gillis, 'Towards a taxonomy of tax reform', in *Tax reform in developing countries*, pp. 7–26, at pp. 19–20.
18 Vito Tanzi, 'The impact of economic globalization on taxation', *Bulletin of the International Bureau of Fiscal Documentation*, 52 (1998), pp. 339–43.
19 Robert Bates and D. D. Lien, 'A note on taxation, development and representative government', *Politics and Society*, 14 (1985), pp. 53–70. Developed countries seem able to collect taxes on capital even in the context of economic globalization: M. P. Devereux, R. Griffith and A. Klemm, 'Corporate income tax reforms and international tax competition', *Economic Policy*, 35 (2002), pp. 451–86; Duane Swank and Sven Steinmo, 'The new political economy of taxation in advanced capitalist democracies', *American Journal of Political Science*, 46 (2002), pp. 642–55.
20 France Stewart, *Adjustment and poverty: options and choices* (London, 1995).
21 A recent discussion that puts this position strongly is Eric M. Zolt and Richard M. Bird, 'Redistribution via taxation: the limited role of personal income tax in developing countries', *UCLA Law Review*, 52 (2005) pp. 1627–94.
22 Kahler, *Orthodoxy and its alternatives*, p. 55.
23 Peter Kjaer and Ove Pedersen, 'Translating liberalization: neoliberalism in the Danish negotiated economy', in Campbell and Pederson, *The rise of neoliberalism*, pp. 219–48, at pp. 220–1.
24 Ibid.; and see Michel Foucault, 'Politics and the study of discourse', in Graham Burchell, Colin Gordon and Peter Miller (eds), *The Foucault effect: studies in governmentality* (Chicago, 1991), pp. 53–72, at p. 59.
25 Sven Steinmo, 'The evolution of policy ideas: tax policy in the 20th century', *British Journal of Politics and International Relations*, 5 (2003), pp. 206–36, p. 224.
26 Steinmo, *Taxation and democracy*, p. 204.
27 For a more detailed discussion of the role of the IFIs in tax reform, see Miranda Stewart, 'Global trajectories of tax reform: mapping tax reform in developing and transition countries', *Harvard International Law Journal*, 44 (2003), pp. 140–90; Miranda Stewart and Sunita Jogarajan, 'The International Monetary Fund and tax reform', *British Tax Review* [2004], pp. 146–75.
28 J. J. Polak, 'The changing nature of Fund conditionality', *Essays in International Finance*, No. 185 (Princeton, 1991), p. 39.
29 World Bank, *Lessons of tax reform* (Washington, DC, 1991), p. 64.
30 Vito Tanzi, 'The changing role of fiscal policy in Fund policy advice', *IMF Seminar Paper* (Washington, DC, 1997), p. 1.
31 G. T. Abed, *Fiscal reforms in low-income countries: experience under IMF-supported programs*, IMF Occasional Paper No. 160 (Washington, DC, 1998), p. 12.
32 See IMF, *Review of technical assistance policy and experience* (Washington, DC, 2002).
33 Richard Goode and Andrew M. Kamarck, 'The International Monetary Fund and the World Bank' in Joseph Pechman (ed.), *The role of the economist in government* (New York, 1989), pp. 231–54, at pp. 232–3.
34 Kahler, *Orthodoxy and its alternatives*, p. 59.
35 Goode and Kamarck, *The IMF and the World Bank*, p. 241.
36 Richard M. Bird, *Tax policy and economic development* (Baltimore, 1992), p. 183.
37 Victor Thuronyi (ed.), *Tax law design and drafting*, 1 (Washington, DC, 1996), 'Introduction', pp. xxvii–xxxi, at p. xxix.
38 Hall, *Policy paradigms*, p. 276.
39 Goode and Kamarck, *The IMF and the World Bank*, p. 241.

40 For more detail, see Parthasarathi Shome (ed.), *Tax policy handbook* (Washington, DC, 1995); Vito Tanzi and Howell Zee, 'Tax policy for emerging markets: developing countries', IMF Working Paper 2000/35 (Washington, DC, 2000), p. 56.
41 Richard Gordon and Victor Thuronyi, 'Tax legislative process', in Thuronyi (ed.), *Tax law design*, pp. 1–14, at p. 4.
42 Thuronyi, *Tax law design*, p. xxix.
43 See Tim Lindsey (ed.), *Law reform in developing and transition countries* (New York, 2006); Katharina Pistor and Philip A. Wellons, *The role of law and legal institutions in Asian economic development 1960–1995* (New York, 1999).
44 See e.g. the models developed by the IMF in recent years (at www.imf.org); an older example is Ward Hussey and Donald Lubick, *Basic world tax code and commentary* (Virginia, 1996).
45 Isabelle and Grunberg, 'Double jeopardy: globalization, liberalization and the fiscal squeeze', *World Development*, 26 (1998), pp. 591–605.
46 Ken Messere, *Tax policy in OECD countries: choices and conflicts* (The Netherlands, 1993), at p. 368.
47 G. R. Olsen, 'The World Bank and the IMF: tax, democracy and shrinking aid in Sub-Saharan Africa', *Forum for Development Studies*, 28 (2001), pp. 147–72, at p. 152.
48 Abed, *Fiscal reforms in low-income countries*, p. 20.
49 See Alan Tait, *Value added tax: administrative and policy issues* (Washington, DC, 1991).
50 Abed, *Fiscal reforms in low-income countries*, p. 20.
51 Milka Casanegra de Jantscher and Richard Bird (eds), 'The reform of tax administration', in *Improving tax administration in developing countries* (Washington, DC, 1992), pp. 1–22, at p. 1.
52 Abed, *Fiscal reforms in low-income countries*, p. 11.
53 As the first African state to achieve independence, Ghana has been much studied. This chapter draws from Douglas Rimmer, *Staying poor: Ghana's political economy 1950–1990* (Washington, DC, 1992); Jeffrey Herbst, *The politics of reform in Ghana, 1982–1991* (Berkeley, Calif., 1993) and Tony Killick, *Development economics in action: a study of economic policies in Ghana* (London, 1978).
54 Killick, *Development economics in action.*
55 Herbst, *The politics of reform in Ghana*, p. 17.
56 Rimmer, *Staying poor*, p. 40. This tax structure was common in many developing countries: Vito Tanzi, 'Taxation in developing countries', in Luigi Bernardi and Jeffrey Owens (eds), *Tax systems in North Africa and European countries* (Deventer, 1994), pp. 1–22.
57 Rimmer, *Staying poor*, p. 113.
58 Killick, *Development economics in action*, pp. 147–8.
59 Rimmer, *Staying poor*, p. 80.
60 Killick, *Development economics in action*, p. 114 and Table 5.4.
61 Ibid., pp. 305, 323 n. 18.
62 Ibid., p. 302.
63 Rimmer, *Staying poor*, p. 133.
64 J. H. Frimpong-Ansah, *The vampire state in Africa: the political economy of decline in Ghana* (London, 1991), n. 17.
65 Herbst, *The politics of reform in Ghana*, p. 35; Ishan Kapur, Michael T. Hadjimichael, Paul Louis Ceriel Hilbers, Jerald Alan Schiff and Philippe Szymczak, *Ghana: adjustment and growth, 1983–1991*, IMF Occasional Paper 86 (Washington, DC, 1991), p. 1.
66 Leite, *Ghana: economic development in a democratic environment.*

67 Eboe Hutchful, *Ghana's adjustment experience: the paradox of reform* (Geneva, 2002), p. 165.
68 Kapur, *Ghana: adjustment and growth*, p. 2.
69 Kwabena Donkor, *Structural adjustment and mass poverty in Ghana* (Aldershot and Brookfield, 1997), p. 132.
70 Donkor, *Structural adjustment*, p. 134; Hutchful, *Ghana's adjustment experience*, p. 35.
71 See especially Donkor, *Structural adjustment* and Lynne Brydon and Kate Legge, *Adjusting society: the World Bank, the IMF and Ghana* (London, 1996).
72 Kapur, *Ghana: adjustment and growth*, pp. 32–5, 36–7.
73 Hutchful, *Ghana's adjustment experience*, n. 67.
74 Ibid.
75 Ghana Budget Statement 1995, in Donkor, *Structural adjustment*, p. 139.
76 Donkor, *Structural adjustment*, p. 194.
77 Fred O. Boadu, Victor K. Nyanteng, Seth Bimpong-Buta and Mark Nadler, 'Ghana: promoting accountability and transparency in government behaviour', in Lucie Colvin Phillips and Diery Seck (eds), *Fixing African economies: policy research for development* (London, 2004), pp. 25–63, at p. 26.
78 Seth Terkper, 'VAT in Ghana: why it failed', *Tax Notes International*, 12 (1996), pp. 1801–16, p. 1804.
79 Kwamina Panford, *IMF–World Bank and labor's burdens in Africa* (Panford, Conn., 2001), p. 24.
80 Ben Ephson, The Wall Street Journal Interactive Edition, 'Ghana's government braced for troubles with VAT reintroduction', Sept 4, 1998 in *Tax Notes International*, 17 (1998), p. 805.
81 See George O. Assibey-Mensah, 'The value-added tax in Ghana', *Public Budgeting & Finance*, 19 (1999), pp. 76–90; Terkper, *VAT in Ghana: why it failed*; Seth Terkper, 'Ghana reintroduces Vat – lessons learned and progress after a year', *Tax Notes International*, 20 (2000), pp. 1253–68.
82 Panford, *IMF–World Bank*, p. 65.
83 Boadu, *Ghana: promoting accountability and transparency*, p. 41.
84 Seth Terkper, 'An examination of Ghana's proposed VAT law', *Tax Notes International*, 9 (1994), pp. 787–92, at p. 788; Terkper, *VAT in Ghana: why it failed*.
85 Terkper, *VAT in Ghana: why it failed*, p. 1803.
86 Terkper, *Ghana's proposed VAT law*, p. 788 and n. 3.
87 Hutchful, *Ghana's adjustment experience*, pp. 36, 38; Donkor, *Structural adjustment*, pp. 120–1.
88 Donkor, *Structural adjustment*, pp. 120–1. Frimpong-Ansah states that the initial programme was not the product of the IMF: *The vampire state in Ghana*, p. 153 and n. 11.
89 Hutchful, *Ghana's adjustment experience*, pp. 50–1 and 150; Herbst, *The politics of reform in Ghana*, p. 119.
90 Terkper, *Ghana's proposed VAT law*, p. 787.
91 Hutchful, *Ghana's adjustment experience*, p. 148.
92 Terkper, *VAT in Ghana: why it failed*, p. 1802.
93 Ibid.
94 Hutchful, *Ghana's adjustment experience*, p. 148.
95 Botchwey went on to convene a review of IMF conditionality that drew attention to deficiencies in structural adjustment processes: Kwesei Botchwey, Paul Collier, Jan Willem Gunning and Koichi Hamada, *Report of the group of independent persons appointed to conduct an evaluation of certain aspects of the enhanced structural adjustment facility, part 2* (Washington, DC, 1998), pp. 20–1.

96 Seth Terkper, 'Interest in the reintroduction of VAT in Ghana', *Tax Notes International*, 13 (1996), pp. 180–1.
97 'Parliamentarians educated on VAT', *Ghanaian Digest*, Aug 4–6, 1997, *Tax Notes International*, 15 (1998), p. 679.
98 World Bank, *Introducing a value added tax: lessons from Ghana*, Premnote 61 (Washington, DC, 2001).
99 Seth Terkper, 'Ghana's professional and trade groups weigh in on VAT debate', *Tax Notes International*, 16 (1999), p. 982.
100 IMF, *Ghana: selected issues*, Staff Country Report (Washington, DC, 2000); Seth Terkper, 'Ghana experiences smooth transition to new 12.5 percent VAT rate', *Tax Notes International*, 21 (2000), p. 30.
101 Seth Terkper, 'Ghana's trade and industry minister-designate Kovi Apraku rules out VAT increase', *Tax Notes International*, 22 (2001), p. 1380.
102 Hutchful, *Ghana's adjustment experience*, p. 243.
103 IMF, *Ghana Country Report No. 05/292* (Washington, DC, 2005), p. 35.
104 Kennedy, *Challenging expert rule*, p. 24.

11
The Flat Tax: Fiscal Revolution or Policy Diffusion?

Joseph J. Thorndike

Since 1994, nine European countries have adopted some type of 'flat tax', a programmatically vague but politically popular approach to fiscal reform. Journalists have chronicled the phenomenon with almost breathless enthusiasm. 'A quiet revolution has been sweeping through countries of the old Soviet bloc', reported the London *Sunday Times* in August 2005. 'The flat tax revolution is sweeping across Europe', declared an Australian newspaper just a week later. 'Flat taxes, once a fantasy of free market ideologues, are sweeping across the European Union', commented another.[1]

'Revolution', it seems, has become the indispensable trope for descriptions of global tax reform. But this cliché obscures more than it illuminates, imposing narrative simplicity on a complex historical process. The flat tax is not a discrete idea or policy agenda 'sweeping' from one nation to the next. The flat tax regimes enacted since 1994 – all of them in central and Eastern Europe – differ widely from one another: some tax income, others consumption; some apply to individuals, others to businesses; some feature low rates, others much steeper ones. Conflating these disparate regimes impedes useful analysis, constructing a unitary programme where none, in fact, exists.

Yet the transnational dynamic of flat tax reform has been real, even if the reified notion of a single flat tax has not. To understand this dynamic, we must treat the flat tax not as a unitary programme, but as a general approach to fiscal reform, including bureaucratic, legislative and ideological elements. Thus defined, we can explain the popularity of flat tax reform, especially among countries trying to navigate the delicate transition from centralized planning to a competitive global economy. Specifically, the flat tax phenomenon has been driven by the imperatives of economic globalization, the realities of post-Communist political adjustment, and the resurgence of neo-liberal ideology.

Policy transfer and the flat tax

Over the past 25 years, scholars in several disciplines have developed a robust literature around the subject of policy transfer, diffusion, emulation and convergence.[2] Several key questions derived from this work can illuminate the flat tax phenomenon, explaining its popularity while accounting for its internal diversity.

What is being transferred? The flat tax phenomenon has not been defined by the transfer of specific taxes, administrative techniques, institutions or policy instruments.[3] Rather, the process of policy transfer surrounding the flat tax has focused on ideas, attitudes and rhetoric. These commonalities are not insignificant. Indeed, they reflect the structural imperatives driving the process. Broadly speaking, this sort of transfer might be described as 'emulation' or 'inspiration', as officials in one country have witnessed policy reform abroad and used it as a model for their own efforts.[4]

Who is orchestrating the transfer? The pivotal actors in the flat tax phenomenon have been elected officials. Searching for ways to cope with the pressures of globalization, they have seized on the flat tax as vehicle for reform. In particular, they have used flat tax reforms to attract and retain foreign capital. The flat tax is a marketing tool, with politicians using it to 'sell' their countries to fickle foreign investors. In this effort, they have received considerable help from non-governmental experts, including experts at neo-liberal think tanks in the United States and Europe.[5] Neo-liberals share a preference for free markets, limited government, mobile capital and robust property rights. They are inclined to embrace, rather than resist, the globalization of economic relationships. And when it comes to taxation, they endorse lower taxes overall, and very low or non-existent taxes on capital income in particular. As a group, neo-liberals constitute an epistemic community, a network of policy experts with broadly acknowledged competence and influence. As Anthony J. Evans has observed, these networks have played an important role in the flat tax phenomenon.[6]

What imperatives and constraints are shaping the transfer of flat tax ideas? Economic globalization – including the ever-increasing mobility of investment capital – has been a vital engine of flat tax reform. Flat tax policies represent an effort to cope with the pressures of a competitive global market for investment capital, especially as these pressures are mediated and magnified by the distinctive problems facing transitional economies.[7] Lawmakers in many countries have used flat taxes to signal investors that their country is business-friendly. Tax competition has been a principal weapon in the battle for foreign investment. Indeed, the world has witnessed a steady decline in marginal tax rates, stretching back at least two decades, as nations have competed for investment and human capital.[8]

Meanwhile, institutional imperatives, including anaemic state capacity in many post-Communist nations, have also prompted flat tax reform. With almost no tradition of voluntary compliance and widespread distrust of government institutions, transitional economies face major hurdles in trying to devise and collect taxes. The flat tax phenomenon is inextricably linked with these transitional struggles.[9]

Taken together, these questions illuminate the convoluted and often confusing process by which the flat tax has spread quickly throughout the transitional economies of Eastern and central Europe. They can account for differences in the flat tax regimes adopted by various countries. And they can help explain the cool reception that flat tax ideas have encountered in both 'Old Europe' and the United States.

Defining the flat tax

There is no single flat tax, but a range of fiscal reforms loosely grouped under this convenient rubric. Journalists have used the phrase to describe a range of disparate revenue tools, including taxes with starkly divergent rates, bases and administrative arrangements. Indeed, anyone seeking to distil the essential character of 'the flat tax' from news accounts will be sadly disappointed.

Defined broadly, the flat tax is as old as taxation itself. Any tax applied at a single rate to any sort of base might reasonably be called a flat tax, and such levies have existed for centuries. Single-rate income taxes meet that definition, as do *ad valorem* and unit-based excise taxes. Church tithes might also fall in this category, depending on the political arrangements surrounding them, especially their degree of voluntarism. Finally, poll or head taxes are also flat since the amount of tax assessed is fixed, regardless of the taxpayer's wealth, income or consumption. All these fiscal devices might be called flat taxes, but they differ dramatically in their incidence, effect and administration.

Still, the 'flat tax' moniker is not devoid of specific meaning. In general, it describes a tax levied at a constant rate on a relatively comprehensive base defined by income or consumption. Many countries have such taxes, including some not generally associated with the flat tax 'revolution'. Flat-rate taxes on corporate income are common around the world. So, too, are flat-rate levies on wage and salary income used to finance social programmes, such as the Social Security payroll tax in the United States.[10]

But most discussions of the 'flat tax revolution' concern broader, more fundamental programmes of fiscal reform. The European flat tax phenomenon is not characterized by narrow taxes dedicated to specific government programmes. Nor is it defined by flat-rate levies on discrete slices of the tax base (such as capital gains) or flat taxes on business income. While European flat tax regimes have often included such single-rate levies, the 'flat tax revolution' has been defined by flat-rate, broad-based taxes on personal income.

Notably, most flat taxes are not actually flat. That is, they do not apply a single rate of tax across a comprehensive tax base. Rather, flat tax regimes are usually dual-rate systems, with a single marginal rate applied to income above a threshold, and a zero rate for untaxed income beneath this exemption. Since all taxpayers, including those with income above the threshold, generally receive the benefit of this exemption, effective rates are progressive overall; the average rate rises with income, as the amount of exempted income shrinks relative to the taxpayer's total income.[11] This type of tax – with progressivity created by an exemption, not graduated rates – is often called 'degressive'. All European flat tax regimes include degressive personal levies, with many featuring large personal exemptions keyed to subsistence requirements, the poverty line, or some other measure of minimum need.

Ideological origins of the flat tax

The flat tax is an old idea, rooted in arguments for proportional taxation that stretch back centuries. It has also been a transnational idea, debated in countries around the world, but especially in Europe and the United States. When applied to the modern flat tax revolution, however, the concept of a 'flat tax' assumes a more distinctive, American cast. Flat tax regimes have been associated politically – if not economically – with a specific type of flat tax proposed by two American economists in the mid-1980s, Robert Hall and Alvin Rabushka. Nonetheless, the ideology supporting flat taxes generally, and the Hall–Rabushka flat tax in particular, springs from older arguments about the relative virtues of proportional and progressive taxation.

In his seminal work on the philosophy of progressive taxation, American economist Edwin R.A. Seligman explored early arguments for proportionality offered by a range of philosophical luminaries, including Thomas Hobbes, Adam Smith and John Stuart Mill. Hobbes, for instance, argued that individuals should be taxed in proportion to the benefits they received from the state, chiefly in the form of protection. These benefits, moreover, were best measured by consumption, not income or property:

> For what reason is there that he which laboureth much, and sparing the fruits of his labour, consumeth little, should be more charged, than he living idly, getteth little, and spendeth all he gets; seeing the one hath no more protection from the commonwealth than the other?[12]

The connection that Hobbes forges between proportionate taxation and the use of consumption as a tax base is not necessary, but the link is common among advocates of single-rate taxation, especially those writing in the latter decades of the twentieth century.

In *The Wealth of Nations*, Adam Smith muddled his stance on progressive taxation. 'It is not very unreasonable that the rich should contribute to the public expense not only in proportion to their revenue, but something more than in proportion', he observed at one point. Later, however, he endorsed proportional rates, suggesting that 'subjects of every state ought to contribute towards the support of the government, as nearly as possible in proportion to their respective abilities, that is in proportion to the revenue which they respectively enjoy under the protection of the state'. In fact, Smith's argument for proportionality seems more consistent with his broader discussion of taxation.[13]

Flat tax supporters often cite John Stuart Mill to bolster their case, recalling his observation that progressive taxes were 'a mild form of robbery'.[14] Notably, however, Mill endorsed degressive taxation, with an exemption to allow for basic necessities. Seligman believed that this deviation from true proportionality vitiated Mill's entire case for flat rate taxes, opening the door to any sort of progressive rate structure. Some more recent scholars have agreed.[15]

While these older arguments over proportional taxation resonate with modern concerns, the flat tax revolution has its substantive roots in the mid-twentieth century. More specifically, it is a product of the American conservative intellectual renaissance that began in the 1950s and reached its zenith in the last two decades of the twentieth century. This revival included an element of libertarian thinking derived from neoclassical economics, including the ideas of Hobbes and Smith. These American libertarians – especially the noted economist, Milton Friedman – went on to inspire the flat tax reforms of the late twentieth and early twenty-first century.[16]

In 1962, Friedman published *Capitalism and Freedom*, the first and most influential statement of his libertarian ideology. In it, he linked progressive taxation to issues of inequality, but resisted moral arguments for the redistribution of market rewards. 'I find it hard, as a liberal, to see any justification for graduated taxation solely to redistribute income', he wrote. 'This seems a clear case of using coercion to take from some in order to give to others and thus to conflict head-on with individual freedom.' Sacrificing freedom for the sake of equality – or a particular form of equality stressing the equal distribution of economic rewards – was simply intolerable. Friedman did allow for the possibility of some limited graduation in the rate structure of the income tax, largely as a concession to 'social standards of equity'. But graduation for the sake of redistribution alone was indefensible.[17]

Friedman preferred a flat-rate income tax coupled with an exemption. He opposed the corporate income tax, preferring to tax corporate profits at the individual level. And he endorsed a wide-ranging rollback in tax preferences, including special treatment for capital gains, the interest on state and local bonds, and income earned by oil, gas and other extractive industries. Using tax preferences to advance social goals or bestow favours violated a crucial canon of equity – equal treatment before the law. Indeed, one of Friedman's principal complaints about existing tax laws was their 'capricious and unequal' incidence.[18]

Friedman considered a flat-rate income tax consistent with the benefit principle of taxation. 'A proportional flat-rate-tax would involve higher absolute payments by persons with higher incomes for governmental services', he suggested, 'which is not clearly inappropriate on grounds of benefit conferred.' More important, the flat tax would discourage punitive taxation of the rich, avoiding 'a situation where any large numbers could vote to impose on others taxes that did not also affect their own tax burden'. Exemptions were legitimate, Friedman believed, as a means to alleviate poverty. He even endorsed a negative income tax: a government subsidy for those below the exemption. Such limited interference in the market was acceptable, he maintained, since it did not derive from the political tyranny of the majority. 'It is very different for 90 per cent of the population to vote taxes on themselves and an exemption for 10 per cent', he explained, 'than for 90 per cent to vote punitive taxes on the other 10 per cent – which is in effect what has been done in the United States.'[19]

Friedman insisted that his flat tax would not disrupt government revenues. A single rate of 23.5 per cent would raise as much money as the existing graduated rate structure, he predicted, assuming that lawmakers also broadened the tax base by eliminating credits, exemptions and other preferences. Moreover, the tax would likely raise even *more* revenue than the graduated system it replaced. By reducing incentives for evasion and eliminating inefficiencies inherent to the graduated rate structure, a flat tax would provide more than enough revenue.[20]

Friedman's flat tax got a cool reception. Even sympathetic observers dismissed the idea as 'radical, impractical, and visionary', he later recalled.[21] But 20 years later, *Capitalism and Freedom* helped inspire Alvin Rabushka and Robert Hall to develop a more detailed version of the flat tax.[22] In 1981, they published an article in the *Wall Street Journal* calling for a 19 per cent, single-rate tax on personal compensation, coupled with a 19 per cent single-rate tax on business profits. Existing US taxes were enormously complicated, they maintained, slowing growth, fostering evasion and costing the country billions in lost revenue. More important, complex and burdensome taxes undermined the moral foundations of American society. 'The benefits of tax reform are not merely economic', they concluded.

> The complexities of the federal tax system now foster contempt for government and make petty criminals out of a large fraction of the population. A simplified tax with low marginal rates would help restore confidence in government and would support the basic honesty of the American people.[23]

The Hall–Rabushka flat tax differed from Friedman's levy on a key point: it was a consumption tax. The flat tax retained much of the administrative infrastructure used to collect the income tax, but it excluded savings and investment from the tax base. In the 20 years since Friedman had offered his plan, consumption taxes had gathered a large and growing cadre of supporters. Economists across the political spectrum were increasingly impressed by the efficiency gains inherent in switching the tax base from income to consumption. The Hall–Rabushka flat tax, meanwhile, became the most famous model for consumption tax reform.

Still, the flat tax remained stuck in the realm of theory, not reality. In 1996, magazine publisher Steve Forbes sought the Republican nomination for president, using the flat tax as his signature issue. After a brief flurry of excitement, his campaign faltered. American voters were uneasy with the notion of a flat tax, embracing weak formulations of the idea (including those allowing retention of popular deductions) but recoiling from more sweeping versions. Throughout the 1990s, the flat tax remained a darling of the American right, and even some liberals found the idea attractive. But it never developed a secure base of popular support. Ultimately, the flat tax would find its first success outside the United States. While Americans were debating the possibilities of flat tax reform, other nations were rushing headlong into these uncharted fiscal waters.

The transfer of flat tax ideas

Loosely defined, the flat tax has been around for more than 50 years. Hong Kong introduced an early version shortly after the Second World War, and the Channel Islands, Jamaica and Bolivia also pioneered single-rate reform. But none of these countries managed to export the idea. Rather, the modern flat tax phenomenon – the transnational movement often described as a 'revolution' – took shape on the shores of the Baltic when Estonia enacted flat-rate income taxes in 1994. Over the next decade, eight countries in Eastern and central Europe followed suit (see Table 11.1). This process of policy transfer was driven by various imperatives and shaped by disparate constraints. In some countries, ideology was central, while in others, the quest for foreign investment took centre stage. Almost elsewhere, the political and bureaucratic legacy of communism played a vital role.

Modern flat tax regimes share important qualities. All are marked by single-rate taxes on income, although rates on different types of income are not always the same (corporate income is often taxed at different rates than personal income). They also share an ostensible commitment to simplicity and a comprehensive tax base, avoiding many of the deductions, credits and other

Table 11.1 European flat taxes, 1994–2005

Country	*Year adopted*	*Individual rate (%)*	*Corporate rate (%)*
Estonia	1994	24	24
Lithuania	1994	33	15
Latvia	1995	25	15
Russia	2001	13	24
Serbia	2003	14	14
Slovakia	2004	19	19
Ukraine	2004	13	25
Georgia	2005	12	20
Romania	2005	16	16

Source: Chris Edwards, 'Catching up to global tax reforms', in *Tax & Budget Bulletin* (Washington, DC, 2005).

tax preferences associated with income taxation. Finally, all flat tax regimes provide for some sort of personal exemption in the individual portion of the income tax, making them degressive rather than truly proportional systems.

But the flat tax regimes differ markedly in the rates they impose, with some much higher than others. Moreover, the regimes are marked by extensive diversity in their fiscal tools beyond the personal and corporate income taxes. Virtually all include some sort of value added tax (VAT), but implementation and rates differ widely. Many flat tax regimes also impose a variety of 'social' taxes designed to fund social welfare programmes, but these, too, differ from one another. Moreover, these social taxes often operate as a parallel system of income taxation, diluting the presumed purity of a single-rate system.

To understand the commonalities and distinctions among various flat tax regimes, we must move beyond the level of aggregate generalization and examine the revenue systems of particular nations in more detail. In this section, we will consider flat tax reform in three countries: Estonia, Russia and Slovakia. These three regimes illustrate the diversity of forces driving flat tax reform, as well as the disparate results that can emerge from these complex dynamics.

Estonia

In 1994, Estonia replaced its graduated income tax with a flat-rate levy on personal and corporate income. Officials were eager to fix a dysfunctional revenue, hobbled by limited administrative capacity and weak traditions of tax compliance. They also sought to attract and retain foreign capital, reversing capital outflows that followed the end of communism.[24] Notably, however, several key Estonian officials also embraced the ideological case for flat tax reform, including a commitment to property rights and private enterprise.

In the early days of independence, Estonia adopted a tax system with graduated rates for personal and business income: 16, 24 and 33 per cent for individuals, and 15, 23 and 30 per cent for businesses.[25] In 1994, lawmakers approved a single, 26 per cent rate for all types of income. In 2000, they exempted retained earnings from the corporate levy, taxing only those profits paid out to investors as dividends. In 2005, Estonia cut the single rate on personal income to 24 per cent and scheduled additional reductions for the future; by 2009, the rate is scheduled to fall to 20 per cent.[26]

Meanwhile, exemptions for the personal tax – already equal to a third of average per capita income – were scheduled to increase over the same period. Estonian officials defended exemptions as a matter of fairness, embracing the rationale for degressive taxation. 'Equality and fairness is one of the guiding principles stipulated by the Estonian Constitution and it is also reflected in the tax laws', the Ministry of Finance declared. Since exemptions provide more relief to the poor than they do to the rich – reducing effective rates most sharply among those at the bottom of the income scale – they helped promote equality.[27]

Estonia also levied an 18 per cent value added tax and a 33 per cent 'social tax' on wages. The latter has been used to fund social welfare programmes, including universal health care. Since social benefits are limited but the social tax is not, high-income taxpayers pay more in tax than they receive in benefits. This arrangement adds another element of redistribution to the tax system, according to Estonian officials, bolstering social equality.[28]

Lawmakers expected the flat tax to compensate for Estonia's limited capacity to collect taxes. Both tax collectors and citizens were unschooled in the operation of a modern tax system, and the country struggled with its first, post-Communist revenue regime. As officials later recalled, 'We inherited this ridiculous Soviet system where everybody spent weeks filling forms, so we changed it to something more convenient for all.'[29] In a 2003 interview, former prime minister Mart Laar agreed. '[T]he truth is that you have to make your tax system as simple as possible because if it is not understood then the people will just avoid it', he said. 'But if people understand the tax system and what it's for, then they are more eager.'[30]

Estonian officials also hoped to attract foreign investors, spurring development and boosting economic growth. By most accounts, they were successful. 'Estonia's liberal policy regime has created a favorable investment climate and made it possible for the country to attract foreign investors, particularly in the telecommunications and banking sectors', concluded the International Monetary Fund (IMF) in 2000. The country saw large capital inflows from nations in the European Union, ranking second in per capita inflows among all transitional economies.[31]

Such practical concerns were vital to Estonian flat tax reform. But ideology also played a pivotal role. Perhaps the most potent agent of change was Laar, Estonia's young prime minister and a voluble champion of free market ideas. As he set out to remake the nation's economy, Laar looked to Milton Friedman. 'The only economics book I had read was Milton Friedman's *Free to Choose*', Laar declared in a 2005 interview. He ignored warnings from government colleagues and international agencies, pursuing the flat tax relentlessly. 'Most experts advised against it and said it was a very stupid idea', he recalled. 'My finance minister said don't do it, the IMF said don't do it. But it's not very easy to convince a young person that he is wrong and I was that type of young person. So I did it.'[32]

Indeed, the Estonian flat tax resembled Friedman's 1962 plan for a flat-rate levy on personal income. It was levied on income, not consumption; and while some forms of capital income were left untaxed, others – including dividends and capital income – were included in the tax base. As a result, the tax differs significantly from the Hall–Rabushka flat tax; it represents a throwback to earlier ideas about proportional income taxation.

Laar considered the flat tax a blow for liberty; 'we had to make clear that if somebody works more and earns more, he will not be punished for this,' Laar recalled. After leaving office, he became a popular speaker on the neo-liberal lecture circuit, championing free market reforms around the world. Echoing Friedman, he insisted on the link between economic and political reform.[33] Still, he marvels at his unlikely success. 'Like the lizard who didn't know he couldn't walk on water and found that he could, we didn't know a flat tax couldn't be done', Laar said. 'We just walked on the water because we did not know that it was impossible.'[34]

Russia

In 2001, Russia replaced its graduated income tax with a flat-rate levy on individual income. This reform was hailed around the world and is widely regarded as a signal success for flat-rate taxation. As with Estonia, the Russian programme was designed to cope with serious problems in the existing tax regime. Also like Estonia, it found some of its most ardent support among neo-liberal intellectuals.

Prior to the 2001 reform, Russia's tax system – adopted after the fall of communism – was primitive and dysfunctional. Steep and sometimes punitive rates encouraged tax dodgers, and revenue officials were hobbled by inadequate legal authority and limited administrative capacity. According to Yegor Gaidar, a key architect of Russian economic reform, the system was doomed from the start. 'When we had no experience with market systems, we thought we could more or less import a tax system from a developed country', he told an American audience in 2002. But tax systems must grow from native soil. 'The national tax systems are a historical product', Gaidar explained. 'The French don't like their tax system, they hate it, but they generally comply. It is part of the general social contract that you have to pay tax. In Russia there is no such social contract.'[35]

A 1997 study found tax compliance anaemic at the corporate level, with almost 29 per cent of total tax liability completely unpaid, and most of the rest being paid in the form of barter or tax offsets for goods provided to the government. Large taxpayers routinely negotiated their tax payments. Overall, taxes as a ratio of gross domestic product fell steadily from 39 per cent in 1992 to 33.5 per cent in 1998. Tax arrears grew dramatically; as a ratio to tax collections over the prior 12-month period, arrears reached 34 per cent in the middle of 1997, compared with 4–6 per cent in Canada, the United States and Australia. One official later estimated that, by 2001, Russians were declaring as little as 25 per cent of their income. Chronic revenue shortfalls left the country struggling to pay its bills. In 1998, Russia defaulted on $40 billion in debt, triggering a near meltdown in the economy.[36]

Tax evasion paved the way for flat tax reform. Russians were willing to sacrifice graduated rates because the ostensibly progressive structure was not working anyway. 'People did not comply', recalled Gaidar. 'People in the lower brackets paid – teachers, doctors. Those who should pay in the higher brackets found ways not to pay. Only the poor paid the taxes.' In 2001, lawmakers adopted a flat-rate tax of 13 per cent on personal income, abandoning the three-tiered graduated system of 12, 20 and 30 per cent. For a relatively small number of taxpayers – those previously in the top two brackets – this provided a windfall. Those in the bottom bracket, however, actually saw a slight increase in tax rates. Overall, the average rate for all taxpayers fell modestly from 14 to 13 per cent. The new system included a higher exemption, but relative to wage levels, it remained steady at roughly 12 per cent.[37]

Meanwhile, the tax rate on certain forms of capital income actually climbed under the new regime, making the Russian reform quite distinct from the Hall–Rabushka flat tax and its exemption for all types of capital income. The rate on dividends doubled from 15 to 30 per cent. The corporate income tax rate – nominally unchanged at 30 per cent – actually rose by 5 per cent as municipalities took advantage of their authority to levy a piggyback rate of 5 per cent on the national tax. Finally rates for social insurance payments were reduced and reconfigured as a 'unified social tax'.[38]

The 2001 reform included a range of administrative changes designed to stem tax evasion. For the first time, taxpayers were assigned a uniform identification number. The law also introduced a withholding system, with taxes on personal income collected at the source. And tax authorities were endowed with robust enforcement tools, including the right to assess taxes indirectly (in the absence of adequate information from the taxpayer), and the power to conduct audits. As several observers have noted, these administrative reforms were a crucial part of the reform package – and a key explanation for its substantial success.[39]

Ideology played a central role in the Russian tax reform. Gaidar acknowledged the important, if still limited, influence of Western economists. 'Yes, I read [Milton] Friedman's books with interest, and also Hayek', he recalled in 2000. 'They were very authoritative for us, but all the same far away from our domestic realities.'[40] But Russia's leading advocate for the flat tax, Andrei Illarionov, was deeply influenced by Western economic thinking. A young economist known for his ardent free market ideology, Illarionov became Putin's chief economic adviser, and he used the post to mount a passionate campaign for radical tax reform. Aligning himself with the ideas of free market icons like Friedman and Ayn Rand, he insisted that political and economic liberty were inseparable. 'Every tariff and every limit on foreign-exchange transactions is a blow to our consciousness', he declared in 2000. 'Every tax acts against our freedom.' Indeed, Illarionov was given to provocative statements. 'The state is a mechanism to steal money from one person and give it to another', he asserted in 2000.[41]

Putin tapped Illarionov to help develop a new economic programme with a team of like-minded reformers. Sequestered outside Moscow in a new think tank, the Centre for Strategic Studies, this team developed a comprehensive reform package, including the new flat-rate tax on personal income.[42] The Baltic states seemed to inspire Illarionov, but the most powerful influence came from the United States. In interviews, he cited the Hall–Rabushka flat tax as his model for Russian reform, despite the many points of divergence between the two models. 'You must honour the inventor, like Thomas Edison and the electric light', he said. Indeed, Rabushka himself regards the Russian reform as a key episode in the transnational process of flat tax reform.[43]

Slovakia

In January 2004, Slovakia jettisoned its progressive income tax – including its five-tiered rate structure ranging from 10 to 38 per cent – and replaced it with a flat-rate tax of 19 per cent. Political leaders also adopted a new flat-rate levy on corporate income and a simplified value added tax, both of which were also set at 19 per cent. As with Estonia and Russia, these changes were driven by administrative necessity and ideology. But in Slovakia, tax competition and the quest for foreign investment were pivotal.

Slovakia's tax reform was prompted by a sense of economic stagnation and governmental failure. 'At that time', recalled two analysts for the Institute for Social and Economic Reform, 'there was a tax system generally considered as unsustainable, too complicated, changing too often, bringing in more exemptions and special rates, and thus distorting the business environment'. The system was unstable and exceedingly complex. As one key advocate declared, 'It was not a stable system, and super complicated for small and medium-sized companies.'[44]

The new tax regime was designed to attract foreign investors. 'It is a strong and positive signal for the inflow of foreign investments', declared finance minister Ivan Miklos. Ministry officials compared Slovakia's new regime with flat taxes abroad, including the well-established Hong Kong system for taxing personal income. Eager to speed the pace of Slovakian growth, they believed a flat tax would attract foreign capital.[45] The reforms were also intended to stem tax evasion. 'This should reduce the incentives for corporations and individuals to engage in tax evasion, which is very high', noted an economist for the nation's largest bank. And as the trade journal *Institutional Investor – Americas* observed, 'It should also pare down an internal revenue bureaucracy whose reputation for inefficiency and corruption is legendary.'[46]

Slovakia's flat tax reflected the rise to power of a new centre-right coalition government in late 2002. Finance minister Miklos was a key advocate, as was his chief economic adviser, Martin Bruncko. 'A few years ago, Martin Bruncko studied the flat tax at Harvard University', observed the *Christian Science Monitor* in an admiring profile. 'Today, the 28-year-old is flying to European cities to promote the idea, which he made a reality in his native Slovakia.'[47]

American conservatives encouraged the Slovak reforms. In Estonia, foreign advocates had cheered the flat tax reform enthusiastically, but their contributions were mostly after the fact. In Russia, they took a more active role, but the strong hand of Vladimir Putin ensured that Russian reforms would be his handiwork. In Slovakia, national leaders directed the flat tax reform, but they had active support from sympathetic partisans around the world.

In a 2003 visit to Bratislava, Steve Forbes predicted that a new Slovakian flat tax would transform the nation's economy. 'Slovakia is becoming a model for other countries in the region', he declared. 'All of Europe needs to follow the example of Slovakia.'[48]

By many accounts, Slovakia's tax reform was instrumental in attracting foreign investment. In 2004, the Slovak Investment and Trade Development Agency reported a 47 per cent increase in foreign direct investment over the previous year; early 2005 data pointed towards a similar trend. The agency attributed the rise to creation of a suitable business environment, including the new tax system. 'Slovak officials say that their flat-tax reform was crucial in securing a $1.3 billion investment last year by Korean auto maker Hyundai', reported *Business Week* magazine. Indeed, auto companies flocked to Slovakia, with Peugeot Citroen, Ford and Volkswagen all investing heavily. Overall, foreign investment in Slovakia increased more than sixfold between 1998 and 2005. Bruncko attributed much of this rise to the new, flat-rate corporate income tax. But he also stressed the importance of low personal income taxes, since they made the country more attractive to employees of foreign firms.[49]

Slovakia's flat tax regime made waves throughout Europe. 'The reform evoked fierce tax competition among Central-European countries spreading further to the west', observed the Institute for Social and Economic Reform. Austria, Hungary and Poland all reduced their corporate tax rates. The Czech Republic trimmed its VAT rate and scheduled a reduction in its corporate income tax. Many international observers praised the reforms; even the OECD endorsed them. But critics, particularly those in high-tax countries of Western Europe, complained that Slovakia's tax cuts were effectively subsidized by the European Union through its economic aid to Slovakia.[50]

Slovak tax officials were surprised at the strong international reaction – both positive and negative – to their flat tax reform. The country was not the first European nation to introduce a flat tax, and technically speaking, the levy was not particularly innovative; 'a flat tax does not amount to a substantial alteration of the economic system that the public consciousness interprets it to be', noted a study by the Slovak Finance Ministry.[51]

But the flat tax was a potent marketing device, as Slovak officials were quick to concede:

> Slovakia is a small open economy operating in the world of a global economy marked by large international flows of investment. Besides, imperfect information about the profitability of investment opportunities is characteristic of economic reality. This means that fundamental analysis is relatively unreliable in the course of making decisions on the allocation of investment and thus is not always the determinant of decisions made by investors. In light of this, phenomena such as a favourable image of a country on the international scene are sometimes decisive to investment.[52]

Other observers echoed this conclusion. Positive reactions to the flat tax were pivotal, aiding the nation in its quest for foreign investment. 'I think this publicity was as important as the tax rate cut itself', commented Robert Prega, an analyst with one of Slovakia's biggest banks.[53]

Indeed, Slovakia's flat tax reform was driven by a quest for foreign investment. As with Estonia and Russia, it was also a response to administrative failure in the nation's existing tax system. But tax competition was the driving force for Slovakian reform, shaping the nation's policy formulation and recasting the European debate over globalization and fiscal policy.

Conclusion

The transnational popularity of the flat tax has not been a revolution. The flat tax regimes of Eastern and central Europe are too divergent to march under this reductive but convenient banner. The popularity of fiscal reform in the flat tax style does, however, constitute an example of policy transfer. Driven by volitional and structural factors, this process has reflected worldwide debate over fiscal policy, tax competition, and the effects of globalization on public finance. At the same time, the apparent success of many flat tax regimes has added fuel to this debate.

Estonia's innovative embrace of flat taxation – including its restructuring of the corporate income tax in 2000 to leave undistributed corporate profits entirely tax free – has been widely hailed as a signal victory in the drive for proportional taxation. Along with its Baltic neighbours, Estonia has been very successful in attracting foreign capital. Russia, too, has been widely praised for its 2001 fiscal reform, which seems to have rescued the country from its revenue crisis of the late 1990s. Slovakia's flat tax regime is too new to allow for meaningful evaluation, but anecdotal reports suggest that lower taxes may have boosted foreign investment. More certainly, the Slovak reforms have fuelled the dynamics of tax competition, inducing other European nations to consider similar reforms.

Indeed, the flat tax phenomenon has been powered by the unstable but ineluctable dynamics of globalization, with flat tax regimes designed to attract and retain foreign direct investment to transitional nations. And while flat tax regimes have been characterized by the introduction of *flatter* rate structures – generally involving not one but two rates – their political history has reflected the quest for *lower* tax burdens, especially on capital. In such cases, calling something a 'flat tax' serves as a marketing scheme, a means to signal foreign investors that a given country is eager to accommodate the needs of global industry and commerce.

But the quest for investment capital has been only part of the story. In addition, the flat tax phenomenon has been shaped by the political and administrative legacy of communism. As Eastern and central European nations have struggled to cope with the transition to a free market, the flat tax has allowed underdeveloped revenue agencies to compensate for their limited administrative capacity. In general, flat tax regimes have been simpler and less administratively burdensome than the systems they replaced. As a result, they have been well suited to nations with nascent fiscal bureaucracies.

Finally, the flat tax phenomenon has drawn aid and comfort from neo-liberal policy entrepreneurs, including the think tanks who employ them and the politicians who seek their advice. In fact, the flat tax revolution – while incoherent at the level of policy – has been remarkably consistent in terms of ideology. Which is not to say that ideology has been the sole driving force, or even the principal commonality among flat tax movements; the pragmatic appeal of flat tax reform has often been decisive. But the shared ideology of flat tax reformers has lent rhetorical and political unity to this inherently diffuse process.

The future of flat tax reform remains unclear. Estonia and Slovakia have continued to debate the fairness of flat tax regimes, with critics insisting that a return to progressive rates would serve the cause of social justice. In Russia, meanwhile, the neo-liberal economic ideology of Andrei Illarionov has struggled against some decidedly illiberal political trends. In late 2005, Illarionov left his post in Putin's government, complaining that political freedom was under attack in a newly authoritarian Russia. Apparently, Friedman's tie between economic and political freedom remains tenuous.

Still, the dynamics driving the flat tax phenomenon are powerful. The downward pressure on marginal tax rates has been a fixture of global economics for decades. Tax competition promises to remain a powerful spur to national tax reform. Efforts to control this 'race to the bottom' have been stymied by strong resistance in low-tax countries. Slovakia, for instance, has stood firm against complaints that its flat tax regime constitutes an unfair form of 'tax dumping'.

Ultimately, however, flat taxes are not the only answer to tax competition. Policy-makers can lower tax burdens, especially on capital, without abandoning progressive rates. Such piecemeal reform is popular in countries where existing tax regimes are functional and well entrenched. Indeed, the flat tax may remain a phenomenon confined to developing and transitional economies.

Notes

1 'A taxing solution', *The Sunday Times*, 21 August 2005, p. 13; Emma Kate Symons, 'Europe steps up rates of change', *The Australian*, 31 August 2005, p. 8; Toby Harnden, 'Pioneer of the "flat tax" taught the east to thrive', *Sunday Telegraph*, 4 September 2005, p. 10; Stephen Castle, 'Flat tax revolution sweeps in from eastern Europe', *The Independent*, 29 April 2005, p. 31.

2 On distinctions among these terms, see David Dolowitz and David Marsh, 'Who learns what from whom: a review of the policy transfer literature', *Political Studies*,

44 (1996), pp. 343–57, at pp. 344–5. For one of the most influential expositions of policy transfer as an analytical model, see David Dolowitz and David Marsh, 'Learning from abroad: the role of policy transfer in contemporary policy-making', *Governance*, 13 (2000), pp. 5–23.

3 On the diversity of tax reform in transitional economies, see Maciej H. Grabowski, 'Reforms of tax systems in transition countries', *Transition Studies Review*, 12 (2005), pp. 293–312.

4 On the different kinds of transfer, including emulation and inspiration, see Richard Rose, 'What is lesson drawing?' *Journal of Public Policy*, 11 (1991), pp. 3–30, at p. 21. See also Dolowitz and Marsh, 'Who learns what from whom', p. 351.

5 'Neo-liberal' can be a pejorative term, especially among critics of globalization, and many apparent neo-liberals prefer to be called simply 'liberals', identifying themselves with neoclassical economic thought in the mode of Adam Smith. But the neo-liberal label avoids confusion with the more modern usage of 'liberal' to describe left-of-centre political ideologies.

6 On epistemic communities, see Peter M. Haas, 'Introduction: epistemic communities and international policy coordination', *International Organization*, 46 (1992), pp. 1–35, at p. 3. On the flat tax epistemic community, see Anthony J. Evans, *Flat tax: ideas and interest*, July–September 2005, http://www.openrepublic.org/open_ republic/20050619_vol1_no1/content/20050619_ft.htm.

7 On tax competition in the EU, see Michael P. Devereux, Rachel Griffith and Alexander Klemm, 'Corporate income tax reforms and international tax competition', *Economic Policy*, 17 (2002), pp. 451–95.

8 On policy competition among states, see Colin J. Bennett, 'How states utilize foreign evidence', *Journal of Public Policy*, 11 (1991), pp. 31–54. For a useful survey of the literature of taxation incentives and their effect on economic growth, see Vahram Stepanyan, 'Reforming tax systems: experience of the Baltics, Russia, and other countries of the former Soviet Union', IMF Working Paper 03/173 (Washington, DC, 2003), pp. 8–10.

9 On the limited bureaucratic capacity of tax agencies in formerly Communist nations, see Jorge Martinez-Vazquez and Robert M. McNab, 'The tax reform experiment in transitional countries', *National Tax Journal*, 53 (2000), pp. 273–98, at pp. 274–6; Liam Ebrill and Oleh Havrylyshyn, 'Tax reform in the Baltics, Russia, and other countries of the former Soviet Union', IMF Occasional Paper 182 (Washington, DC, 1999).

10 Sinclair Davidson, 'A flat tax for Australia?', Association of Chartered Certified Accountants (Sydney, 2006), p. 14.

11 For a succinct explanation, see Joseph Bankman and Thomas Griffith, 'Social welfare and the rate structure: a new look at progressive taxation', *California Law Review*, 75 (1987), pp. 1905–66, at footnote 6.

12 For a summary of Hobbesian taxation, including this quotation, see E. R. A. Seligman, 'Progressive taxation in theory and practice', *Publications of the American Economic Association*, 9 (1894), pp. 7–222, at pp. 87–8.

13 Ibid., pp. 93–4.

14 See, for instance, F. A. Hayek, *The constitution of liberty* (Chicago, 1960), p. 308; 'A brief history of the flat tax', *American Enterprise*, 6 (1995), p. 61. Notably, Mill dropped this line from later editions of his work. See Miriam A. Ellis, 'Variations in the editions of J. S. Mill's "Principles of political economy"', *Economic Journal*, 16 (1906), pp. 291–302, at p. 299.

15 For Mill's views on taxation, John Stuart Mill, *Principles of political economy with some of their applications to social philosophy*, 7th edn (London, 1909), Book V, ch. 2.

For Seligman's critique, see Seligman, 'Progressive taxation in theory and practice', pp. 154–6. See also Barbara H. Fried, 'Symposium: federal tax policy in the new millennium: the puzzling case for proportionate taxation', *Chapman Law Review,* 2 (1999), pp. 157–95, at pp. 161–2.

16 On the conservative revival in America, including its libertarian element, see George H. Nash, *The conservative intellectual movement in America since 1945* (Wilmington, Del., 1996).

17 Milton Friedman and Rose D. Friedman, *Capitalism and freedom* (Chicago, 1982), p. 174.

18 Ibid.

19 Ibid., pp. 174–5.

20 Ibid., p. 175.

21 Milton Friedman and Rose D. Friedman, *Tyranny of the status quo*, 1st edn (San Diego, 1984), p. 63.

22 Evans, *Flat tax: ideas and interest*; Alvin Rabushka, 'The free market at work in Hong Kong', *Wall Street Journal*, 18 January 1980, p. 8.

23 Alvin Rabushka and Robert E. Hall, 'A proposal to simplify our tax system', *Wall Street Journal*, 10 December 1981, p. 30. For a more detailed exposition of their plan, see Robert Ernest Hall and Alvin Rabushka, *The flat tax*, 2nd edn (Stanford, Calif., 1995).

24 On capital flight, see International Monetary Fund, *Transition economies: an IMF perspective on progress and prospects* (Washington, DC, 2000) at http://imf.org/external/np/exr/ib/2000/110300.htm.

25 On Estonia's first post-Communist tax system, introduced in 1990, see 'Estonia: the transition to a market economy', *World Bank country study* (1993), pp. 20–2.

26 Stepanyan, 'Reforming tax systems', p. 26.

27 Republic of Estonia, Ministry of Finance, 'Questions and answers: Estonian flat income tax system' (Tallinn, 2005), p. 3.

28 Ibid., p. 4.

29 Radek Sikorski, 'Land of the free – Estonia', *National Review*, 24 February 1997.

30 Fredo Arias-King, 'Just do it: interview with Mart Laar', *Demokratizatsiya*, 11 (2003), at http://www.findarticles.com/p/articles/mi_qa3996/is_200310/ai_n9310159; Republic of Estonia, 'Questions and answers', p. 4.

31 René Weber and Günther Taube, 'Estonia moves toward EU accession', in *Finance and Development* (Washington, DC, International Monetary Fund, 2000).

32 Paul Belien, 'Walking on water: how to do it', *Brussels Journal*, 27 August 2005, available at http://www.brusselsjournal.com/node/202; Harnden, 'Pioneer of the "flat tax" taught the east to thrive'. Dilanian, 'Derided in the U.S., flat tax is a winner in eastern Europe'. See also '"Radical . . . but not radical enough": an interview with Mart Laar,' *City paper: Baltics worldwide* (1997), available at http://www.balticsworldwide.com/larr.htm.

33 Mart Laar, 'How Estonia did it', in ed. Gerald P. O'Driscoll Jr., Edwin J. Feulner and Mary Anastasia O'Grady (eds), *2003 Index of economic freedom* (Washington, DC, 2003), pp. 35–7.

34 Harnden, 'Pioneer of the "flat tax" taught the east to thrive'. '"Radical . . . but not radical enough". On Laar and the transnational epistemic community supporting free market reform, see Evans, *Flat tax: ideas and interest.*

35 Leslie Evans, 'Yegor Gaidar: Russia has done better than you think', UCLA Asia Institute (Los Angeles, 2002), available at http://www.asiamedia.ucla.edu/article.asp?parentid=1964.

36 Gale and Gaddy, 'Demythologizing the Russian flat tax', pp. 984–6; Jason Bush, 'From each according to . . . oh, never mind', *Business Week*, 26 May 2003, p. 41; International Monetary Fund, 'Russian Federation: selected issues and statistical appendix', IMF Country Report 02/75 (Washington, DC, 2002), p. 61.
37 Gale and Gaddy, 'Demythologizing the Russian flat tax', p. 985; Anna Ivanova, Michael Keen and Alexander Klemm, 'The Russian flat tax reform', IMF Working Paper (Washington, DC, 2005), p. 6.
38 Gale and Gaddy, 'Demythologizing the Russian flat tax', p. 985; Ivanova, Keen and Klemm, 'The Russian flat tax reform', pp. 4–6.
39 Gale and Gaddy, 'Demythologizing the Russian flat tax', p. 986.
40 Public Broadcasting Service, 'Commanding heights: interview with Yegor Gaidar', transcript from television documentary (2002), available at http://www. pbs.org/wgbh/commandingheights/shared/minitextlo/int_yegorgaidar.html#3.
41 'Reformist on a rampage: a flat tax of 13%, and a cleaned up reputation for repaying debt', *Business Week*, 17 June 2002, p. 60; Catherine Belton, 'Putin's adviser extols Ayn Rand', *Moscow Times*, 26 April 2000; Steve Stephens, 'Russian adviser can teach U.S. lessons about a free economy', *Columbus Dispatch*, 11 December 2000, p. B1.
42 Angela Charlton, 'Think tank embraces capitalism to revive the Russian economy; President Putin's team of dreamers entertains drastic fiscal notions', *Globe and Mail*, 5 May 2000, p. B6; Leon Aron, 'A second go at a "second economic revolution"?', *Russia Outlook: AEI Online*, 1 July 2000, available at http://www.aei.org/publications/pubID.11844/pub_detail.asp
43 John Fund, 'High taxes wither away', *New York Sun*, 1 March 2005, p. 9; Bush, 'From each according to . . . oh, never mind'.; Stephens, 'Russian adviser can teach U.S. lessons about a free economy'. Carol Matlack et al., 'Europe circles the flat tax', *Business Week*, 26 September 2005, p. 59. On the differences between the Hall–Rasbushka tax and the Russian flat tax regime, see Ivanova, Keen and Klemm, 'The Russian flat tax reform', p. 4. Alvin Rabushka, 'The flat tax at work in Russia', 21 February 2002, *The Russian Economy*, available at http://www.russianeconomy.org/comments/022102.html.
44 Peter Goliaš and Robert Kicina, 'Slovak tax reform: one year after', Institute for Economic and Social Reforms (Bratislava, 2005), p. 3; Marta Iurianova, 'Flat tax favors business', *Slovak Spectator*, 6 October 2003, available at http://www.spectator.sk/clanok-14018.html; Andreas Tzortzis, 'Flat-tax movement stirs Europe', *Christian Science Monitor*, 8 March 2005, p. 1.
45 Jonathan Kandell, 'The year of accession: Slovakian overdrive', *Institutional Investor – Americas*, 12 February 2004.
46 Tzortzis, 'Flat-tax movement stirs Europe'.
47 Dewey Smolka, 'U.S. media mogul hails Slovak tax plans', *Slovak Spectator*, 21 July–3 August 2003, available at http://www.slovakspectator.sk/clanok. asp?cl=13455.
48 Goliaš and Kicina, 'Slovak tax reform: one year after', p. 10.
49 Kandell, 'The year of accession'; Mathew Reynolds, 'Once a backwater, Slovakia surges', *New York Times*, 28 December 2004, p. 1. Matlack et al., 'Europe circles the flat tax'; Goliaš and Kicina, 'Slovak tax reform: one year after', p. 11.
50 Zdenko Krajcí and Ludovít Ódor, 'First year of the tax reform or 19 per cent at work', Financial Policy Institute, Ministry of Finance of the Slovak Republic (Bratislava, September 2005), pp. 77–9.
51 Ibid.
52 Marta Iurianova, 'Two years on, flat tax pros and cons still debated', *Slovak Spectator*, 6 February 2006, available at http://www.slovakspectator.sk/clanok-22389.html.
53 Tzortzis, 'Flat-tax movement stirs Europe'.

Index